Public Broadcasting and Political Interference

Public broadcasters, like the BBC and the Italian broadcaster Rai, are some of the most important media organisations in the world. Politicians are often tempted to interfere in the workings of these broadcasters and when this happens, the results are highly controversial, as both the Blair and Berlusconi governments have discovered.

Public Broadcasting and Political Interference explains why some broadcasters are good at resisting politicians' attempts at interference, and have won a reputation for independence – and why other broadcasters have failed to do the same. It takes a comparative approach of broadcasters in different countries, including the United Kingdom, Italy, Spain and Sweden arguing political independence for public service broadcasters is important because of its contribution to democracy allowing voters alternative sources of information which allow them to choose between electoral alternatives.

The book will be of interest to policy-makers, scholars and students of political communication, broadcasting and the media.

Chris Hanretty is Lecturer in Politics at the University of East Anglia, Norwich, UK.

Routledge research in political communication

1 **Political Campaigning in Referendums**
   Framing the referendum issue
   Claes H. de Vreese and Holli A. Semetko

2 **The Internet and National Elections**
   A comparative study of web campaigning
   *Edited by Nicholas W. Jankowski, Randolph Kluver, Kirsten A. Foot
   and Steven M. Schneider*

3 **Global Political Marketing**
   Edited by Jennifer Lees-Marshment, Jesper Strömbäck and Chris Rudd

4 **Political Campaigning, Elections and the Internet**
   Comparing the US, UK, Germany and France
   Darren G. Lilleker and Nigel A. Jackson

5 **Public Broadcasting and Political Interference**
   Chris Hanretty

Public Broadcasting and Political Interference

Chris Hanretty

Routledge
Taylor & Francis Group

LONDON AND NEW YORK

First published 2011
by Routledge
2 Park Square, Milton Park, Abingdon, Oxon OX14 4RN

Simultaneously published in the USA and Canada
by Routledge
711 Third Avenue, New York, NY 10017

Routledge is an imprint of the Taylor & Francis Group, an informa business

British Library Cataloguing in Publication Data
A catalogue record for this book is available from the British Library

Library of Congress Cataloging-in-Publication Data
Hanretty, Chris.
    Public broadcasting and political interference / Chris Hanretty.
    p. cm. – (Routledge research in political communication)
    Includes bibliographical references and index.
    1. Public broadcasting–Political aspects–Case studies. 2. Public
broadcasting–Europe–Case studies. I. Title.
    HE8689.7.P82H35 2011
    384.54–dc22

                                                              2010050850

ISBN: 978-0-415-66552-0 (hbk)
ISBN: 978-0-203-81372-0 (ebk)

Typeset in Times
by Wearset Ltd, Boldon, Tyne and Wear
Printed by TJI Digital, Padstow, Cornwall

Contents

List of figures and tables viii
List of acronyms ix
Preface xi

PART I
The broad picture 1

1 Introduction 3
 1 Setting the scene 3
 2 What are public service broadcasters? 4
 3 What is political independence? 5
 4 Why does political independence matter? 6
 5 Why do other things matter less? 7
 6 What is my explanation of political independence? 8
 7 How do I demonstrate these claims? 9
 8 Outline of the book 10

2 The broad picture: testing rival theories of independence on
36 public broadcasters 11
 1 Measuring independence by proxy 11
 2 What explanations exist already? 15
 3 My explanation 18
 4 Data and model 32
 5 Summary 40

PART II
Specific cases 43

3 Italy: the absence of Caesars 45
 1 Fascism and the post-war period (1924–1960) 47

2 *The Bernabei era (1961–1974)* 53

3 *Reform to reform (1975–1992)* 57

4 *New hopes dashed (1993–2008)* 68

5 *Conclusion* 78

4 Spain: huge steps forward?   81

1 *From dictatorship to transition (1923–1977)* 81

2 *The early democratic years (1977–1996)* 82

3 *From Aznar to Zapatero* 86

4 *Conclusion* 87

5 The United Kingdom: "treading delicately like Agag"   89

1 *From foundation to competition (1922–1955)* 89

2 *The years of Butskellism (1954–1979)* 105

3 *From Thatcher to Blair (1979–2005)* 115

4 *Conclusion* 123

6 Ireland: importing experience   125

1 *From 2RN to television (1926–1960)* 125

2 *Refoundation, confrontation (1960–1976)* 128

3 *1976 until the present day* 131

4 *Conclusion* 134

7 Sweden: "disturbing neither God nor Hitler"   136

1 *An abundance of caution (1922–1955)* 138

2 *Diplomats and exegetes (1955–1969)* 148

3 *The centre does not hold (1969–)* 156

4 *Conclusion* 161

8 Denmark: being driven to the left?   164

1 *Establishment until the 1950s (1922–1955)* 164

2 *The 1950s until Vänstervridning (1957–1974)* 166

3 *The professionalization turn? (1980–)* 172

4 *Conclusion* 175

PART III
Comparisons and conclusions   177

9 Comparing the six broadcasters   179

1 *The market and professionalization* 179

2 *The journalists* 182

3 Management 183
4 Rules 184
5 Conclusion 188

10 Conclusions   189
1 Reassessing independence 189
2 Reassessing legal protection 191
3 Reassessing the causal chain 192
4 Implications for reform 193
5 Continued relevance 195

Notes   197
References   202
Index   211

Figures and tables

Figures

2.1	Schematic representations of journalists	22–3
2.2	Union formation as a function of market size	31
2.3	Predicted versus actual values	39
3.1	Rai timeline	46
5.1	BBC timeline	90
7.1	SR/SVT timeline	137
10.1	PSB audience shares, 1998–2008	196

Tables

2.1	Independence of PSBs worldwide	14
2.2	Index of legal protection	36
2.3	Linear regression model of independence	38
9.1	Comparison of countries	180

Acronyms

AGCOM	Autorità per le garanzie nelle comunicazioni
AN	Alleanza Nazionale
Ansa	Agenzia Nazionale Stampa Associata
BBC	British Broadcasting Corporation
BJTC	Broadcast Journalism Training Council
CBC	Canadian Broadcasting Corporation
CLNAI	Comitato di Liberazione Nazionale per l'Alta Italia
CPIV	Commissionare parlamentare per l'indirizzo generale e la vigilanza dei servizi radiotelevisivi
DC	Democrazia Cristiana
DR	Danmarks Radio
DS	Democratici di Sinistra
EIAR	Ente Italiano Audizione Radiofoniche
GAC	General Advisory Council
IRI	Istituto per la Ricostruzione Industriale
ITA	Independent Television Authority
ITN	Independent Television News
MSI-DN	Movimento Sociale Italiano – Destra Nazionale
NCTJ	National Council for the Training of Journalists
PCI	Partito Comunista Italiano
PP	Partido Popular
PSB	public service broadcaster
PSI	Partito Socialista Italiano
PSOE	Partido Socialista Obrero Español
Rai	Radiotelevisione Italiana
RNE	Radio Nacional de España
RTÉ	Radio Telefís Éireann
RTVE	Radiotelevision Española
SJF	Svensk Journalistföreningen
SR	Sveriges Radio
SVT	Sveriges Television
TOR	rate of turnover
TT	Tidningarnas Telegrambyrån

TVE	Television Española
TW3	That Was The Week That Was
UCD	Unión de Centro Democrático
UR	Sveriges Utbildningsradio
URI	Unione Radiofonica Italiana
VUL	political vulnerability index

Preface

This book is about public service broadcasters (PSBs), and why some PSBs are more independent of the government of the day than others. It is also about the impact of rules – legal rules which stipulate what politicians can and cannot do in relation to public broadcasters; and broadcasters' rules, which give "regulatory values" for journalism, allowing certain practices and discouraging others. Where legal rules constrain politicians, they will have no opportunity to interfere in the broadcaster; where broadcasters' rules tightly constrain journalists (or are widely believed to do so), politicians will have reduced motive to interfere in the broadcaster. This book therefore stands at the junction of political science and media studies. This junction is becoming increasingly crowded, as students of the media embark upon sophisticated comparative typologies of media systems which are based upon, and in part derived from, typologies of political systems (Hallin & Mancini, 2004). If there is an "institutional turn" within media studies – and much recent work on the impact of media systems suggests as much – then it is only fitting that public broadcasters should also be investigated as part of this trend. They are the most highly structured sort of media organization, and at the same time the most political. This book holds lessons not just for those who consume and those who produce the media, but also for those who manage large arm's-length organizations and who structure those organizations through the drafting of legislation. Where the background conditions are propitious – in the present case, where the pre-existing market for news is large – skilled managers can incorporate existing professional strictures and use them as a way of structuring the organization internally and defending it externally. Where the background conditions are less favourable, civic-minded legislators can craft legislation so as to partially insulate public broadcasters, or other public bodies, from political interference. My argument that these twin factors – the degree of legal protection afforded the broadcaster, and, through the development of a large market for news, the pursuit within the broadcaster of rules governing content – increase the independence of public broadcasters is demonstrated by two very different and contrasting methods. In the first part of this book, I consider the broad picture and examine the independence of PSBs worldwide, testing a number of explanations of their independence statistically. In the second part of this book, I go on to consider six broadcasters in depth and chart their histories, paying particular attention to the development of internal rules and occasional episodes of political interference. In the last part of the book, I synthesize the conclusions of both my statistical findings and the findings from more historical research, and attempt to indicate how, in future, public broadcasters might be made more independent. Some of this book draws on previously published research. The statistical model of Chapter 2 was previously published in "Explaining the De Facto Independence of Public Broadcasters", *British Journal of Political Science, 40*(1) (2010), pp. 75–89. The discussion of the value of pluralism in the Italian broadcast media subsequently became an article in its own right, published as "The Concept of Pluralism in Italian Public Media", *Modern Italy, 16*(1) (2011), pp. 19–34.

I have incurred considerable intellectual and personal debts whilst writing this book, which began as a PhD thesis at the European University Institute. Many of those intellectual debts can be gleaned from the copious references to histories of the Spanish, Italian, Irish, British, Swedish and Danish broadcasters I study in this book. Many others are not to be found in the text. I should therefore like to thank: Tom Quinn (RTÉ), Cristina Jurca (TVR), Ingrida Veiksa (LTV), Tina Malavasic (RTVSLO), Margit Desch and Wolf Harranth (ÖRF), Tiiu Siim (ERR), Heike von Debschitz (ZDF), Grethe Haaland (NRK) and Diane Ferguson (CBC), Börje Sjöman at the Sveriges Radio Dokumentarkiv and Ursula Haegerström, Margareta Cronholm and Erik Fichtelius (SVT); David Hine and Nigel Bowles for convincing me of the value of further study; Michael Tatham, Chiara Ruffa, Costanza Hermanin, Sergi Pardos-Prado, Johan Davidsson, Jeppe Dørup Olesen, Bart van Vooren, Niki Yordanova, Elias Dinas and Lúcio Tomé Féteira, all colleagues from the EUI; Per Mouritsen at Århus University and Alexa Robertson at Stockholm University; and Anker Brink Lund, Adrienne Héritier, Gianpietro Mazzoleni and Alexander Trechsel, who read and improved this work in an earlier incarnation. This book is dedicated to my parents.

Part I
The broad picture

1 Introduction

1 Setting the scene

In February 2005, the Swedish public broadcaster Sveriges Television (SVT) began running an advertising campaign entitled "Fri Television". The campaign was designed to highlight that SVT's programming was both free at the point of use and free from political pressure, and included clips of Russian president Vladimir Putin and Italian prime minister Silvio Berlusconi, implicitly comparing free SVT with un-free media in other countries. The campaign provoked strong reactions – not from Swedish viewers, rather from the Italian government. Sweden's ambassador to Italy was invited to the foreign ministry to explain the situation. At the same time, Italy's ambassador in Stockholm visited the foreign ministry there in order to make clear Italy's demand that SVT stay out of "Italian internal affairs", a request which Moderate Party parliamentarian Gustav Fridolin likened to "the demand of a dictatorship".[1] According to deputy foreign minister Laila Freivalds, the government made it clear to the Italian delegation that the government could in no way interfere with SVT's output,[2] and the matter was eventually dropped.

The mutual incomprehension demonstrated during this episode – the Swedish incomprehension that the Berlusconi government would ask the government to intervene and expect it to be successful, and the Italian incomprehension that the Swedes would demonstrate such qualms – suggests that there are differences in Europe when it comes to public media. In some countries, governments habitually bully broadcasters; in others, governments do not. The argument of this book is that we can explain these differences in the political independence of public service broadcasters (PSBs) without having to resort to descriptions of Italian irascibility or Swedish stoicism, or indeed any other kind of explanation couched in terms of national character or "the way things are done here". "The way things are done" certainly matters, but these folkways in turn depend on more fundamental characteristics of the polity. In particular, I argue that they depend on two broad factors: the growth and self-regulation of the market for news, and the legal protection given to the public broadcaster. The larger the market for news, the greater the degree of professionalization amongst journalists in general, and amongst broadcasters in the public broadcaster in particular.

The greater the degree of professionalization, the more reduced the motive to interfere. The greater the legal protections given to the broadcaster, the more limited the opportunities for interference. And the more reduced the motive, and the more circumscribed the opportunities for interference, the greater the degree of independence.

2 What are public service broadcasters?

Because there is considerable debate about the rationale for public service broadcasting, there is considerable debate about the type of content which can be described as "public service broadcasting". Usually this is content which is under-supplied by the market, and which either has considerable intrinsic merit (high culture) or serves widely shared state interests and aims (news and current affairs programming promotes an informed citizenry; popular entertainment reflects and propagates national culture). This considerable debate has meant that "public service broadcasters" have sometimes been implicitly defined as just those broadcasters which happen to offer public service broadcast content. This is surely a necessary criterion for identifying PSBs, but it is not sufficient. Private, free-to-air broadcasters may offer a wide range of meritorious programming, but may do so from a sense of *noblesse oblige*. They do not stand in the same relation to the state as, say, the British Broadcasting Corporation (BBC) or Radiotelevisione Italiana (Rai) do.

I therefore define a PSB as a broadcaster which:

- has as a stated aim the provision of a broad range of content which is socially useful;
- is funded in large part by the state through general taxation revenue or a special hypothecated tax (licence fee);
- principally broadcasts to residents of the same state that funds it;[3] and,
- has the highest posts in the broadcaster appointed by state organs.

This definition excludes certain broadcasters which are commonly described as PSBs, such as Channel 4 in the UK and, since 2005, TV2 in Denmark. These broadcasters have considerable obligations imposed upon them by the state; but this is true of many commercial companies, and the special problems of public service broadcasters, as I define them, often do not apply to them.

I am not interested in all PSBs, only those which operate in democratic regimes. There are two reasons for this. First, totalitarian regimes, by definition, lack an understanding of the public as distinct from the state. It is for that reason that we talk about "state broadcasters".[4] Second, even if a state-funded broadcaster operating in a non-democratic regime were to become independent (and this is unlikely), this would be such an unusual occurrence that it would be unlikely to come about by the same means by which PSBs in democracies become independent. A second qualification is that with two exceptions – the Belgian broadcasters RTBF and VRT, which were formerly the same national broadcaster – I consider only national public service broadcasters. There are a number of regional public service broadcasters, but the value of studying them may be limited where, as is the case in Germany, these regional PSBs operate in a normative and/or economic framework set at the national level by parent organizations or federal legislation. Applying these criteria results in a sample of 49 broadcasters from across the world. These PSBs are listed in Table 2.1 Some choices – such as listing the Office de Radiodiffusion Télévision Française and France Télévisions (twice) separately – may seem like double counting. Rather, these broadcasters have been counted separately because they underwent significant changes in the degree of legal protection, which, as we shall see below, is a key factor in explaining political independence.

3 What is political independence?

Independence is a relationship between two bodies. It does not make sense to talk of the independence of PSBs in absolute terms. Instead, we must talk about the independence of public broadcasters from some other source of power. In this book, I concentrate on political independence: independence from politics, rather than economic independence (often itself regarded as a desirable characteristic for PSBs) or independence from society. In particular, I focus on independence from the classic institutions of representative democracy: legislatures, executives and political parties. By political independence, I mean:

- the degree to which PSBs employees take day-to-day decisions about their output or the output of subordinates, without
- receiving and acting on the basis of instructions, threats or other inducement from politicians, or the anticipation thereof;
- or considering whether the interests of those politicians would be harmed by particular choices about output.

I use "interference" and "intervention" to describe threats or inducements from politicians which cause or attempt to cause PSBs' employees to act in a particular fashion. Independence is related to, but different from, political pressure. The absence of pressure over time is a sufficient condition for independence, but not a necessary one. A broadcaster might face considerable pressure yet still be independent. Indeed, successfully resisting such pressure might lead it to become more independent still, as the repeated use of organizational rules designed to govern complaints by politicians gives those rules greater authority ("the iron is made hot by the striking", as John Reith would say – see p. 91). It is important, therefore, not to conflate these two concepts.

Independence is also different from impartiality. A broadcaster which has low levels of independence is almost always partial. This partiality may be of two kinds (Humphreys, 1996, pp. 155–158). Sometimes low independence broadcasters are partial towards one particular party or group of parties: this is the case where control of public service broadcasting is seen as one of the spoils of victory in a bipolar system characterized by alternation in government. Some-times low independence broadcasters are partial towards a much larger set of parties, perhaps the entire set of parties represented in parliament: this is the case where control of public service broadcasting is part of the maintenance of a cartel of political parties (Katz & Mair, 1995; Bischoff, 2006, pp. 112, 117). In theory, however, an independent broadcaster could also be partial if, as is pos-sible, journalists have ideological commitments which shape their work. As we shall see in the chapters discussing SVT and Danmarks Radio (DR), independent PSBs which are perceived to be partial are often punished by politicians. Impar-tiality is therefore a good strategy for maintaining independence, but the link is a causal one, rather than a conceptual one.

4   Why does political independence matter?

First, PSB independence matters because of its contribution to democracy. Even on the least demanding theories of democracy (Dahl, 1971), voters must have alternative sources of information which allow them to choose between electoral alternatives. If a PSB has a monopoly, and low levels of independence make it favour the government of the day, voters' ability to choose between alternatives is impaired, and democracy weakened. Even where PSBs are but one amongst many providers of political information, the "partiality in and greater availability of government-controlled media" is used by many scholars as an indicator of limited democracy (Coppedge & Reinicke, 1991, p. 50). The same argument applies, however, if the media is controlled by a cartel of political parties rather than just those parties who compose the government.

Second, PSB independence matters insofar as political pressure designed to secure changes in coverage can be seen as a corrupt practice. There is no univer-sal injunction against parties using public funding or public institutions to elect-oral advantage: in most established democracies, parties receive public funding in order to fund campaign expenditure. Nor is there an injunction against parties spending public money to fund programmes that produce disproportionate elect-oral rewards for that party. In the first case, however, this funding is in principle available to all parties who meet certain requirements; and in the second case, the primary benefit accrues not to the party, but to recipients of government welfare programmes. This argument has a broader application than our first argument for politically independent PSBs. If we consider public broadcasters with marginal audience shares which operate in competitive media markets, it is hard to claim that the PSB's lack of independence significantly impairs demo-cracy in that country: other sources of information exist, and dominate the public broadcaster. However, precisely because many of these public broadcasters have been marginalized due to persistent government interference (the case with the Greek and Turkish broadcasters), it is difficult to claim that the primary benefici-ary of these stations' continued existence is the viewing public, rather than, say, the government's prospects of re-election. Since independence need not result from obvious and overt pressure, and since the line between spending designed primarily to benefit the public and spending designed primarily to improve re-election prospects is rarely clear, this argument is less strong than the argument for the political independence of public broadcasters as a contribution to democracy. Nevertheless, it taps an important objection to excessive political influence over PSBs.

Third, PSB independence matters because those who have experience of the alternative tend not to like it, and because, to paraphrase the Dane, nothing is good or bad but public opinion makes it so. The limited independence of the Italian public broadcaster Rai has led to numerous though ineffective public protests. Even those politicians who have traditionally benefited from Rai's low levels of independence have now promised to guarantee greater political independence from both government and parties represented in the legislature. The abortive 2007 reform of Rai sought specifically to grant it autonomy "from the parties", not just from the government (Gentiloni, 2007, §2.6). The expression of this desire may have been a form of lip-service, but even lip-service shows that political independence is *thought* to be a good thing.

5 Why do other things matter less?

This book attempts to explain the political independence of public broadcasters, narrowly conceived. It does not attempt to explain broadcasters' independence from politics more broadly (for example, the degree to which politicians set the permissible strategies of public broadcasters operating in competitive markets), nor broadcasters' economic independence or distinctiveness. Both choices can be challenged. In seeking to explain independence in day-to-day decisions about output, I purposely ignore the degree to which politicians influence or determine the strategic decisions of PSB executives about which services to fund and how to allocate resources. Politicians do influence such choices, either through primary legislation or, increasingly, through service contracts (Coppens & Saeys, 2006). This influence, and the effect it has on the broadcaster's operational autonomy, has no intrinsic interest for us. To give a concrete example: few people care whether politicians or broadcasters decide if and how minority-language programmes are funded. People care about the decision to fund such programmes, rather than the identity of those who take that decision.

Politicians' influence over strategic issues might matter to us if it affected the broadcaster's day-to-day independence from politics. Just as with the dichotomy between politics and administration, it is often difficult to distinguish between strategic action and day-to-day tactics. Legal instruments designed to give politicians influence over strategic matters might instead be used to pressure the broadcaster's day-to-day affairs. With this in mind, my index of legal protection (see Table 2.2) includes items that tap the degree to which politicians regularly take strategic decisions about the broadcaster's operations. This does not mean that this kind of operational autonomy is also valuable, or that I am also trying to explain operational autonomy – merely that, as an empirical matter, broadcasters which enjoy limited operational autonomy also enjoy limited political independence. I also ignore the economic independence of PSBs. Habermasian and Marxist supporters of public broadcasting have argued that public broadcasting can "foster a set of social relations, distinct from and opposed to economic values and relations" (Garnham & Inglis, 1990, p. 111); that these values have intrinsic value; and that public broadcasting should be strengthened insofar as it contributes to these values. I take no position on whether PSBs do further these values, and whether these values are desirable. Ignoring issues of economic independence to concentrate on political independence is only defensible as long as broadcasters' levels of economic (in)dependence do not cause levels of political (in)dependence. This might be the case if, for example, broadcasters who operate in lightly regulated but competitive media markets, who are not large vertically integrated hegemons and who have revenue streams which derive, in large part, from commercial sources (advertising or programmes sales revenue) happen also to be prone to political interference (perhaps from economically right-wing parties), and if the direction of causality ran from the broadcaster's economic position to its susceptibility to political interference.

Certain aspects of the broadcaster's economic position – in particular its funding source – are already accounted for, since they feature in my index of legal protection. Other economic aspects, such as audience share, can also be accounted for relatively easily, and prove not to be significant in the statistical model of independence provided in Chapter 2. The most obvious routes by which broadcasters' economic independence might affect their political independence are thus accounted for.

6 What is my explanation of political independence?

My argument is easily understood. In order to interfere in public broadcasters, politicians must have motive to interfere and the opportunity to do so. Where politicians lack either, they will not interfere, and the broadcaster will be independent. The principal opportunities to interfere come from politicians' legally sanctioned role in determining aspects of the broadcaster's operation, and in staffing the top levels of the broadcaster. After all, it is because politicians have these opportunities that we are particularly interested in broadcasters' independence from politicians, rather than their independence from other groups of elites. Where the legislation governing the broadcaster grants politicians an extensive role vis-à-vis the broadcaster, politicians' opportunities to interfere will be extensive, and political interference may result. Conversely, where the relevant legislation grants the broadcaster significant legal protection, politicians will have fewer opportunities to interfere, and so the broadcaster will be more independent, irrespective of whether politicians also have motives for interfering.

A broadcaster may still be independent even if it enjoys limited legal protection. Where politicians believe that journalists are non-partisan, or that the broadcaster has rules concerning output which tightly constrain the manner in which content is produced, then there is little sense in interfering in the broadcaster: even were the current stock of journalists to be replaced, a new set of journalists would only follow the same strictures, and produce similar output, to not net benefit. Even where politicians judge that there is some benefit in interfering in the broadcaster, the politicians may defuse such interventions by promising to revise the rules (so that the kind of content which prompted the politician's objection never arises again), or to offer to adjudicate the complaint by reference to existing rules (so that the immediate sting is taken out of the objection). Such a strategy, however, does not occur to all broadcasters; it is more likely to be deployed either in countries where journalists themselves have embarked upon a "professionalization project", or in countries where media markets are sufficiently large to support press agencies with a rigid house style. Consequently, broadcasters in less developed media markets – such as those in the south of Europe – will be unable to pursue this strategy, and will instead have to rely on the capacity of legal rules to protect them from politicians' interventions.

7 How do I demonstrate these claims?

I demonstrate these arguments by two means. In Chapter 2, I test statistically a number of competing explanations of the political independence of PSBs – my own, in terms of the degree of legal protection enjoyed by the broadcaster and the size of the market for news; and rival explanations, in terms of party-system polarization and the partisanship of the bureaucracy. In the chapters that follow, I analyse the histories of broadcasters in six countries – the Italian and Spanish broadcasters Rai and Radiotelevisión Española (RTVE); the British and Irish broadcasters the BBC and Radio Telefís Éireann (RTÉ); and the Swedish and Danish broadcasters SVT and DR – in order to assess the link between market size and professionalization, and between professionalization and greater independence. Each of these means borrows strength from the other. The statistical chapter is used to eliminate rival explanations; the historical chapters are used to demonstrate links which cannot easily be quantified (such as the link between market size and professionalization), and to demonstrate the kind of causal connection which statistical tests can rarely uncover. My explanation of PSB independence is therefore based on comparisons between countries. It is not primarily intended to explain over-time variations in independence within one country. Nor, as the references to many excellent histories of these broadcasters attest, is it intended to give an original or comprehensive account of these broadcasters' relationship with politics. This kind of comparison is the principal strength of this book. Much empirical work on politics and the media studies single countries. Single-country studies can furnish insightful analyses, and can demonstrate causal claims couched in particular terms, but they are always open to the Kiplingesque objection ("What should they know of England, who only England know") – that whilst certain features might be vaunted as bulwarks of independence in a given country, those same features have either no effect in other settings, or are even actively harmful to independence. This work, by offering a comparative explanation, will be of relevance to all those in countries which are similarly situated to the ones described in this book. In the last chapter, I give some recommendations for PSB reform, recommendations which are applicable across a wide range of contexts.

Nevertheless, comparison trades depth for breadth. The country chapters in this book are all based, to varying degrees, on combinations of archival research, interviews and original language sources. Yet there are aspects in the histories of each broadcaster which are themselves worthy of a monograph. The comparative explanation I provide cannot readily account for the unusually conflictual relationship between Danmarks Radio and Danish politicians, nor for the unusually quiescent relationship between early "state" broadcasting in Ireland and Irish politicians. This is as it should be: all worthwhile explanations are reductive, and all reduction implies a loss in fidelity. The current vogue in political science for researchers, whether quantitative or qualitative in orientation, is to acknowledge the uncertainty and sources of error in their inferences. Accordingly, the penultimate chapter in the book revisits some of the predictions made in the light of the statistical results in Chapter 2.

8 Outline of the book

In this chapter, I have introduced the main arguments of the book – that broadcasters will be more independent if the legislation governing them grants them considerable legal protection, and if the broadcaster has embarked on a "professionalization project". The next chapter tests these arguments statistically, and also allows us to examine other rival explanations of political independence in terms of the partisanship of the bureaucracy and the polarization of the party system. Chapters 3 to 8 build upon the statistical findings of Chapter 2, and demonstrate what statistical results could not – namely that there is a strong link running from the size of the market for news, through professionalization, to greater independence. Each country chapter is itself part of a paired comparison: thus, longer chapters on Italy, Britain and Sweden are followed by shorter chapters on Spain, Ireland and Denmark, which act as checks on many of the inferences drawn. These country chapters are divided into three broad periods, which typically run from the foundation of the broadcaster to the post-war period; from the post-war period until the late 1970s and the end, in many countries, of the Keynesian consensus; and from that point until the present day. Within each period, I examine the history of the period, the key values of the broadcaster, the concrete rules it developed during that time, its structure and recruitment of staff, and cases of political interference during the period. In the last two chapters, I summarize the key findings of the country chapters. I rank the six broadcasters in terms of their degree of political independence, and examine whether the predictions made by the statistical model hold. I close by asking whether my arguments about past differences between countries can help us analyse current changes in media markets, and to better legislate for the future.

2   The broad picture

Testing rival theories of independence
on 36 public broadcasters

After defining the political independence of public broadcasters, and restricting
the analysis to those national-level public broadcasters operating in democratic
regimes, we can now turn to analysing and explaining the degree of political
independence that public broadcasters have. I start this chapter by proposing a
proxy measure for political independence, based on the turnover of chief executives of these broadcasters. This gives us an indication of which broadcasters are
more independent from the government of the day, and which are less so. I then
turn to existing explanations of public service broadcaster (PSB) independence,
in terms of party-system polarization and bureaucratic partisanship. After indi-
cating why these explanations are unsatisfactory, I then offer my own explanation of PSB independence. I do so by examining the motivations of each actor in
turn – politicians, journalists and managers – and suggest that legal protection
and the size of the market for news should have positive effects on PSB independence, with the latter factor in turn affecting independence through its consequences for journalistic professionalization and the spread of companies who
sell news wholesale: press agencies. Having described both my own explanation
and rival explanations, I turn in the last section of this chapter to test these explanations statistically, using data on 36 broadcasters worldwide. I close by discussing the fit of my statistical model of independence, and what it implies for the
historical chapters that follow.

1 Measuring independence by proxy

Just as there have been few comparative explanations of PSB independence,
there are few comparative measurements of independence. This is understandable. Given the definition of political independence above (p. 5), any "measure"
of independence would require a running reconstruction of the decisions of hun-
dreds of journalists throughout the PSB. Although journalists' own descriptions
of their work and answers to survey questions could carry us some way along
this path, they are unlikely to furnish us with measurements of independence
which can be applied with confidence to compare and/or rank PSBs in several
countries. I therefore use a proxy variable based on the turnover of the chief
executive of the broadcaster.

The practice of measuring the political independence of an institution by the turnover of its chief executives comes from the literature on central bank independence. Cukierman (1992) and Cukierman and Webb (1995) developed two proxies for independence: the rate of turnover (TOR) of central bank governors, and the political vulnerability index (VUL). TOR is equal to the reciprocal of the average tenure of the central bank governor in years. VUL is the percentage of government changes which were followed within six months by a change in the central bank governor. In adapting these indexes for the case of public broadcasting, I have calculated the turnover of the chief executive of the broadcaster. In countries with a dual board structure (supervisory board and executive board), this is the director-general or intendant. In countries with a single board structure (France, Bulgaria, Canada, Portugal, South Africa), it is the president of the broadcaster. Because higher values of TOR and VUL indicate lower independence, I average these two figures and subtract the result from one to get a proxy measure for independence, I:

$$I = 1 - \frac{TOR + VUL}{2}$$

Data on government changes is taken from Budge, Woldendorp and Keman (1998), Müller-Rommel, Fettelschoss and Harfst (2003) and subsequent issues of the *European Journal of Political Research*. Data on the turnover of chief executives has been taken from broadcasters' websites and a Lexis-Nexis news search.

The logic behind the use of TOR is as follows. Where chief executives are in office for a very short period of time, they lack knowledge of the broadcaster, and consequently lack capacity to defend it. By contrast, where the chief executive has been in office longer than one legislative term – and perhaps longer than many of the members of that legislature – then she will know more about the broadcaster and will be better able to defend it. Certainly, where the broadcaster is run by a string of short-term executives, it is likely to be in a dependent position vis-à-vis politicians. This is certainly the case with Hungarian broadcaster MTV, none of whose directors-general have served a full term, and where 6 of 14 directors have served less than a year in office.

The logic behind the use of VUL is as follows. If, following a new government, there is a change in the chief executive, then either the chief executive reached the end of her term, or left early. If she reached the end of her term, it may be that the terms of chief executives are designed so as to coincide with changes in government (the case with the Spanish system until 2006 and the current Estonian system).[1] If this is the case, then one may reasonably assume that the chief executive is, in some sense, the expression of a government choice. If the terms do not coincide by design, then the fact that they did so coincide may create this impression in any case. If, on the other hand, the chief executive left early, she was either constrained to resign, or did so of her own accord. If she was constrained to resign, then this most likely represents the introduction of some new constraint connected to the government. If she did so of her own accord, this may reflect a belief that the government should have a "clean slate" to influence the forthcoming selection of a chief executive.

The logic behind aggregating these two measures in a single proxy is twofold: first, the two measures may capture different aspects of political dependence; aggregating them may therefore allow us to pick up on certain aspects of independence which would not be noticed were just one indicator used.[2] Second, insofar as each indicator involves error, aggregating two measures can reduce the error present (Costner, 1969).

There are three principal advantages of this measure. First, the necessary data is readily available for a large number of cases. Table 2.1 shows independence scores for 36 broadcasters, with a total of 266 chief executives included. The temporal span of the data in many cases extends from either the broadcasters' foundation or first appointment under a democratic regime. Second, the measure permits statistical analyses of independence, not only because the measure is numerical and continuous, but also, following on from the previous point, because the large number of cases for which data is available means that linear regression analysis can be carried out.

Third, the measure correlates well with our pre-theoretical judgements of the independence of various PSBs, and with more direct measures of independence according to public opinion. Polls conducted in Denmark, Britain, Canada, France and Italy show that broadcasters with higher scores were more likely to be perceived as independent by the public. Of the respondents, 42% and 38% believed that the BBC and DR respectively were independent of the government (MORI, 2004; Danmarks Radio, 2006); a slightly lower percentage (35%) believed the Canadian Broadcasting Corporation (CBC) to be independent of the Canadian government (COMPAS, 1999). Some 22% of respondents thought that the French media in general was independent of political interests; in a subsequent question, France Télévisions was neither substantially more trusted nor substantially less trusted, suggesting that if a question had been asked about independence, France Télévisions would not score substantially better (CSA & Marianne, 2003). Finally, older internal polling for Rai showed that only 4.1% of respondents believed Rai to be "outside of politics", which I take to be equivalent to "politically independent" (Istituto Eurisko & Montesi, 1988). These responses match the broadcasters' ranking and relative distance according to Table 2.1. There are, however, a number of pitfalls with this measure. The first is that the measure always implies some dependence, since no broadcaster will have a "perfect score". Chief executives may retire from work, die in office or be poached by other television competitors – all reasons which are unrelated to the broadcaster's independence, but cause some increase in values of TOR or VUL. However, this will not affect the relative position of the broadcasters if, for example, the incidence of unrelated causes such as death, retirement or poaching is the same across all broadcasters.

A second related problem is that the measure loses discriminatory power above a certain point. BBC directors-general who have retired have done so after 7 or 10 years; SRG-SSR directors who have retired have done so after 20 years;

Table 2.1 Independence of PSBs worldwide

Country	PSB	Acronym	Independence
Argentina	Canal 7 Argentina	C7	n/a
Australia	Australian Broadcasting Corporation	ABC	0.91
Austria	Österreichischer Rundfunk	ORF	0.85
Belgium	Vlaamse Radio- en Televisieomroep	VRT	0.87
Belgium	Radio-Télévision Belge de la Communaute française	RTBF	0.79
Bulgaria	Bâlgarska Nationalna Televizija	BNT	0.27
Bulgaria	Bâlgarsko Nationalno Radio	BNR	0.56
Canada	Canadian Broadcasting Corporation	CBC	0.86
Chile	Televisión Nacional	TN	0.89
Croatia	Hrvatska Radiotelevizija	HRT	n/a
Cyprus	Cyprus Broadcasting Corporation	Cy/CBC	n/a
Czech Rep.	Cesky Rozhlas	CR	n/a
Czech Rep.	Ceská Televize	CTV	0.64
Denmark	Danmarks Radio	DR	0.89
Estonia	Eesti Raadio	EE/ER	n/a
Estonia	Eesti Televisioon	EE/ETV	0.82
Finland	Oy Yleisradio	YLE	0.92
France	France Télévision	FT	0.72
Germany	Zweites Deutsches Fernsehen	ZDF	0.91
Greece	Elliniki Radiophonia–Tileorassi SA	ERT	n/a
Hungary	Magyar Televizió	MTV	0.36
Iceland	Ríkisútvarpi	RUV	n/a
India	Prasar Bharati	BCI	n/a
Ireland	Radio Telefís Éireann	RTÉ	0.88
Israel	Israel Broadcasting Authority	IBA	0.79
Italy	Radiotelevisione Italiana	RAI	0.81
Japan	Nippon Housou Kyoukai	NHK	0.87
Korea	Korean Broadcasting Service	KBS	n/a
Latvia	Latvijas Valsts Televizija	LT	0.75
Lithuania	Lietuvos Radijas ir Televizija	LRT	0.53
Malta	Public Broadcasting Services Ltd.	PBS	n/a
Netherlands	Nederlandse Omroep Stichting	NOS	n/a
New Zealand	Television New Zealand	TVNZ	0.78
Norway	Norrikskringskasting	NRK	0.93
Poland	Polskie Radio SA	PR	0.75
Poland	Telewizja Polska	TVP	0.75
Portugal	Radiotelevisão Portuguesa SA	RTP	0.57
Romania	Societatea Româna de Televiziune	RO/TVR	0.65
Serbia and Montenegro	Radiotelevizija Srbije	RTS	n/a
Slovenia	Radiotelevizija Slovenija	RTVSLO	0.68
Slovenia	Slovenská Televizia	SK/STV	0.39
South Africa	South Africa Broadcasting Corporation	SABC	0.59
Spain	Television Española SA	TVE	0.56
Sweden	Sveriges Television Ab	SVT	0.86
Switzerland	SRG SSR idée suisse	SRG-SSR	0.96
United Kingdom	British Broadcasting Corporation	BBC	0.89
USA	Corporation for Public Broadcasting	CPB	0.75

but this difference, whilst it affects the value of TOR, is unlikely to reflect genuine differences in independence instead of greater competition for the first of these jobs. Third, the choice to count only changes of chief executive officer which happen within six months of a change in government is partly arbitrary. There are no good reasons why a change of chief executive 179 days after a change in government should be an indicator of dependence, whilst a change of chief executive 181 days after a change in government should not. In particular, where term lengths are very short, the government may wait until the next round of appointments before it intervenes. Following the election of the Berlusconi government in May 2001, it took nine months before the mandate of the then-current board, appointed by a previous left-wing government, expired. Yet the extraordinary levels of turnover at the top management (Hanretty, 2006, ch. 4) suggest that such turnover was "political", even if it fell outwith Cukierman and Webb's six-month window.

Additionally, the measure does not take into account anticipated reactions. Only one President of the US Corporation for Public Broadcasting (Martin Rubenstein) has resigned within six months of a change of US President or change in control of Congress, but three (John Macy, Donald Ledwig and Robert T. Coonrod) have resigned in the July preceding closely fought presidential elections (of which two resulted in a change of president). It is difficult to say whether these resignations were anticipated reactions; but interregna at the head of a public broadcaster facing an incoming Congress or executive opposed to it may be just as politically debilitating as interregna which come after the Congress or executive is re-elected.

Fourth, the measures concentrate on the chief executive in each PSB, prescinding from the fact that not all directors-general have the same power within their organization. If, for example, the director-general in a dual-board PSB enjoys little decision-making power, and if real power is instead concentrated in the supervisory board, then a better measure of independence might be the replacement rate of the supervisory board following changes in government. This objection is not particularly troubling: in PSBs with powerful boards, changes of boards might also occur following changes of government, but this does not preclude a change in director-general.

2 What explanations exist already?

Surprisingly little comparative work has been written about the politics of public broadcasting. Whilst there are a number of comparative works which deal with public service broadcasting – including many jeremiads lamenting its death (Tracey, 1998) – only a few (Etzioni-Halevy, 1987; Qualter, 1962; Smith & Ortmark, 1979) deal with the comparative politics of public service broadcasting. Different reasons can be given for this lack of scholarly interest. American social scientists (the most numerous kind) may ignore public broadcasting because it has negligible impact there. European social scientists may be distracted by non-political but European developments, such as the European

Union's attitude towards public service broadcasting as a potentially market-distorting form of state aid. Media scholars in general tend to concentrate either on the macro (global) or micro levels, ignoring the meso level of comparative study of nation-states and their media. Correspondingly, there are few factors which have been cited as explaining the degree of political independence of PSBs. In this section, I discuss four factors which have been mentioned in previous research: bureaucratic partisanship, party-system polarization, corruption and the rule of law, and public involvement.

2.1 Bureaucratic partisanship

The one factor which has been cited in a comparative work on public service broadcasting is the partisanship of the bureaucracy. "Since a public national broadcasting corporation exists in the same normative framework and in the same political arena as the government bureaucracy, it is likely to have some features in common with it" (Etzioni-Halevy, 1987, pp. 8–9). Etzioni-Halevy hypothesises that "countries that have party-politicised bureaucracies are also more likely to have party-politicised public broadcasting corporations as compared with other countries where the bureaucracies have become largely nonpartisan" (1987, p. 9). Suppose that, subsequent to the establishment of a public broadcaster, politicians engage in a search for appropriate models to guide their behaviour towards the broadcaster, using an availability heuristic (Tversky & Kahneman, 1973). Given that PSBs in certain respects resemble government departments more than corporations, politicians may use the same model that they use to govern their relationships with bureaucrats in their subsequent relationship with broadcasters. Where the model of politician–bureaucrat relations involves party-politicization, politicians will be used to giving partisan orders to bureaucrats, and will subsequently give such orders to broadcasters (and will expect them to be carried out). Where instead the model of politician–bureaucrat relations involves "professionalized" bureaucracy, politicians will be used to having bureaucrats disallow certain orders as incompatible with basic norms of professional conduct, and will thus not make partisan requests of broadcasters, and/or will accept broadcasters rebuffing such requests.

Conversely, the broadcaster might adopt the model of behaviour found in the bureaucracy. Tjernström (2000) argues that, in its early years, SVT's predecessor Radiotjänst modelled itself on the Swedish Telegrafstyrelse, a quasi-state institution which ran Radiotjänst's distribution network. It is plausible to see this imitation as a source of independence, insofar as Radiotjänst was able to cultivate a bureaucratic coalition to prevent nationalization (Hadenius, 1998, pp. 46–47). Unfortunately for this argument, Etzioni-Halevy (1987) found no support for the general hypothesis in her study of four PSBs (the BBC, the Australian Broadcasting Corporation, the Israeli Broadcasting Authority and the German ARD).

2.2 Party-system polarization

Hallin and Mancini claim that there is a link between "polarized pluralism" – a type of party system characterized by significant extreme or anti-system parties at either end of the political spectrum, buttressing a number of centrist parties (Sartori, 2005, p. 116) – and greater "political parallelism and instrumentalization". This is because "the notion of politically neutral journalism is less plausible where a wide range of competing world views contend" (Hallin & Mancini, 2004, p. 61). Their view is echoed by PSB journalists and managers. Rai's London correspondent wrote that,

> [w]hereas in Britain, the existing agreement of "90% of the people on 90% of the issues" (Sir Winston Churchill's figures) leaves ample scope to "non-controversial" political broadcasts, the disagreement between government and pro-Communist opposition runs deep to the foundations of the national constitution which makes it very difficult, and often impossible, to plead absolute impartiality.
>
> (Orlando, 1954)

Or, again, for Giovanni Cesareo and other Marxist commentators:

> In truth, equidistance is a sheer abstraction in a society divided into opposing classes … In this situation one cannot help but stand for one of the two sides: it is for this reason that "objectivity" and "impartiality" are only masks of the domination of those who are in power.
>
> (Cesareo, 1970, p. 132)

The sentiment is not restricted to Italy. Oliver Whitley, chief assistant to the BBC director-general, claimed that "the nation divided always has the BBC on the rack" (quoted in Briggs, 1979, ch. 1). Nevertheless, there remain many problems with this explanation. First, it is not clear precisely what kind of polarization is required. Mancini and Hallin refer not to polarization per se but to polarized pluralism, a type of party system defined by a number of variables (including prolonged periods of government by the same party or same set of parties, which may have its own effects on independence). Second, certain measures of polarization which concentrate on manifesto policy proposals suggest that there were low levels of polarization in Italy (author's calculations using data from Budge, Klingemann, Volkens & Bara, 2001, according to the method of Sigelman & Yough, 1978; cf. Evans, 2002, pp. 168–169).

Third, it is not obvious that the argument holds outside two polar cases of the UK (at least during the period of Butskellite consensus) and Italy. Finland has often been cited as a case of polarization (and polarized pluralism), but Finnish broadcaster YLE does not show the same levels of political dependence as Rai (Raunio & Wiberg, 2003; Evans, 2002, p. 162). Fourth, Hallin and Mancini are extremely charitable in interpreting which countries share the characteristics of polarized pluralism, given that they "apply it to countries such as Spain and Portugal, which had a form of polarized pluralism only during brief periods of democracy early in the twentieth century" (2004, p. 61). Fifth, the explanation may hold within countries across time, but not across countries. Thus, points of great conflict between government and broadcaster may occur in times of national polarization, but these may be fluctuations around a baseline level of conflict or independence which has little or nothing to do with polarization.

2.3 A note on the role of the public

In his classic study of the Tennessee Valley Authority, Philip Selznick (1949) demonstrated how that authority protected itself from other over-powering federal agencies by co-opting the grass-roots. The Tennessee Valley Authority's grass-roots were better organized than the amorphous audience of the PSB, but there remains a sense in which the independence of the public broadcaster can be preserved by mobilizing the public in the same way. Should the broadcaster be subject to political interference, the broadcaster could mobilize public outrage in order to force the politicians to back down. However, it is not obvious either that interference in the broadcaster need be visible to the public, or that the public should value the independence of the broadcaster over other benefits. Attempts to interfere may be made at a relatively dry, institutional level – as Sveriges Radio's director-general Olof Rydbeck noted, "One could hardly 'mobilise the storm troopers' – SR certainly had millions of listeners and viewers, but they were totally uninterested in SR as an institution" (Thurén, 1997, p. 110). Conversely, where interference has been overt and particular, public outrage has often been lacking. This is the case in Italy, where those movements which have protested most strongly against Berlusconi's interference in Rai – the so-called *girotondisti* – have been movements of limited breadth recruited principally from the middle classes, and particularly from academic and cultural milieux. The role of the public in this book is therefore fairly limited.

3 My explanation

3.1 What do politicians want?

By politicians, I mean individuals who hold elected office, typically, but not exclusively, at national level. Only these individuals have both the necessary interest in intervening in the work of the PSB and the necessary rights to intervene in the PSB through effective measures. Non-elected individuals, such as party press officers, also intervene in PSBs, but I assume that they act on behalf of politicians.

We can typically locate politicians in some kind of political space. We are usually familiar with these *n*-dimensional spaces in our respective polities. One common space has two axes, one which runs between left- and right-wing political positions, and another which runs between authoritarian and libertarian political positions. Call each politician's position in this space his/her *ideal point*.

Most politicians are vote-seekers, and act purposefully so as to maximize or satisfice their vote share, given their ideal point. That is, they choose from the set of possible actions that action which will result in the greatest additional number of votes won. By implication, politicians do not act vis-à-vis a broadcaster because they are angry, or because they just feel like it. As vote-seekers, politicians are only interested in the PSB insofar as it actually affects, or is perceived to affect, their share of votes.[3]

Of the variety of types of output produced by public broadcasters, news and current affairs is the category most obviously linked to politics and thereby to voting. Hereafter when I talk about "broadcast output", I refer exclusively to news and current affairs. Other types of output, including comedy and drama, are "political", and do have an impact on politics (Baumgartner & Morris, 2006), but I leave them out in the name of parsimony.

Broadcast output, understood in this sense, actually affects vote shares, though not by very much. In the United States, DellaVigna and Kaplan (2007) showed that the introduction of Fox News into certain media markets caused an increase of between 0.4 and 0.7% in the share of votes won by Republican candidates. In Italy, Sani and Legnante (2001) have shown very strong associations between Rai and Mediaset viewership and voting for the centre-left and centre-right respectively.

Irrespective of the truth or falsity of these findings, broadcast output is *perceived* to affect vote shares. This is particularly true for politicians, who typically over-estimate the impact of the media relative to the general population and relative to academic scepticism about the direct relationship between media and votes (Johansson, 2004; Krauss, 1998, p. 681). Thus, politicians will even be interested in broadcasters like PSBs which disdain the influence wielded by channels like Fox.

In a certain sense, we can "map" broadcast output onto the same political space inhabited by politicians. That is, for the example political space mentioned above, there is such a thing as more right-wing content or more left-wing content, more authoritarian content or more libertarian content. Attempts have been made to map newspaper (Ho & Quinn, 2008) and television (Groseclose & Milyo, 2005) output onto a common political space with moderate success, but it seems entirely plausible to imagine that broadcast output can be informally mapped onto some political space and that politicians do in fact map content in this way. If one grants that broadcast output can be mapped in this way, then one can also readily grant that broadcast output which is close to the ideal point of a certain politician or group of politicians increases the vote-share for that politician or group of politicians, other things being equal. That is, left-wing content translates to votes for left-wing parties.[4]

From these assumptions about politicians' goals and media content, it follows that politicians act towards the PSB so as to move the output it produces closer to their ideal point. Unfortunately for politicians, they cannot unilaterally shift the PSB's output. At the most basic level, politicians cannot write the news themselves, but must rely on others to do so. More generally, three factors intervene between politicians and broadcast output: the flow of events, the type of journalists at the PSB and the managers who supervise them. By events, I mean things that happen in the real world that have some connection to politics, and which serve as the input for any kind of news production process. Examples of events, from most dramatic to least dramatic, include elections, cabinet reshuffles, political scandals, passage of legislation, reports on economic conditions, reports on social conditions, and so on. There is a steady stream of events, and these events can be more or less favourable for an individual politician or group of politicians. To some degree, politicians and their aides can create events, but they compete with other potentially more dramatic and less artificial events.

We normally have expectations about the kind of coverage that will result from a given event, and whether it will be favourable for a given group of politicians or will reflect negatively upon them. If some event happens which we naively think will reflect badly on the government and will reflect well on the principal opposition party – for example, if the government is forced to abandon a new policy and revert to an old policy introduced by the opposition when in government – then it seems likely that the content produced from this event will be closer to the opposition's ideal point than the government's (assuming, of course, that content can be mapped in this way).

Politicians are no different from us in this respect: they too have expectations about content. These expectations are not wishful thinking: that is, they are not systematically biased by the desires of the politician in question. By bias, I mean bias away from the kind of content which would be produced by an ideal observer in the sense given by Roderick Firth, as a spectator who is "omniscient ... omnipercipient ... disinterested ... [and] dispassionate" (Firth, 1952, pp. 333–340) and who, one supposes, has unlimited newsprint or screen-time to fill.[5] Due to lack of information or expertise, politicians' expectations about content might never be exactly the same as those of an impartial spectator, but they are often not far away. If the output of a PSB can be shifted very far from this point, then intervention becomes worthwhile; but if journalists do, in fact and in perception, hew fairly close to the line ploughed by an impartial observer, then intervention becomes fruitless. If they are to evaluate intervening in the PSB's work, they need to know how far output can be nudged from that notional content produced by an impartial observer – and that requires knowing about the beliefs and practices of journalists and managers.

3.2 What do journalists do?

There are such things as journalists: machines for turning events into broadcast content. There are two ideal types of journalists: partisan journalists and nonpartisan journalists. Distinguishing between different types of journalists on the basis of their job orientation is a well-established tradition in media research, and a number of typologies have been produced. The number of types in these typologies is not always the same, but the key distinction I wish to make here is similar to Donsbach and Patterson's distinction between the "neutral journalist ... who does not routinely and consistently take sides in partisan or policy disputes [and] the advocate journalist [who] takes sides and does so in a consistent, substantial and aggressive way" (2004, p. 265). Partisan journalists have ideal points in the same political space inhabited by politicians, though they need not be the same ideal points as any particular politician. Thus, if politicians could staff the broadcasters with partisan journalists who shared their ideal points, and could be assured of no interference by management, then they could nudge content away from the notional content that would be produced by an impartial observer. By saying this, I do not mean to imply that non-partisan journalists do not have ideal points in the same political space, only that these ideal points are not relevant. After all, journalists are, by the nature of their job, heavily involved in and interested by public life. It would consequently be abnormal if they did not have some policy preferences.

> He would be a bad journalist if he took no interest in the world around him and an unlikely human being if that interest did not father opinions; but in the office he has to stand back from the opinions, distance himself and keep them out of his work ... [Non-partisan journalists] suppress [their] views and it is an effort.
>
> (Taylor, 1975, p. 3)

We can think of journalists as having production functions which turn events into output. These production functions differ according to the type of journalist. For non-partisan journalists, output is a function of the position that the event "has" (E), and of the rules that the journalist is obliged to follow (r). This function is not exact, because the practice of journalism is not exact. Many contingencies affect broadcast output: the fact that the treasury minister could not be found to explain in front of camera the decision s/he had taken; that the broadcast item was cut from three to two minutes, requiring the statement from the Green Party also to be cut; that the presentation given by the opposition party was aesthetically appealing; and so on. We can therefore think of the output which is actually produced as a single draw from lots of possible outputs.

Because we are describing the production function of non-partisan journalists, we know that there is no ideal point which affects the journalist's judgement, and so we can describe the production function as a draw from a distribution centred on E. The non-partisan journalist is thus much more likely than not to produce output that is very close to the "theoretically conceivable condition of unbias". This does not tell us whether the output actually produced on a given occasion will be far away from E or not. The journalist may be inexperienced and produce very variable output; this may on a number of occasions result in output which is very far from the output which would be produced by a more experienced observer (see Figure 2.1(a)), and which would be perceived

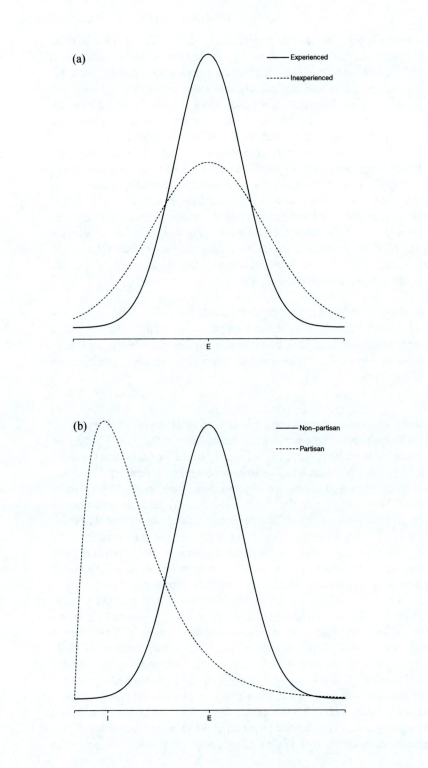

(a)

Experienced
Inexperienced

E

(b)

Non-partisan
Partisan

I   E

(c)

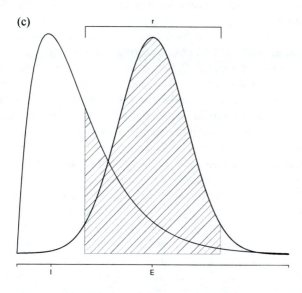

Figure 2.1 Schematic representations of journalists.

by politicians as evidence of journalistic partisanship. Whether output is in fact far from *E* or not depends upon the rules that the journalist is obliged to follow, to which I return below.

The production function for the partisan journalist also depends on the event to be covered, and the rules that she is obliged to follow. Again, the production function can be thought of as a draw from numerous possible treatments of the event – a given distribution with a given mean. Here, however, the distribution of possible treatments of the event is not centred on *E*, but somewhere between that position and the ideal point of the journalist (*I*). Precisely where the centre point of this distribution would be is not specified: perhaps it is at the ideal point (particularly if *E* and *I* are close), or perhaps it is half-way between the two points (see Figure 2.1(b)). The key argument I wish to make is that some draws from these distributions will be judged "out of bounds" by the rules the broadcaster sets. More particularly, I wish to claim that these rules disallow treatments of events which diverge from the treatment that would be given by an ideal observer, and thereby constrain output. This kind of situation is depicted visually in Figure 2.1(c). The figure shows the two distributions from which the partisan and non-partisan journalist respectively draw their coverage. However, only part of that coverage – the shaded part – is "ruled in" by the rules at work in the broadcaster. Since higher values of *r* reflect more constraining rules, the line becomes shorter the more constraining rules are. The rules I am talking about are rules which typically enjoin certain values on journalists (fairness, impartiality, objectivity, neutrality, truthfulness, etc.), forbid certain practices (impersonation of others, stealing of documents, naming of minors), and set up some structure by which to arbitrate these values (complaints committees, ethics boards, ombudsmen, even courts).

How might these rules work to constrain output to within a reasonable distance of E? One classic example is the two-source rule, namely that any claim must be backed up two sources. Suppose that journalists gather interviews with government officials to ascertain the motive for war in Iraq. Suppose further that one irate source claims that the sole motive for war is George W. Bush's anger at Saddam Hussein's attempted assassination attempt of Bush's father. Were this claim to be included in a treatment of the decision to invade, it would result in output which was extremely critical of the US government, and probably be interpreted as far to the left. (This claim is very likely untrue; but what is more important is that if it had been true, more people within the US government would likely have said so). Thus, the two-source rule prevents departure from E due to the willingness of some people to say anything to be featured in the news.

Another common rule is to require journalists to solicit comment from all parties to a dispute. Were only some parties heard in a discussion of some issue, it might prevent relevant facts from being aired. (Nowadays it is more common to hear this rule cited, not to justify the participation of a given individual, but rather to give a reason for their lack of participation: "the minister was asked to appear on the show but declined to do so", which also serves a protective function.) We can therefore be more precise about the production functions described above. Suppose that there is some set of rules r, which varies in scope (covering more or fewer issues) and in rigidity (permitting more or fewer practices with respect to a particular issue, or being more specific about how an issue should be treated). The greater the value of r, the more possible treatments far away from E will be discarded. We can think of a partisan journalist's production function as a draw from a normal distribution centred somewhere on the line EI, but where draws which are more than r's length away from E are discarded.

3.3 Management

Journalists do not act alone, but are recruited and organized by managers. By the management of the broadcaster, I mean those who sit on the board of the broadcaster, as well as either the chief executive officer of the broadcaster or the members of any executive board. The management of the broadcaster ordinarily has multiple goals which are common to many executives in organizations: these include esteem, operational autonomy and personal or organizational income.

The management of the broadcaster determines the stock of journalists, and affects broadcast output by promoting, demoting, recruiting or dismissing journalists. Management can thus move output closer to a given point in policy space by promoting or recruiting partisan journalists who have ideal points close to that particular point, or by demoting or dismissing partisan journalists who hold ideal points far from that point. Management has approximate knowledge of which journalists are partisan, and the direction of their partisanship. Selective personnel changes of this kind will be ineffective in moving output closer to a desired point in policy space if many journalists are non-partisan, or if rules are highly constraining. The resulting output will continue to approximate the kind of output produced by a disinterested observer. Conversely, selective personnel changes will be effective where all or some journalists are partisan and rules provide only loose constraints. Selective personnel changes of this kind are not normally conducive to management goals as listed above. Those passed over resent it; those rewarded attribute their rise to their political patrons, not to management. Management must therefore be induced to move output closer to a particular point in policy space, or must be replaced by suitably motivated individuals through politicians' power of appointment. If managers are to resist attempts by politicians to move output to a closer point, they must know how to prevent the kind of interventions that would negatively affect goals such as operational autonomy and personal or organizational income.

3.4 Politicians' interventions, and how to pre-empt them

Interventions consist of sanctions, rewards and appointments. A sanction is any action which decreases management goal-satisfaction, including reductions in management esteem, operational autonomy and personal or organizational income. Conversely, a reward is any action which increases management goal-satisfaction (esteem, operational autonomy and personal or organizational income). Interventions are of two types: actions which politicians may undertake because the law grants elected officials the right to perform that action, and all other actions. Call this second type of intervention an "informal intervention".

A number of informal interventions are possible: politicians may write letters to the PSB criticizing coverage; may request to meet members of management and discuss particular issues with them; may organize licence-fee non-payment campaigns; may refuse to appear on PSB programmes; and so on. These methods of intervening may have certain psychological effects on the broadcaster: no one likes to be thought badly of, and executives or journalists might try to avoid such criticism in future by making sure that no similar event prompts politicians' ire. However, these informal interventions are likely to depend for their effectiveness on the politicians' ability to take further, legal, actions which may have far more potent effects on the broadcaster. For this reason, informal intervention is likely to be a poor strategy for inducing the broadcaster to produce output at close to the politician's ideal point; intervention through actions stipulated in law is instead likely to be a dominant strategy. I henceforth concentrate on "formal" interventions. Interventions of this type are not always possible, or consequential: the law may limit the frequency or magnitude of such actions. Other things being equal, the more the law limits the frequency or magnitude of sanctions, rewards or appointments, the more independent the broadcaster will be. This degree of legal protection is discussed further in section 4.3.

Where politicians believe that all journalists are non-partisan, or that rules are highly constraining, the management of the broadcaster can claim that the news produced by the broadcaster is dictated by the nature of the events themselves.

Consequently, there is no benefit to be had by intervening, since any new personnel, or any new pressure, could not alter the kind of output produced; politicians therefore refrain from intervening. Politicians' beliefs about the partisanship of journalists are not formed through the same process as management beliefs about the partisanship of journalists, and thus the two sets of beliefs are likely to diverge. In particular, politicians may falsely believe that journalists are more partisan than they actually are. Politicians' beliefs about the partisanship of journalists come from three sources. First, politicians keep track of the kind of output they expect given a particular event (expected output), and the actual output produced concerning that event. Politicians attribute the difference between expected output and actual output to journalistic partisanship. Second, politicians may have more direct knowledge of journalistic partisanship through their personal contacts with journalists. Third, politicians may infer that journalists are partisans on the basis of previous action by (other) politicians. That is, if politicians intervened in the broadcaster at some previous time, those politicians must have believed journalists to be partisans, and this is a good reason for believing journalists to be partisan. If politicians believe that journalists are partisan, they will consider intervention in order to secure output closer to their ideal point. They may do so even if they believe that journalists are co-partisans: they may intervene in order to reward these individuals. Or, they may do so if they believe journalists within the broadcaster are partisan, but that their sympathies are divided equally between all parties. Let us say that if intervention is possible (and legal protection means that this is not always the case), and if politicians believe journalists to be partisan, intervention will be attempted.

Attempted interventions are *defeasible*. An intervention is based upon beliefs about expected output, journalistic partisanship and the degree to which rules constrain. If management can demonstrate that these beliefs are in error, the claim can be defeased. Specifically, an intervention is defeasible if the management causes politicians to believe that:

1   journalists are less partisan than politicians think they are, or
2   rules constrain more than politicians think they do, or
3   their expectations about output conditional on some event were implausible.

Direct evidence of journalistic partisanship is hard to convey, in particular if it is evidence that journalists are non-partisan. Recall that according to the definition given above, non-partisan journalists are typically journalists who abstain from taking positions. In response to management claims that no evidence has been found that a given journalist or group of journalists has taken a position in the past, politicians might well respond that "absence of evidence is not evidence of absence".[6] Conversely, evidence that rules constrain is relatively easy to convey. In particular, explicit collections of rules can be distributed to politicians in order to demonstrate the rules followed by the broadcaster (see pp. 111–151). A demonstration that rules constrain defeases a politician's intervention by convincing him or her that there cannot be large differences between the output that would be produced by an ideal spectator and the actual output of the broadcaster, or that if there is a difference, this difference is not due to the partisanship of journalists, since this partisan impact would be dampened by constraining rules.

It is more common for these rules to arise in the context of a specific item to which politicians object. Here the argument is slightly different, and the emphasis on the constraining effect of rules is less. Typically the broadcaster argues that the purportedly objectionable coverage was in conformity with a rule followed by the broadcaster and, insofar as it is in conformity with this rule, it is not objectionable. (Implicit in this argument is the counterfactual: had the coverage not been in conformity with the rule, you would have been right to object to it; but had it not been in conformity with this rule we would not have broadcast it anyway.) In any case, this argument is not sound, for it relies upon the unspoken major premise that "whatever is in conformity with the broadcaster's rules is unobjectionable".

Politicians' responses to such a defence are deeply unsatisfactory. First, they may use non-rational means, and repeat their objection in a louder voice or with greater drama; but the more vociferously the politician repeats his or her objection, the more this objection resembles pure power-politics and the naked promise of future sanctions or rewards. As O'Neill notes,

> There are strong social norms against an explicit threat, and violating them infuses the target with new attitudes and utilities beyond the motives inherent in the objective situation ... An individual under an ultimatum is likely to stiffen, since acquiescing means a loss of face.
>
> (1991, pp. 95–96)

Thus, using non-rational means may be counterproductive. Second, politicians may challenge the minor premise of the argument, namely that the coverage was not in conformity with the cited rule. This, however, is a difficult claim for the politician to make, since it relies on the assertion that the politician knows how to apply the broadcaster's rules better than the broadcaster itself does. This claim can occasionally be made on those (relatively) rare occasions when the politician in question has worked in the broadcaster (see p. 122), but it is otherwise unlikely to be convincing. Additionally, even where the coverage does seem to violate a certain rule or at least not uphold it, the broadcaster may be able to cite additional rules which permit exceptions. Whilst I would not argue that the rules PSBs develop are as detailed as jurisprudence or public administrative procedure, it seems that the politician in this situation is placed "more and more into the position of a dilettante" facing "the unavoidably increasing weight of expertly trained officials" in Weber's (1991, p. 89) classic phrase. Third, the politician may challenge the major premise – that the rules the broadcaster has generally produce desirable effects. Cognitively speaking, this task is tremendously difficult, and requires the politician to think in synthesis about the broadcaster's approach to its entire work. Moreover this strategy may not be tenable where the politician has previously accepted the specific rule, or the rule-set of which it forms part. Politicians may then be accused of inconsistency: "you favoured this rule [or rule-set] six months ago when it favoured you, but now that it acts against you, you reject it, and are therefore hypocritical." Sometimes this strategy is linked with greater knowledge of what politicians actually committed to (see p. 129); it is, however, likely to be unsuccessful when deployed against emerging parties who have not accepted the rule-set. If an intervention cannot be defeased – that is, if there is no evidence that management can bring to bear which would convince politicians that the gap between the output they expected and the actual output was not due to journalistic partisanship – then the intervention can be *defused*. An intervention is defused where management admits that mistakes were made, but that such mistakes were made not because of journalistic partisanship, but because of inadequately constraining rules; and where management promises that the rules will be revised to ensure that mistakes of this nature will not occur again. Defusing an intervention pre-empts sanctioning: by constraining journalists even further, the management signals to politicians that any subsequent intervention will likely be ineffective because any selective changes in personnel desired by the politicians will be rendered null and void by the dampening effect of rules. In order to avoid interventions which could potentially reduce goal satisfaction, managers who value any of the goals discussed above – esteem, operational autonomy and personal or organizational income – should encourage the development of rules constraining output. Yet in order to do this, management must be aware of the option to develop such rules, and must gain the consent of journalists. The first requirement – that managers be aware of the option to develop such rules – sounds trivial, but is not. Literature on organizational decision-making has shown how solutions often emerge from a garbage-can process, where the availability of suitable examples dominates. Management is more likely to be aware of the option of developing such rules where analogous rules have already been developed by other content providers or journalistic associations. The second requirement – that management gain the consent of journalists – is also affected in the same way: journalists are more likely to consent to such rules where other similarly placed journalists in other media organizations have also consented to such rules, or where journalists as a whole have consented to such rules. Whether other journalists have agreed to such rules, it shows journalists in the public broadcaster that their peers have evaluated the consequences of rule-adoption and found them to be positive. That is, journalists must see the benefit of adopting rules. Part of the reason for journalists adopting such rules is that they understand the role that these rules play in defending the broadcaster, and thus defending many factors which indirectly affect them, such as the broadcaster's funding stream. In other words, they understand that the rules may ultimately become a source of protection for them. Protection requires that the same body which creates, revises or otherwise maintains the rules continue in office for a certain time. If management is subject to constant turnover, there is no guarantee that rules implemented one year will not be ripped up the year after. The need to convince journalists also suggests that rules developed by politicians and imposed on the broadcaster cannot play the role that the theory requires of them. There are two reasons for excluding such rules. The first of these relies on the generalization that rules imposed by outsiders, particularly for complex tasks, are generally less well followed than rules developed independently (Locke, 2000, pp. 416–417). The second is that rules imposed by some group of politicians may not find favour with all politicians. They therefore fail to play the role taken on by independently developed rules, since there is little guarantee that journalists who follow such rules will not be left out in the cold if these rules are torn up by an incoming government.[7]

3.5 How do these rules come about?

Above I hypothesized that rules analogous to the kind of rules employed in PSBs were more likely to have been developed in a given country the larger[8] the market for news in that country. More particularly, I argue that this proceeds through two different paths: first, the larger the market for news in a given country, the more likely journalists in that country are to embark on a professionalization project, producing rules which raise their status. Second, the larger the market for news in a given country, the more likely it is that news wholesalers – press agencies – will develop, and form a homogenized news product produced precisely through rules governing content.

3.5.1 Through journalists' professionalization project

First, the larger the market for newspapers, the greater the division of labour. In the market for newspapers, the historical expansion of the market meant that the job of typesetting the newspaper became separate from the job of writing, editing and publishing it. Later, the job of writing and editing – that is, the journalistic part of the process – was separated from the job of publishing the newspaper. Consequently, as the market grew, the more it became appropriate to talk of "journalists" instead of owner-editors or publishers. Second, the larger the market – that is, the larger the number of newspapers sold, relative to population in absolute terms – the larger the number of entrants, assuming that fixed costs are present and are otherwise equal, and that firms enter the market until marginal revenue equals marginal cost. The larger the number of entrants, the larger the absolute number of journalists required to produce content for these entrants. Third, the larger the market, and the larger the accounting profit of the players in the market, the more wages for journalists will be able to support full-time journalists. High circulation of Scandinavian newspapers enabled market players to accumulate economic resources and "therefore to offer the journalists decent salaries that made it unnecessary for them to seek other sources of income" (Høyer, Hadenius & Weibull, 1975, quoted in Hallin & Mancini, 2004, p. 170). Retallack (1993, p. 184) notes that journalism in Germany at the beginning of the 19th century was almost always "a secondary occupation or *Nebenberuf*, that almost never yielded sufficient income on its own", but that this changed rapidly such that by 1848 those pursuing journalism as a primary occupation outnumbered those pursuing it as a secondary occupation by three to one. Fourth, the larger the absolute and relative numbers of journalists, and the more journalists perceive themselves as journalists instead of editors or publishers, the greater their awareness of potential shared interests and the need for some structure to pursue them. In the era when a single journalist wrote the entire content of a newspaper and engaged with a publisher to do so, any question of broader interests could easily have been subsumed under the rubric of the entirely individual personal relationship between the journalist in question and his publisher. Because journalists' shared interests were only partly concerned with financial remuneration, and were also concerned with non-financial incentives such as status, journalists have not always organized by forming trade unions; or, if they did, these trade unions were atypical, in that a primary concern was not the development of a mechanism for collective wage-bargaining and for dictating the terms of labour, but rather developing standards to govern what they produced. That is, they began a project of professionalization.

By professionalization, I mean the process by which those who practise a particular occupation, in order to secure both economic and social interests (in particular, an increase in social standing), form themselves into a group, standardize and systematize the knowledge they use in their occupation, and restrict or limit entry to the group, often through requiring entrants to adopt this same, standardized, systematized knowledge (Sarfatti Larson, quoted in MacDonald, 1995, p. 11). This process is most clear – and has been most successful – in the fields of law and medicine, occupations which are very clearly based on "advanced, or complex, or esoteric, or arcane knowledge" (MacDonald, 1995, p. 1).

To apply this concept to journalism may seem less appropriate given that (1) knowledge of how to report current events is less obviously complex or esoteric than, say, law;[9] or that (2) the entry requirements to journalism are typically less demanding than the entry requirements for either medicine or law. It may seem particularly inappropriate in countries like Britain, where a plurality of journalists prefer to describe their occupation as a "craft", rather than as a "profession" (Delano, 2002). Nevertheless, journalists have embarked upon this process of professionalization across Europe, succeeding to different degrees. Indeed, the concept of professionalization – and degrees of success in professionalizing the occupation of journalism, form one of the key *differentia* in the leading typology of media systems (Hallin & Mancini, 2004).

The references to standardized knowledge should make clear the link between professionalization and rules. These rules are adopted by journalists not because they serve to restrict entry, but rather because they help in boosting journalists' status. As Weber (1991, p. 208) noted, voluntary submission to rules can boost status:

> Strict discipline and control, which at the same time has consideration for the official's sense of honour, and the development of prestige sentiments of the status group, as well as the possibility of public criticism, work in the direction of strict mechanization ... A strong status sentiment among

officials not only agrees with the official's readiness to subordinate himself
... status sentiments are the consequence of such subordination, for internally they balance the official's self-feeling.

This link has been explicitly noted in studies of journalism. The insistence on a
body of advanced, or complex, or esoteric knowledge becomes "a prominent
component of news journalists' occupational ideology", linked in part to the
concept of professionalism (Aldridge & Evetts, 2003, p. 558). Professionalism
serves journalists' needs for prestige – which are greater than before thanks to
the influx of graduate and postgraduate trainees. "It is a discourse of self-control,
even self-belief, an occupational badge or marker which ... enables workers to
justify and emphasize the importance of their work to themselves and others"
(Aldridge & Evetts, 2003, pp. 556, 555). Thus, journalists in countries with large
markets for news, who had formed associations like the Swedish Publicistklubben or the Austrian Presseclub Concordia, developed rules which had as their
primary function an increase in the social standing of journalists. They were, in
every sense, "honour courts", where journalists could demonstrate the binding

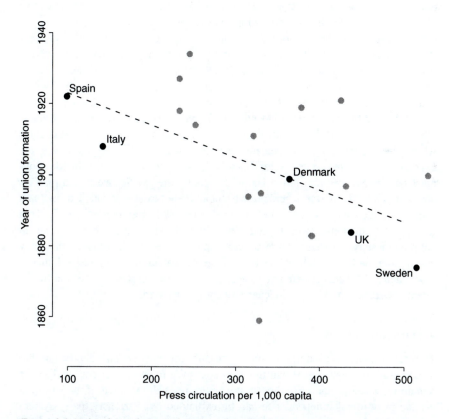

Figure 2.2 Union formation as a function of market size.

commitments they had contracted amongst themselves, and thereby demonstrate their merit.

The link between the size of the market and the formation of professional associations can be seen in Figure 2.2, which shows the relationship between press circulation, in daily newspaper copies per 1,000 population in 1975,[10] and the date of formation of a journalists' association or union.[11] The correlation is moderate to strong ($r=-0.52$), and negative as expected. Bigger markets for news – on a per capita basis – do lead to earlier union formation. We may therefore use the size of the market for news as a very loose proxy for union formation, and the pursuit, by journalists, of a professionalization project.

3.5.2 Through press agencies

With the expansion of the market of news and consequent division of labour, opportunities arose for intermediaries who could act as "wholesalers" of news. These intermediaries – press agencies – invested to create networks of correspondents who could cover a breadth of events which could not be matched by any single newspaper. They made money on their investment by selling the same copy, produced by their correspondents, to multiple news outlets. In order to be attractive to a variety of outlets, the news produced by press agency correspondents had to meet certain demands, including not being "slanted" lest it conflict with either the particular editorial or implicit slant of a given newspaper, or the expressed desire of a given newspaper not to provide such slanted information. It was also, however, desirable that this news be relatively homogeneous in its structure: in other words, that it be regular. Press agencies therefore had certain rules of composition which were followed by their correspondents, which made agency copy regular, structurally homogenous and thus relatively easy to sell to competing newspapers. Thus, where press agencies exist, it becomes possible for a PSB to draw on, or cite the example of, rules for content established by press agencies. We see this development both in Sweden and in the United Kingdom, the two largest media markets considered here. However, where press agencies do not exist – or where, as in Spain and Italy, these agencies existed but operated not according to market incentives but to support from non-democratic regimes – such development is not possible. In between these two extremes there are cases of countries which, although they may have media markets which are relatively large per capita, either lacked a domestic news agency (Ireland) or had a news agency which was more of a consortia of different newspapers and less an independent entity (Denmark).

4 Data and model

Thus far, we have settled upon a proxy measure for independence, and a number of potential explanations of that independence. We must now operationalize the remaining variables, and use those numbers to assess how much of the variation we see in political independence can be explained by, variously, party-system polarization, bureaucratic partisanship, the size of the market for news, and the degree of legal protection afforded the broadcaster. At the same time, we can test whether these factors have a statistically significant effect, or whether we can remove them from our models.

4.1 Polarization and bureaucratic partisanship

To operationalize polarization, I use the unweighted range of party left–right scores for each country for parties reported in Huber and Inglehart (1995). Huber and Inglehart's measures are used in preference to other data, since they track party position rather than policy stands: to the extent that polarization is thought to affect independence negatively, it is through the broadcasting of extreme politicians' statements, rather than politicians' extreme policy proposals. To operationalize the partisanship of the bureaucracy, I use data from the International Institute of Management Development, which includes in its survey of business executives a question on whether "public service ... is [or is not] independent from political interference" (International Institute for Management Development, 2006, p. 376). Scores range from 1 to 6; higher scores indicate lower partisanship. Values for the partisanship of the bureaucracy were imputed in three cases using the mean.[12]

4.2 Size of the market for news

To measure the size of the market for news, I use data on press circulation per 1,000 population from 1975. The year 1975 is used because there is reliable data available for this year, since later data would in certain cases be later than the early years of the broadcaster (thus implying reverse causation), and because there is some comparable data for countries which did not exist in 1975.[13] Newspaper circulation is used because newspapers are the medium that concentrates most on news instead of entertainment generally, because markets in radio and television have for much of the period been state monopolies or otherwise restricted markets, and because newspapers have had a historical role in setting norms for journalism, both in general and through operating as recruitment pools for companies in other media. Because newspaper circulation in communist countries was artificially inflated, I also use a dichotomous control variable to account for this inflation.[14]

4.3 Legal protection

Above, I argued that politicians' interventions ultimately rely for their efficacy on the legal possibilities open to politicians by virtue of their office. Here I expand on the two types of legal possibility: sanctioning and rewarding the broadcaster.

   We can construct three broad categories of legal possibility for sanctioning:

- psychological sanctions which result from repeated parliamentary oversight;
- *ex ante* restrictions on the operation of the broadcaster which reduce organizational autonomy and can be used as bargaining chips; and

- *ex post* sanctions such as reductions in funding levels or the threat of reappointment.

Parliamentary and governmental oversight plays a dual role in the literature on principal–agent problems in politics. Typically, it is cited as an example of how politicians can compel their agents – bureaucrats, executive agencies, etc. – to release information, thus reducing the asymmetry in information between the two. This reduces the agent's ability to shirk, since politicians can now deploy sanctions more judiciously in the light of better information. Oversight also, however, plays a role in sanctioning. Aggressive or repeated questioning which implies criticism negatively affects personal and organizational esteem and reputation. Where agents value these goods, they may try to prevent such questioning in the future by a number of strategies: by avoiding the particular type of content which prompted the questioning; by pursuing bland and inoffensive content which could not prompt any such questioning at all; or by pursuing content in other fields which is favourable to the questioner, thereby currying his or her favour. The psychology of accountability suggests that such conformist strategies "become the likely coping strategy ... when audience views are known prior" to decision-making (Lerner & Tetlock, 1999, p. 256): political committees, with committee members' views tagged neatly by their respective party labels, are thus likely to promote conformity instead of a more self-critical attitude. Where parliamentary or government oversight is more frequent, there is greater opportunity to pursue such aggressive questioning, and thus to inflict sanctions. We should therefore expect PSB independence to be lower the more frequent oversight is, other things being equal. Additionally, where parliamentary or government oversight is in person, rather than written, the psychological effect of questioning is greater.

A second form of sanctioning mechanism comes through the stipulation of *ex ante* controls on the broadcaster: administrative procedures which limit in advance agents' room for manoeuvre. There are both discretionary and non-discretionary *ex ante* controls. Common non-discretionary controls on PSBs' freedom of operation include content quotas, recognition of unions and worker representation, and requirements for citizen input. Common discretionary controls include the requirement for ministerial permission before borrowing more than a certain amount, or before subcontracting particular services to separate companies. Both types of *ex ante* controls are found in the rational choice institutionalist literature, but they play different roles. Non-discretionary *ex ante* controls, if they are at all relevant to the principal's control of the agent, are attempts to privilege a particular political position by "stacking the deck" (Moe, 1990, p. 226 fn 14); they contribute to the "locking-in" of the preferences of a particular principal or set of principals. There is no sanctioning element. Discretionary *ex ante* controls, however, function as sanctioning mechanisms in the normal way. Ministers may withhold ministerial permission as a way of punishing the broadcaster for having broadcast material harmful to the government. Or, approval may be given pursuant to the removal of personnel, or a change in programme policy, thereby turning these *ex ante* controls into a bargaining tool. Consequently, the greater the *ex ante* controls, the lower the independence of the PSB.

The third form of sanctioning comes from threats to personal or organizational income by refusing reappointment or by cutting funding. When the threat of non-reappointment is not available (because reappointment is disallowed by law), agency-shirking can be greater. Or, where the threat of non-reappointment is not immediate (because terms in office are long), or not threatening (because office-holders are typically in their last career, or the politicians have nothing to offer them), agency-shirking can be greater. Similarly, where budgets are assured for a number of years and contain no discretionary element, the potential for agency-shirking is greater.

Politicians may not need to deploy sanctions where they have substantial discretion in appointment. Given substantial discretion, principals may be able to appoint broadcasting executives who share their ideal point. Again, where these individuals have considerable power over the output of the PSB, the result may be diminished PSB independence.

So far, I have discussed "politicians" as if their identity and interests were clear. In the language of principal–agent theory, PSBs have multiple (often collective) principals, who change over time. In the simplest possible case, a single government minister in office for perpetuity may use the entirety of sanctioning mechanisms described above. In the most complex case, different constellations of actors – parliamentary committees, parliaments, ministers, cabinets – use differing sanctions according to differing decision-making rules, involving normal majorities, pluralities or super-majorities, each of which would be frequently rescinded by changes in the composition of parliament or of government. In general, we can say that

- the greater the number of veto players – actors whose consent is required for sanctioning or rewarding – the less politicians in general can sanction;
- the longer the legally mandated period between decisions which may be used to sanction or reward, the less politicians in general can sanction.

Note that these principal–agent problems are replicated within the broadcaster. Appointing or sanctioning a particular individual will only lead to decreased independence if that individual has some influence within the broadcaster; yet appointments to the broadcaster typically only concern the supervisory board or, in extremis, the chief executive officer. Consequently, even if politicians manage to appoint to the board of the broadcaster individuals who share their ideal point, they cannot be sure that this ideal point will subsequently be implemented.

To operationalize these different aspects of legal protection, I have developed an index of protection (Table 2.2) built on previous work by Gilardi (2002, 2005) and Elgie and McMenamin (2005). Items in the second column – "Appointments" – are largely drawn from Elgie and McMenamin, comprising three indicators (tenure, appointing body and mode of dismissal) for the first and

Table 2.2 Index of legal protection

Sanctions	Appointments

Reporting to government:
  no reporting requirement: 1
  annual written reporting: 0.66
	Appointing body for first executive group
	  management board members: 1
	  complex mix of executive and legislature:
	    0.75

annual in-person report: 0.33
  greater than annual in-person reporting: 0
Reporting to parliament:
  no reporting requirement: 1
  annual written reporting: 0.66
  annual in-person report: 0.33
  greater than annual in-person reporting: 0
Borrowing:
  unrestricted: 1
  requires ministerial permission: 0
New operations, sub-contracting:
  unrestricted: 1
  requires ministerial permission: 0
State participation:
	the legislature: 0.5
	  the executive collectively: 0.25
	  one or two ministers: 0
	Tenure of first executive group:
	  more than six years: 1
	  six years: 0.8
	  five years: 0.6
	  four years: 0.4
	  less than four years: 0.2
	  no fixed term: 0
	Dismissal of first executive body:
	  dismissal not possible: 1
	  dismissal for non-policy reasons: 0.5
	  dismissal at appointing body's
	    convenience: 0

independent foundation: 1	Appointing body for second executive group

non-majority state participation: 0.5
total or majority state participation: 0
	management board members: 1
	  complex mix of executive and legislature:
	    0.75

Term of service contracts:
  greater than six years: 1
  six years: 0.8
  five years: 0.6
  four years: 0.4
  three years: 0.2
  less than three years: 0
Mechanisms for altering funding:
  automatically uprated licence fee: 1
  discretionally uprated licence fee: 0.75
  advertising: 0.5
  pluriannual grant from parliament: 0.25
  annual grant from parliament: 0
	the legislature: 0.5
	  the executive collectively: 0.25
	  one or two ministers: 0
	Tenure of second executive group:
	  more than six years: 1
	  six years: 0.8
	  five years: 0.6
	  four years: 0.4
	  less than four years: 0.2
	  no fixed term: 0
	Dismissal of second executive group:
	  dismissal not possible: 1
	  dismissal for non-policy reasons: 0.5
	  dismissal at appointing body's
	    convenience: 0

second executive bodies. An example of a first, or upper, executive body is the former Board of Governors of the BBC or the Fernsehrat of ZDF; an example of a second executive body is the post of director-general, intendant or, more rarely, a multiple-member executive board.[15]

The first indicator – appointing body – is an indirect measure of the number of veto players involved, from a single minister to combinations of the legislature, executive and civil society. The second indicator – tenure – gives the periodicity with which politicians may either sanction (refusal to reappoint) or appoint.[16] The third indicator gives the ease with which the particular sanction of dismissal can be applied.

Items in the first column concern sanctions or rewards exclusively. The first two items – reporting to government and reporting to parliament – refer to the psychological sanctions of repeated questioning, with greater effects assumed from in-person reporting than from written reporting, and from more frequent reporting than infrequent reporting. The next three items – borrowing, new service permissions and state participation – are discretionary ministerial decisions which may be used as bargaining chips in order to extract concessions, or as sanctions for past actions; the periodicity, however, of these decisions depends on whether the broadcaster chooses to submit the issue for ministerial consideration. State participation is the most ambiguous of the three: one law[17] prevents the relevant minister from voting in the AGM, which might be thought to undermine the use of this legal provision as a sanctioning or rewarding mechanism; in other countries, the powers given to shareholders naturally varies according to national provisions on joint-stock companies. The fourth item – the term of service contracts – is, again, a measure of the periodicity with which regulatory approval can be turned into a sanctioning device. Finally, the last item, the mechanisms for altering funding, is a measure of the discretion enjoyed by politicians in setting the broadcasters' year-on-year funding.

I have chosen to average each of the two columns and take the average of these two figures as my operationalization of legal protection. Alternate specifications of the index of de jure independence do not change the results appreciably. Gran and Patterson (2006) argue that the de facto independence of agencies depends not on the mean value of legislative guarantees of independence, but on the minimum, since politicians will attack the "weakest link". Yet countries which score highly on Appointments also score highly on Sanctions; the correlation between the two terms is 0.91. The specification also matches expert attempts to insulate PSBs from political pressure: the score for one model law on public broadcasting would be the second-highest in the sample, beaten only by Switzerland (Rumphorst, 1999).

4.4 Model

In order to test our hypotheses about the impact of party-system polarization, bureaucratic partisanship, the size of the market for news and the degree of legal protection, I use multivariate regression analysis. This provides us with a relatively simple statistical model of independence. Table 2.3 shows the results of this analysis. The first column of data shows the full model, with all four main explanatory variables and one interaction term included. This full model is over-specified: with five explanatory factors and only 36 broadcasters, the ratio of variables to observations is too high. Additionally, because our dependent variable is bounded between 0 and 1, the model has some problems with heteroskedasticity: the errors in the model are more tightly clustered as we approach public broadcasters with near-perfect scores. The value of the Breusch-Pagan test for heteroskedasticity is 12.50, which, on five degrees of freedom, is significant at the 0.05 level.

The full model does, however, show that party-system polarization and the partisanship of the bureaucracy are not significant predictors of PSB independence. In neither case do these variables even remotely approach standard levels of statistical significance. I therefore removed both of these variables from the model, leaving the reduced model shown in the second column of data. In this reduced model, all three terms – the two main terms and the one interaction term – are significant at the 0.05 level, and all coefficients are in the predicted direction: the bigger the market for news, and the greater the legal protection, the higher the independence of the broadcaster. The model performs reasonably well: the problems of heteroskedasticity faced by the previous model disappear (Breusch-Pagan value of 3.5 on 3 d.f., $p=0.321$); there are no problems with outlying observations driving the results (value of Cook's distance less than 0.25 for all cases); and the model explains more than half of the variation in PSB independence.

If the model is broadly correct – and if the unexplained variance is not the result of some other systematic factor – then the prospects for designing independent PSBs are relatively good. Assuming average press circulation, an increase from no legal protection to full legal protection would result in an increase from negligible to almost total de facto independence. Of course, no public broadcaster has no legal protection; every piece of legislation studied here grants the broadcaster some protection. However, even if we consider just those values of legal protection which we see in the data, a change between the minimum score for legal protection (0.15) and the maximum (0.82) would still result in a huge increase in PSB independence.

We can understand the substantive significance of these coefficients better if we apply them to a real-world example of PSB reform. In Spain, the Zapatero

Table 2.3 Linear regression model of independence

	Full model	*Reduced model*
Intercept	−0.02 (0.26)	−0.12 (0.24)
Legal protection	0.36* (0.17)	0.41* (0.17)
Press circulation	0.09† (0.05)	0.13** (0.04)
Polarization	0.00 (0.01)	
Bureaucratic partisanship	0.03 (0.02)	
Circulation × post-communist	−0.03*** (0.01)	−0.04*** (0.01)
N	36	36
R^2	0.61	0.57
adj. R^2	0.55	0.53
Resid. sd	0.12	0.12

Notes
Standard errors in parentheses.
† significant at $p<0.10$; *$p<0.05$; **$p<0.01$; ***$p<0.001$.

government, following a report by a committee of sages, drafted a new law on RTVE establishing a single-tier board of 12 members nominated by the parliament for a non-renewable six-year term, one of whom would be the president of the new corporation. The reform scores much higher than the previous law of 1980 (0.8 compared to 0.5). The likely effect of the law on RTVE's independence will be positive: from an independence score of 0.49, the mean predicted independence score would rise to 0.78 (SD=0.068), fulfilling the intent behind the legislation of liberating RTVE from excessive governmental control.

Because this work combines broad statistical analysis with in-depth historical analysis, it is useful to examine more closely the "predictions" or retrodictions that the model makes for our six cases (Lieberman, 2005). Figure 2.3 plots the predicted versus actual values of the model for all broadcasters in this sample. The figure also plots a 45° line where predicted values match actual values. Cases above the line are cases where the broadcaster is more independent than our model suggests; cases below the line are cases where the broadcaster is less independent. It seems that Spain and Italy after 1993 are less independent than

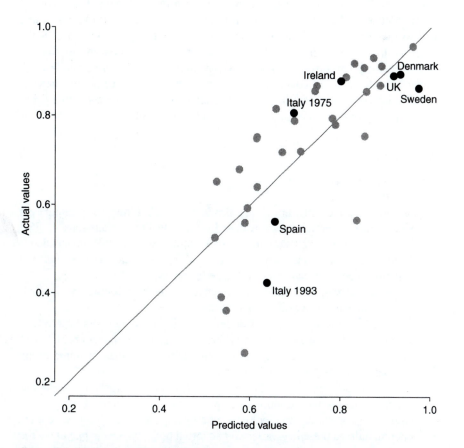

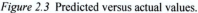

Figure 2.3 Predicted versus actual values.

we might expect; the same is true, to a lesser degree, of Sweden and Denmark. Conversely, Italy between 1975 and 1993, and Ireland, are more independent than we might expect. It is worth bearing in mind that this interpretation assumes that our proxy measure of independence is accurate, and sufficiently fine-grained to pick up, for examples, differences between Rai during one period and Rai during a somewhat later period. The historical chapters that follow allow us to test whether this proxy indicator is indeed reliable. To foreshadow what comes next: it is true that the Irish public broadcaster RTÉ is more independent than one would have predicted by examining the Irish market for news and the degree of legal protection given to RTÉ; this is largely a result of highly efficient borrowing of practices from the BBC. However, the mispredictions in Italy and Denmark are faults of the proxy indicator: whilst directors-general rarely changed during the period 1975–1993, they were effectively immobilized by highly political battles on the board of the broadcaster, a board which had acquired much more power as a result of the 1975 reforms. The "poor" showing from 1993 onwards is only poor when one starts from this rather misleading benchmark. In Denmark, our proxy indicator also overstates the degree of real independence, and so the gap between the predictions made by the model and real-world performance is even more instructive. The goal, therefore, in the chapters that follow will be to trace the causal path sketched out in this chapter, and to identify carefully the links between market size, "professionalization" projects, codified rules governing output and attempts to defuse and defease political interference. These historical chapters will also provide us with a richer understanding of how independent these broadcasters really are.

5 Summary

Thus far, I have:

- provided a proxy measure of independence which allows us to compare a wide range of broadcasters, and to test statistically explanations of PSB independence; detailed a number of rival explanations of PSB independence in terms of party-system polarization and bureaucratic partisanship, and explained certain weaknesses of these explanations;
- set out a theory of PSB independence which starts from politicians', journalists' and managers' incentives and behaviour;
- detailed how rules can be used to defease politicians' attempts to interfere, by showing that the kind of output they criticize is not objectionable, or to defuse attempts at interference, by introducing new rules or adjudicating complaints on the basis of existing rules;
- argued that such rule development will only occur in larger media markets either where journalists embarked upon a "professionalization project" or where press agencies emerged furnishing largely homogeneous news copy;
- operationalized these key variables and tested both my own explanation and rival explanations statistically.

Readers who are completely convinced of the way in which I have operationalized these independent and dependent variables, and who believe in the accepta-
bility of using multivariate linear regression to test causal claims, may wish to
stop here. Those readers who are instead sceptical of these explanations should
continue to the historical analyses which take up the next part of this book.

Part II

Specific cases

As large organizations with considerable impact on the politics of their respective countries, public broadcasters are intrinsically interesting. Nevertheless, I have chosen six broadcasters as having particular interest in light of our own desire to know more about political independence. This part of the book charts the history of those six broadcasters – Rai, RTVE, the BBC, RTÉ, SVT and DR. These countries are clustered geographically; but this clustering is also found when researchers attempt to classify media systems: two broadcasters have been drawn from each of Hallin and Mancini's (2004) three media system types (the Polarized Pluralist or Mediterranean type; the Liberal or North Atlantic type; and the Democratic Corporatist or Central European type). I concentrate on the broadcaster in the larger of the two countries in each cluster – Rai, the BBC and SVT – and dedicate more space to recounting and analysing their histories. With some exceptions for Italy and Spain, each chapter offers a history of the public broadcaster (and where applicable, its predecessor companies) divided into three broad periods – from its foundation in the early 1920s until the early post-war period; from the early post-war period until the 1970s; and from the 1970s until the present day. Within each period, I discuss first the broad historical setting of that period, before going on to discuss the key rhetorical commitments emphasized by the broadcaster, paying particular attention to those commitments which describe "regulatory" values in journalism – values like impartiality, objectivity and pluralism. I then examine the concrete rules designed to embody those regulatory values, before examining the structure, organization and recruitment of news departments within the broadcaster. I close each period by considering notable cases of political interference. These episodes are not intended as "measurements" or "indicators" of political independence, nor could they be: like an iceberg, much of political interference is hidden below the water-line, and we do not even have the guarantee that the ratios of seen to unseen episodes is constant across broadcasters. Nevertheless, these episodes, and in particular some of the more egregious cases from Spain and Italy, allow us to understand differences between broadcasters and within broadcasters over time.

3   Italy

The absence of Caesars

Never say objectivity doesn't exist. It's the alibi of those about to bullshit you.

Ottone (1996)

Less partisan Rai boards have often been dominated by intellectuals. One consequence is that these individuals occasionally offer useful, unguarded insights into the functioning of the broadcaster. Medieval historian Franco Cardini, a member of the board of Rai between 1994 and 1996, thought that Roman history could provide an appropriate remedy for Rai's problems of excessive turnover and dispersion of power:

> What Rai needs is a relatively long period of real government … A period of dictatorship followed by an extremely tough mayor, as ancient Rome and the medieval cities did. A period in which one could truly reform, in the etymological sense of the word: re-form.
>
> (Cardini & Riccio, 1995, pp. 50, 91)

Yet dispersion of power and limited term-length have not always been problems of Rai. For the first 30 years of its existence (1944–1974), Rai was a relatively centralized organization with power concentrated around the managing director or the director-general. These figures were able to impose codes governing content, or to exhort journalists to greater professionalism. Executives like Filiberto Guala (managing director, 1954–1956) and Ettore Bernabei (director-general, 1961–1974) did not always do so in order to increase the broadcaster's independence, but at least in the latter case a modicum of independence was obtained, even at the cost of numerous compromises with the dominant Christian Democratic Party.

It is unclear whether Guala or Bernabei's successors could have used the machinery they developed, and the centralization they achieved, for less partisan ends. They did not have the chance: after Bernabei's departure in 1974, a major reform of Rai divided the broadcaster into multiple competing entities, and inaugurated the instability and dispersion of power accentuated by the "temporary" reform legislation of 1993 and lamented by Cardini. This dispersion of power, and in particular the limited term in office of both the board and the director-general (two key components of the index of legal protection discussed in Chapter 2), might not matter for the independence of the broadcaster if journalists were bound by a strong commitment to professional norms, or if Rai had been able to build on non-partisan agency copy; but neither of these conditions holds. The dominant value in the media, that of pluralism, has an essentially political genesis, and imposes no restrictions on content; attempts to introduce other regulatory values such as objectivity or impartiality, or to introduce written codes of conduct, have been unsuccessful since boards and directors-general have not been able to push reforms through in the limited time available to them.

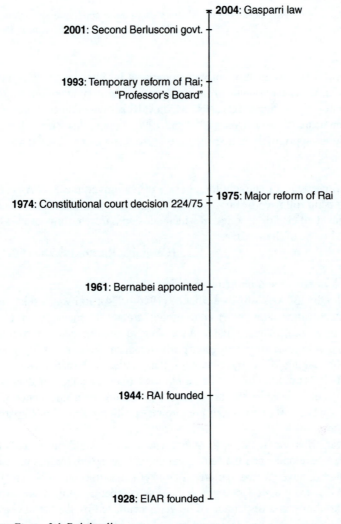

Figure 3.1 Rai timeline.

Rai is thus an excellent demonstration of my argument that an independent broadcaster must have a modicum of legal protection and the basis for professional codes capable of governing broadcast output.

I consider four periods in Rai's development: the period from the first radio broadcasts in Italy in the 1920s to the appointment of Ettore Bernabei as director-general in 1961, including the transformation of the fascist radio company Ente Italiano Audizione Radiofoniche (EIAR) into Rai (1); the period from Bernabei's appointment until the reform of 1975 (2); the period from that reform until the collapse of the established party system in 1993/1994 (3); and from 1993 until the present day, including the "temporary" reform of 1993 and the current Gasparri law of 2004 (4). Within each section I briefly consider the history of the period, including developments in the media market (*.1), before moving on to discuss the key rhetorical commitments of Rai (*.2), its concrete rules as they developed (*.3), the structure, organization and recruitment of news staff (*.4) and alleged cases of interference during that period (*.5).

1 Fascism and the post-war period (1924–1960)

1.1 The setting

The Italian media market before radio offered little promise for independent broadcasting. There were few potential consumers of printed news: in 1861, almost three-quarters of the Italian population was illiterate, and universal (>95%) literacy did not arrive until the 1950s (Banks & Databases International, 2007; Castronovo, Giacheri Fossati & Tranfaglia, 1979, p. 10). As a result, sales were limited: the *Corriere della Sera* was by far Italy's largest newspaper at the start of the First World War, with daily sales of over 200,000 copies – but this was only a fifth of the circulation of the London-based *Daily Mail*, which had a number of similarly situated competitors (Griffiths, 2006, p. 133). For most Italian newspapers, costs could not be covered by sales and advertising revenue alone (Mazzanti, 1991, p. 49). Consequently, non-profit-oriented actors – the political parties, industrialists, the Catholic Church – stepped in and operated their own newspapers as means of pursuing influence rather than making profit. Given proprietors' wishes, "political and ideological militancy became ... a winning card as far as entering the profession was concerned" (Becchelloni, 1991, p. 14).

Journalists and editors in the larger newspapers of the North might have attempted to gain autonomy by professionalization – and indeed attempts in this vein were made by Luigi Albertini, editor of the *Corriere* (Asor Rosa, 1981, p. 1245) – but professionalization was halted by the Fascist regime. This was for two reasons: first, any pretence at objectivity was not credible in a regime of censorship; and second, the Fascists, in their bid to control entry to their journalistic profession, created an Order of Journalists, membership in which was compulsory for all practising journalists, which is still the case today (Barile, 1989). In many other countries, journalists have professionalized as part of a project in order to secure a state-granted monopoly on the exercise of their profession, allowing the profession to pursue social closure and extract monopoly rents: in Italy, journalists achieved this by accident. There was consequently less incentive to purse a professionalization project.

Nor was the market large enough to sustain a dedicated press agency without government subvention. During the Fascist period the sole press agency was the Agenzia Stefani, a quasi-official body which relayed releases from the government press office: the first radio broadcaster, the Unione Radiofonica Italiana (URI), was obliged to take all its news from this source (Cannistraro, 1975, p. 229). After the Second World War, and on the suggestion of the Allies, a co-operative press agency, the Agenzia Nazionale Stampa Associata (Ansa) was set up with participation of all major newspapers; but from 1949 onwards Ansa was subsidized by the Prime Minister's Office and subsequently by the Foreign Office, ostensibly in order to relay Italian news around the world, but in practice privileging government voices in all agency copy (Murialdi, 1980, p. 237).

As in other European countries, radio broadcasting was initially carried out by private operators granted an exclusive state concession. The URI was granted an exclusive licence to broadcast in December 1924, but in 1928 it was replaced by a new body, the EIAR, which became state property by 1933, and which was funded by licence fee (Zeno-Zencovich, 1983). Agenzia Stefani's stale news releases became increasingly propagandistic during the course of the 1930s, and the amount of propaganda broadcast by EIAR grew (Cannistraro, 1975, p. 255).

Following the Allied liberation of Italy, Rai (Radio Audizioni Italiane) was founded on 26 October 1944.[1] The new organization inherited the EIAR's concession and structures, apart from in the North where the radio services run by the Comitato di Liberazione Nazionale per l'Alta Italia (CLNAI) continued until December 1945. Commenting on the decree establishing Rai, Chiarenza (2002, p. 33) notes that "all political forces, with no exceptions, could find nothing better to do than dust off the legal schema used for the EIAR, limiting themselves to substituting Fascist political control with control by the new executive." The company was run by a director-general and managing director, both of which were appointed by the major shareholder, the Istituto per la Ricostruzione Industriale (IRI), and thus by the government of the day.

1.2 Key rhetorical commitments

In its early years Rai was in theory committed to impartiality and objectivity. These terms were used in 1947 legislation establishing a parliamentary committee to supervise the broadcaster,[2] and again towards the end of this period when the Constitutional Court heard its first challenge to the constitutionality of Rai's television and radio monopoly.[3]

These commitments were initially reiterated by Rai management: the board declared in October 1945 that Rai's news bulletins

> must be absolutely impartial, and must not have a preference for any of the parties ... those responsible within the company should take care that the

radio news bulletins always meet these demands, and that they are never partial, either through omission or through the order in which news is given. As with all ideals, it is possible that this ideal will not be met, just as it is human for not everyone to be satisfied with our bulletins' performance in this respect.

(Chiarenza, 2002, p. 30)

Objectivity and impartiality – or the lack thereof – were also terms used when Rai was criticized. Shortly after the board issued the statement above, Mario Scelba, Minister of Posts and Telecommunications, and thus the minister within the government who was, in some sense, "responsible" for Rai, sent a telegram to Rai's president, criticizing Rai's news service as "manifestly partial". In another attempt by the Christian Democratic party, Democrazia Cristiana (DC), to intimidate Rai into changing its coverage, the party's newspaper, *Il Popolo*, "deplored the absence of objectivity within Rai" (quoted in Veltroni, 1990, p. 86).

These terms, however, fell into disuse as the DC's control over Rai grew, particularly after the election of 1948. By 1956, Piccone Stella, head of Rai's news division, felt able to tell the parliamentary committee charged with monitoring Rai's objectivity that the concept was "in an absolute sense, both a noble aspiration and a naive abstraction" – and thus, by implication, not something to worry too greatly about (Chiarenza, 2002, p. 83).

1.3 Concrete rules

Rai could not do as Radiotjänst did and adopt codes first developed by professional associations: the Order of Journalists was in limbo following the war, and had narrowly avoided being shut down by Allied forces (Murialdi, 1980, p. 183). There was strong opposition to the idea that the Order could or should develop such codes: Luigi Einaudi, first president of Republican Italy, argued that

> The Order becomes a ridiculous piece of nonsense from the moment one supposes that it can give a judgement on technical approaches, professional ability, or the duration of traineeships offered ... There is no Order for poets and there cannot be an Order for journalists.
>
> (quoted in Farinelli, Paccagnini, Santambrogio & Ida Villa, 1997, p. 323)

Nor could Rai rely on press agency copy to shape its output, as the BBC did. The company was not part of the co-operative that ran Ansa, and did not take copy from the agency. Instead, it initially (1944) sought to restrict its news announcements to official press releases put out by the authorities. The decision led to the resignation of the first editor of the radio news, Corrado Alvaro (Monteleone, 1999, p. 199).

Some written codes did exist, but these did not attempt to translate the requirements of impartiality and objectivity into concrete guidelines for content. Rather, they were primarily stylistic or moralistic in character:

At that time in Rai there was lying around, not just in the news-desks but also in the other rooms where non-journalistic programmes were prepared, a booklet, a manual for writing for radio edited by no less than [novelist] Carlo Emilio Gadda ... Gadda's manual was certainly well done, but the simple rules, the dry pronouncements of Piccone Stella were the indispensable instrument for regulating any prose destined to fly through the ether.

(Mazza & Agnes, 2004, p. 34)

In addition to Gadda's style manual, there was also a "self-regulatory code", often spoken of as secret, but which was in fact mentioned in board minutes of 1953 (and reprinted in Gismondi, 1958). The code, however, was used to justify interventions by management who "intervened only, but extremely firmly, to safeguard aspects concerning morality and good manners, which were to be identical with those models which the Catholic world claimed to be those of the entire country" (Chiarenza, 2002, p. 60).

There was, therefore, no code which would constrain journalists' output, as viewed in political space; no rules enjoining them to greater impartiality or objectivity, and thus no commandments which could be cited by the broadcaster to those who accused it of being biased. Those codes which did exist were designed for an implicit partisan purpose. Yet one might still wonder whether these codes might not have served a purpose in regulating Rai's contact with politicians, and whether the structures designed to enforce them might not have served some other purpose had they been radically rewritten. Certainly, Biagio Agnes – then a journalist, and later (1982–1990) director-general of Rai – thought they were useful to the company:

One might say this was an excess of prudery. No, rather it was a minimal example of codes, of rules that those who worked in Rai had to keep in mind, and which were formulated supposing the existence of other, unwritten codes, other rules of mutual respect which, for their part, the politicians should have stuck to.

(Mazza & Agnes, 2004, p. 32)

1.4 Structure, organization, recruitment in news

These codes, developed in 1953, found organizational expression in a complex system of oversight committees developed by Filiberto Guala. Guala was a fervent Catholic who, on his first visit to Rai staff in Turin, boasted that he had come to "hunt down pederasts and Communists" (Cesareo, 1970, p. 35). These committees cut out the old *aziendalisti* – those employees who had been with the company in its previous incarnation as EIAR – and involved all the main players in news; these committees supplemented the normal control of news, which was unified in one division, reporting to the director-general.

Monitoring journalists, however, was less essential as the DC gradually tightened its grip on the personnel decisions of the broadcaster. As the company expanded (with the first television broadcasts beginning in 1954), a steady stream of journalists came from the Christian Democratic daily *Il Popolo*: Rodolfo Arato, director-general from 1956 onwards; his successor, Ettore Bernabei; and Vittorio Chesi, director of radio news from 1965.

Recruitment from DC publications can be considered a "normal" method of recruitment resulting from a structural feature of the market for news – namely, the presence of numerous party organs. Recruitment through other methods consciously designed to place partisan sympathizers within the broadcaster was also practised. Often this took the form of bi-directional movement between the press offices of ministers or parties, and Rai. The leadership of Rai set an example: after Giuseppe Spataro, a DC deputy and subsequently communications minister, the next president of Rai, Cristiano Ridomi, was recruited from the prime minister's press office. Such practices were, however, commonplace throughout the broadcaster. As Chiarenza (2002, p. 112) describes it, "hirings were almost always determined by political and clientelistic pressure, independent of any clear objective … in most cases the journalists came from the secretariat of the parties or their press offices; rarely from journalistic experience in the daily newspapers." This placement could be honed thanks to the practice of seconding journalists to political posts: according to Cesareo (1970, p. 96),

> the practice entered into use at the time of the Tambroni government, in 1960, when the head of domestic services for the television news was "seconded" to the prime minister's office, and assumed the functions of Tambroni's personal private secretary. From then, it has grown such that the press offices of the Prime Minister, of the Interior Ministry, of the Ministry for State Participation, of the parties participating in Rai's management … regularly borrow … journalists employed by the Corporation.

In addition to representing a source of free labour, these practices allowed the parties (1) to assess the reliability of certain journalists in general, (2) to create on the part of these journalists a sense of gratitude, and (3) to generate a roster of potential acceptable nominees for future posts.

Although much could be achieved by hiring in a period of natural growth, the DC was not afraid to remove journalists it thought were not sufficiently reliable. The editor of the television news bulletin, Massimo Rendina, was removed from the broadcaster, allegedly upon the direct request of then-prime minister Antonio Segni, for being insufficiently anti-communist, despite his Catholic newspaper background (Chiarenza, 2002, p. 85). This tactic, however, could only be used rarely, as it tended to produce discontent amongst the smaller parties in the DC-led coalition governments of the period.

1.5 Political interference

As should be obvious by this point, Rai during its first 15 years was effectively controlled by the Christian Democratic Party, especially in its news output. The

DC's degree of control was openly admitted in a parliamentary debate towards the end of the 1950s, when the minister responsible for Rai, Lorenzo Spallino, answered a question on control of Rai by claiming:

> Naturally it is the board of Rai which decides [loud shouts from the left]. Well, if you're not too upset by it, the DC decides. Or does this also upset you? Do you dislike it that the Italian people should have given a majority to the DC? The Italian people decides when it sends to the Parliament men who are inspired by the principles of Christian Democracy [applause from the centre]. This is the reality of things, even if you dislike it.
>
> (quoted in Veltroni, 1990, p. 99)

This control had concrete effects on the broadcaster's output. Content analysis demonstrated the DC's disproportionate share of news items and reportage:

> From an analysis of the political speeches given on Sundays in the last three months of 1950 and transmitted on radio, Christian Democratic speakers were given 105 separate news items for a total of 1,099 lines, whilst the communists were given 13 news items, and the Republicans just five.
>
> (Monteleone, 1999, p. 238)

Rai employees tacitly admitted to acting in the DC's interests. Following a 1949 letter from then-junior minister Giulio Andreotti, inviting the broadcaster to exercise the most "prudent" discretion in matters of domestic or international controversy, the broadcaster replied that:

> as far as the invitation to abstain from broadcasting news items which could give rise to worrying repercussions of a political nature, we make so bold as to note that, both in internal as well as in international political news, as in economic and trade union news, Rai – conscious of the responsibility it holds – already exercises severe self-censorship [*una severa opera di autodisciplina*].
>
> (Monteleone, 1999, p. 238)

Nonetheless, in terms of organization, Rai's structure was functionally sound, and the same structures which permitted easy censorship also permitted the broadcaster to supply a coherent product. The formal rules employed by the broadcaster may have been inspired by Catholicism, but were no more prudish and no more ridiculous to modern eyes than the rules employed by other broadcasters at this time, born of the need to demonstrate "a safe pair of hands" to their respective governments. It was only through the permanence of the DC in power that such rules became identified with propagandistic use of the public broadcaster.

2 The Bernabei era (1961–1974)

2.1 The setting

The 1960s brought greater openness to Italy. In religion, the Second Vatican Council (1962–1965) liberalized the Church's position on numerous issues. In politics, the failure of the Tambroni government meant the beginning of an opening to the left under Amintore Fanfani, and coalition governments including the Italian Socialist Party (Partito Socialista Italiano, PSI) as an external component. This opening to the left was mirrored in Rai by the appointment, in 1961, of Ettore Bernabei as director-general. Bernabei, like Arata before him, had been editor of *Il Popolo*, and was an acolyte of Fanfani. Under his leadership, Rai gained greater independence from the Christian Democrats, and greater independence from politics in general – but only because at the same time it became dependent on a wider range of parties, who would push for ever greater recognition and ever larger shares of appointments, until the reform of 1975, which followed Bernabei's reign, formalized this nascent spoils system.

2.2 Key rhetorical commitments

Though Bernabei had a similar background to previous directors-general, and thus might have been expected to continue subordinating the needs of the audience to the diktat of party, Bernabei understood the need to produce entertaining and uplifting television content. One of Bernabei's contemporaries, Enzo Biagi, has argued that the television produced by Bernabei "was some of the best television produced in the world, easily withstanding the comparison with the most celebrated broadcasters such as the BBC" (Mazza & Agnes, 2004, p. 8). If entertaining television was sought, greater professionalism was needed. This was the key value of the Bernabei period, but it was not a value which was found in written documents, but rather based on Bernabei's own recruitment and commissioning decisions.

This was particularly the case in news. Prior to Bernabei the model for the television news had been the cinema newsreels of the 1930s and 1940s, featuring video footage of events whilst an off-screen voice commented. Additionally, the dominance of the DC within the broadcaster meant that many of the events shown were trivial – footage of ministers at opening ceremonies or giving speeches – whilst non-trivial events featuring the Communist Party were ignored.

Bernabei disagreed with this kind of news not because he objected, ideologically, to the over-representation of Christian Democrats and the exclusion of Communists, but rather because he was convinced, politically, that this model lacked credibility (Pinto, 1980, p. 29). Thus, in order to present a credible message which benefited the party, it was paradoxically necessary to gain some autonomy from it – and possibly independence at some later stage. Yet, it was not possible to realise any autonomy for Rai without the company forming, from the inside, certain strongly professionalised social profiles who, precisely in virtue of the quality of their work, and in contrast to those following traditional roles, obtained a strong degree of self-regulation strictly connected to the director-general's project.

(Pinto, 1980, p. 30)

2.3 Concrete rules

This demand for professionalism did not translate into written rules governing output: the process of creating the television news bulletin was entirely conventional by the standards of many European broadcasters, with morning meetings, items contributed, followed by subsequent editorial meetings to decide on running orders. The only control exercised over content was the control exercised by the editor and deputy editor, who decided whether a piece was worthy of broadcast or not. Yet control was entrusted to these individuals because they all enjoyed strong fiduciary relationships with Bernabei and the management of the broadcaster. The strength of this fiduciary relationship was often based on the fact that Bernabei had taken strong interest in recruitment matters and had often had to pay a high price (recruiting other not so talented but well-connected journalists in order to balance out "non-political" hires) in order to hire these individuals. As Pinto writes,

> [The management] based their action on the recognition of the professionalism of the individual journalist, seen as political professionalism in the key posts of the company, and as technical capacity in the technical and production positions, but, at the same time, they employed this *fatally individual professionalism* to reconfirm and render structurally insuperable their own hegemony.

> (1980, p. 89; emphasis added)

An "individual" professionalism was acceptable to most socially aspirational journalists, since it echoed well-worn tropes about the journalist's job being intellectual – and hence highly individual – work.

At the same time, however, the absence of any codified or structural professionalism had negative consequences for the broadcaster. First, it could not outlast the departure of the particular individuals who had contributed to the company's professionalism. Second, it could not outlast the director-general who was responsible for this professionalization, and who was the fulcrum of the fiduciary relationships which underpinned it. Third, the absence of formal components meant that the contradiction between a commitment to professionalism on the one hand, and, on the other, the latent desire to demonstrate that the Christian Democratic Party was at the centre of the political life of the country, was left unexamined.

2.4 Structure, organization, recruitment in news

Despite this, Bernabei's professionalization project did succeed in gaining the broadcaster greater autonomy. This is clearest in news, where, given Bernabei's dim assessment of the then-existing model,

> the company therefore faced the problem of a comprehensive re-qualification of the entire news and current affairs sector ... In 1962 the task of building a modern *telegiornale* [news bulletin], with the newspapers of the North as a reference point, was entrusted to Enzo Biagi. *The choice, both of the journalist in question, and of the reference point, was not coincidental.*
>
> (Pinto, 1980, p. 29)

In future years, Biagi's reputation would grow still further. Nevertheless, it was still sufficient at that time to allow Biagi to put a series of conditions to Bernabei, including the ability to rebuff political pressure as far as content was concerned. And thus, for a time the *telegiornali* became less staid. It is perhaps an oblique compliment that even Marxist commentators like Giovanni Cesareo felt obliged to damn Biagi with faint praise, for favouring the interests of the dominant class out of false consciousness rather than conscious intent, pursuing "the classic line of journalism which is falsely 'independent'" (Cesareo, 1970, p. 44).

Equally, the choice of a Northern reference point was important because the market for news had always been larger in the North than in the South. Even in the brief period where the two Rai networks had been split between those in the South and the partisan-controlled networks in the North, the Northern radio news had been fresher, unburdened by the legacy of EIAR and with access to foreign press agencies who chose bases in Milan (Monteleone, 1999, p. 200).

The "Biagi experiment" was successful, in that "for a time – and to the great relief of millions of Italians – the continual appearances of ministers, deputies and senators of the majority, forever intent on cutting ribbons, laying corner-stones, and opening conventions, became less" (Chiarenza, 2002, p. 103). Not only was the content of better quality, it also served as a rallying point for the defence of the broadcaster: when justice minister Guido Gonella (ironically the first President of the Order of Journalists when it was re-founded in 1963) attacked Biagi's management of the television news,

> [a]ll of Rai's journalists joined with Bernabei against Gonella, releasing a communique where they affirmed that their jobs needed to be carried out in "full independence", and the obligation to provide objective news could not be passed over for "elements of political and moral corruption". Rai's board was to protect "their right to defend themselves against any attack and speculation concerning their professional dignity."
>
> (Pinto, 1980, p. 34)

Unfortunately, whilst Biagi's presence and the new impetus he gave to television news could win a modicum of independence for the broadcaster, and offered the potential for resistance to political interference, Biagi was still working under considerable constraints – particularly as far as staffing was concerned. One of the means by which Bernabei had secured the possibility of hiring talented journalists and producers who were not connected to the Christian Democratic Party (like Biagi) was his promise to simultaneously hire other journalists and managers who were not necessarily talented, but who enjoyed good political connections. Over time, this practice was extended to include those close to the PSI and the Social Democrats (the Liberals and the Republicans had already procured a limited number of posts within the company).

Because of the importance of this hiring strategy to the political standing of the company, not even Bernabei could permit Biagi to hire as he wished:

> Amongst the guarantees which Biagi had not obtained (and perhaps had not even thought to ask) was the possibility of choosing capable journalists ... and not necessarily [journalists] drawn from the press offices and the youth secretariats of the political parties.

Consequently, the Biagi experiment ended quickly, as Biagi "soon realised the impossibility of setting a new course with such human resources ... and, at the first occasion, resigned" (Chiarenza, 2002, p. 103).

This was the paradox of Bernabei's system, which Biagi so quickly grasped: employees were encouraged to do a better job, as evaluated by considerations internal to the craft, but only conditional on their acceptance that staffing decisions are subject to considerations which are instead external and political-clientelistic in nature. The latter was the price to pay for greater autonomy in certain areas; the former was the method for achieving it.

2.5 Political interference

During Bernabei's period in office the nature of political interference in Rai changed. Before Bernabei it was difficult to speak of interference per se: the broadcaster's low levels of political independence were due to the fact that most journalists were biddable or otherwise convinced to work as agents of the dominant Christian Democrats; interference was consequently not necessary to secure coverage favourable to the party.

Under Bernabei, however, journalists were no longer unambiguously agents for the DC: some claimed to have no political agenda, whilst others, working in the same unified news apparatus, had been recruited on the basis of their (differing) partisan sympathies. Consequently, the overall direction of output was less clearly towards the DC. Cases of intervention were increasingly cases in which politicians thought that journalists had overstepped the line. Rai, however, proved increasingly unable to respond to such interventions, and attempts to provide guarantees – whether to the politicians or to the journalists

– were fruitless. Aldo Sandulli, a former president of the Constitutional Court, was appointed president of Rai in 1969 in order to act as a "guarantor": but he was unable to prevent a fight developing between the board vice-president Italo de Feo and journalist Sergio Zavoli, who had drawn criticism for a current affairs programme on the Italian penal code. Sandulli resigned that same year.

3 Reform to reform (1975–1992)

3.1 The setting

The 1975 law which reformed Rai was long overdue. Legislation to replace the 1947 governmental decree – which remained the legislative basis for Rai's continued operation – had been promised since 1969 (Chiarenza, 2002, p. 148), and the charter between Rai and the state had been renewed annually in the expectation that new legislation would shortly fill the vacuum. Despite numerous exploratory talks, debate deadlocked around five key issues: the relationship between supervisory and management roles (in large part inspired by Bernabei's management of the broadcaster); the relationship between the executive and the broadcaster; guarantees of objectivity; the legal structure of the broadcaster; and, finally, programming issues.

The Constitutional Court forced the parliament's hand, and in part made its task easier, with an extremely bold ruling in summer 1974.[4] The Court had been asked to rule on whether Rai's monopoly over national television broadcasting was incompatible with constitutional provisions on freedom of enterprise (Arts 41, 43) and freedom of expression (Art. 21). As in its previous judgments,[5] the Court held that bandwidth limitations meant that untrammelled private enterprise in broadcasting would quickly lead to natural monopoly and a consequent risk that citizens' right to receive information of various kinds – also inferred from Art. 21 – would be impaired. The Court once again affirmed that "the State monopolist is institutionally situated so as to enjoy the most favourable conditions of objectivity and impartiality necessary to surmount the difficulties imposed by the natural limitations of the medium" (§2d), and yet at the same time laid out a series of conditions which the state had to meet in order that its conduct be constitutional.

The Court insisted in its judgment that it was passing no judgment on how Rai had in fact been managed up until that point, and that the conditions it laid out were made "with respect for the discretionality the legislator enjoys in choosing the most appropriate instruments to ensure the pursuit of the two fundamental objectives [discussed in the ruling]" (§8) – but by the standards of the court, its ruling represented an astonishing incursion into the legislator's domain in a field where its jurisprudence has rarely been of the highest calibre (Volcansek, 2000).

Of these seven conditions the Court laid out, four in particular are important for our purposes:

- that programmes be influenced by "impartial criteria" respecting "the fundamental values of the constitution, and the richness and multiplicity of
strands of thought" (§8b);
- that journalists be held to a "greater objectivity" and be in position "to carry
out their duties within the framework of professional codes" (§8b);
- that "the executive organs of the body managing [the concession] (whether
this be a public body or a private concessionary owned by the public purse)
not be constituted in such a fashion as to represent, directly or indirectly, the
preponderant or exclusive expression of the executive power, and that their
structure be so as to guarantee their objectivity" (§8a);
- that "for the implementation of the above-mentioned directives and issues
of control relating to the same, adequate powers should be given to the Parliament, which institutionally represents the entire national collective"
(§8c).

The judgment makes almost no explicit reference – and few implicit references
– to the value of pluralism, which, as we shall see, was judged to be the motivating principle behind the 1975 reform. Rather, the values more often evoked by
the Court are traditional "liberal" values of objectivity and impartiality. As far as
organization is concerned, although the Court is concerned about the influence
of the executive, it is remarkably sanguine about the potential impact of parliamentary control over the broadcaster.

Although Rai was immediately affected by the Court's criticism of its governance, over the long term it was affected more by the court's decision, in that
same judgment, to permit local cable television. Whilst a national private television network would represent a threat to the free formation of public opinion, the
Court held that private enterprise at the local level would not be damaging in the
same way. The decision permitted a number of private enterprises to experiment
in the new market for local television via cable and local terrestrial. Because of
the considerable capital expenditure involved in supplying content capable of
competing with Rai, local networks quickly coalesced to form de facto regional
or national networks. One such national network was run by Silvio Berlusconi's
company Mediaset, which bought out its two principal competitors, the publishing houses Rusconi and Mondadori, in 1982 and 1984 respectively, leaving Berlusconi with a monopoly of private television. Berlusconi's friendship with
Socialist Party leader Bettino Craxi (prime minister, 1983–1987) effectively
obstructed legislation regulating commercial television. Berlusconi's channels
consequently operated in a normative vacuum, and were not subject to many of
the public service obligations placed on other European commercial television
stations. In particular, not only was there no obligation to broadcast news and
current affairs programming, there was a ban on its broadcast, and the Mediaset
channels only started experimenting with news in 1991, barely three years before
Berlusconi's entry into politics. Had commercial news flourished, it might either
have shown up Rai's own news coverage, or, had it been similar, demonstrated
that Rai's criteria of news selection were criteria which would be followed by

most operators. Instead, Italy's major commercial channels produced news which disproportionately featured Berlusconi's own party and members of his governing coalition.

Were the influence of commercial television on Rai limited to news, it would scarcely merit mention; at the same time, however, the growth of unregulated commercial television meant that Rai's public service ambitions of pedagogy, moral uplift and national unification had to be put on hold in order to secure ratings, and thereby advertising revenue. At the time of the 1975 reform, however, these developments were still unforeseen.

3.2 Key rhetorical commitments

3.2.1 Pluralism

The specifics of the Constitutional Court's ruling are key because of the importance the value of pluralism acquired during the course of the parliamentary debate prior to the passage of the 1975 reform and in subsequent rulings of the Constitutional Court. Roberto Zaccaria, a leading jurist in the field of telecommunications (as well as former president of Rai and parliamentarian), has defined pluralism as "the most important constitutional value in the field of telecommunications" (Zaccaria, 1998, p. 126). Yet the basis for this importance is not self-evident. Pluralism is not a constitutional requirement: or rather, there is nothing in the text of the Italian Constitution which refers to pluralism or any similar concept; and the process of elucidation of the "constitutional value" of pluralism appears mysterious. The 1974 decision does not use the term "pluralism" in connection with the media. It does mention the "social pluralism" found in Italian society, which the media ought to reflect; but the term is used as descriptively, not as indicative of any value-claim, still less any inference from the text of the Constitution. The same holds for the court's (two) references to a "plurality of sources of information" – again, the word is used as a descriptive term. Thus, any support for the idea that pluralism in the media is a constitutional value cannot be based on what the Constitutional Court did in its 1974 decision, nor indeed on any other Court decisions around that time.

The stated aim of the law, as revealed in the parliamentary debates prior to its passage, was to implement the (supposed) principles of the Court's sentence. The majority opinion of the committee which reported on the draft bill[6] summarized the "decalogue" of commandments issued by the Court in its decision, but did so incorrectly, falsely attributing to the Court a request for "*l'obiettività dei programmi di informazione e il pluralismo di pensiero nei programmi culturali*", a phrase which is nowhere found in either of the Court's landmark decisions of 1974. The same error was made in the plenary: Gianfranco Merli (DC), speaking for the majority, argued that

> certain arguments … justify the choice of pluralism, *which is at the base of the Constitutional Court's judgement* … The concept of pluralistic information as

a duty and thus as a service, which affects all means of communication, *as the Court has recently held in its judgement*, causes us to revisit the reform of Rai.
(debate of 13 March 1975, col. 20903; emphasis added)

Why, if the Court had not, in the text of its decision, made pluralism the fundamental constitutional value in the field of the media, did the parliament act as if it had? Legislators may have uncovered a value "hidden" in the Court's decision; or they may have made a mistake; or, as is most likely, they have "discovered" pluralism in the Court's ruling in order to win greater legitimacy for a value that had essentially political roots.

In order to make this case, it is necessary to establish the context in which the reform law was passed. As already noted, the concession granted to Rai was due to expire; the Court's judgment only increased the pressure for quick parliamentary passage of some law on Rai. Quick parliamentary passage, however, was not something that the fourth Moro government – a minority government formed by the DC and the small Republican party – could guarantee. The DC was in a poor state following the failure of the "No" campaign in the previous year's divorce referendum, and what parliamentary energy the party could muster was employed in the passage of the public order law, the *legge Reale* (Ginsborg, 1990, p. 371). Consequently, any reform legislation capable of being approved in short order would have to win the support, not just of a parliamentary majority, but of a sufficiently large majority to prevent parliamentary obstructionism.

The Partito Comunista Italiano (PCI) was disposed to form part of this supermajority. By 1975, the party had embarked on the process of moderation that would lead it, two years later, to the historic compromise and parliamentary support for a DC-led government. Overt parliamentary obstruction of an important piece of reform legislation would have seemed incongruous with this new dash for respectability.

At the same time, the PCI remained a Gramsciite party, which viewed television as "an instrument for the conditioning of the subaltern classes along the lines of a bourgeois model" (Chiarenza, 2002, pp. 166–167). Abetting the DC in the reform of such an instrument would seem antithetical to the party's interests. Consequently, it was necessary that the reform be portrayed as furthering a value which could be shared by the PCI.

Pluralism was just such a value. Part of the move towards the historic compromise was terminological. As Alessandro Pizzorno put it,

> The PCI needed to declare its ideological conversion. "Democratic" it was by definition. "Liberal"? This would have been a bit much. "Pluralism" was a relatively fresh term. Few knew what it meant: it would therefore be discussed for quite some time, if only to find out what it meant.
>
> (Ufficio Stampa della Rai, 1976, p. 248)

The value was equally palatable to the DC, harking back to the arguments made in debates in the Constituent Assembly concerning the "pluralistic society", which some DC politicians supported as a "middle way" between "the two false and opposing doctrines of individualism ... and collectivism" (Matteucci, Bobbio & Pasquino, 1976, p. 721).

Consequently, the value of pluralism was sufficiently politically convenient – and vague – as to allow the approval of the reform, which occurred, with an ample majority on 26 March 1975.

3.2.2 Objectivity and impartiality

The dominance of pluralism is particularly surprising when one realizes that other values which have been repeatedly employed in other Western democracies as regulatory values in the media – the values of objectivity and impartiality – were not only present in the Court's 1974 ruling, but were given greater emphasis. The "objectivity" and "impartiality" of information were each mentioned five times in the 1974 judgment. These values were not reducible to pluralism, nor could they be considered manifestations thereof: "so-called pluralism of information, whilst having a relationship with objectivity, nevertheless cannot substitute for it" (Fragola, 1983, p. 197). The jurisprudential basis for these values was also less tendentious than that supporting the value of pluralism, even if it rested on a rather bald assertion by the court: "objectivity" and "impartiality" were two character-istics which a state monopoly in television would have to meet if it were to qualify as a service of general interest in the sense of Article 43 of the Constitution – pre-sumably because the public had a "general interest" in information of this kind.

Furthermore, the Court was able to cite references to these concepts in previ-ous rulings;[7] had it wished, it could have cited legislation of 1947 establishing the parliamentary supervisory committee in public broadcasting, which was to act so as to secure "the objectivity and impartiality of information".

Yet even by the time of the legislative work on the reform of Rai – and in conformity with the view expressed above that privileging pluralism served a political purpose – a majority of parties had chosen to emphasize the concept of pluralism in preference to these other values. It was left to deputies of the neo-fascist Movimento Sociale Italiano – Destra Nazionale (MSI-DN) to point out that impartiality and objectivity had been neglected:

> It was said: a plurality of voices, autonomy, independence. Yet the Com-mission, and with this the majority, has not sought to include the other characteristics which were by contrast indispensable and binding in the judgement of the constitutional court, or the objectivity, the impartiality and the completeness of information. These three conditions are interdependent, connected, and cannot be cut off from each other: free information has a value insofar as these three conditions are found. And yet in the legislative proposal the concept is not found: there are only scattered references.[8]

Why was objectivity so difficult a concept for the various parties to agree on? First, many Marxists argued that objectivity was, in theory or in practice, a bourgeois concept used to maintain hegemony and avoid the fall of capitalism to its own internal contradictions. For Lidia Serenari,

> objectivity does not exist in a society divided into classes: either one speaks for the class in power or for the class opposing it. The fiction that one can speak for all, ignoring class, is typically bourgeois in that it aims to avoid the accumulation of contradiction and class conflict, instead consolidating the current situation.
>
> (quoted in Chiarenza, 2002, p. 169)

The PCI, perhaps seeking to demonstrate a certain degree of moderation in the debate, tried to admit some role for objectivity, but on its own terms, leading to the following contradiction in terms from a Central Committee meeting of 1970: "objectivity, to have any commonly acceptable meaning, must refer to the democratic and antifascist principles of the Constitution" (quoted in Chiarenza, 2002, p. 172). The Socialists, by contrast, adopted a different tack in a 1970 report:[9]

> the principal error that has been and is made when discussing Rai is precisely the wish that every broadcaster be impartial. If one continues on this road one inevitably finishes bogged down in mechanisms of censure. As far as impartiality is concerned what counts is the result in terms of reception [of information]; which, in a regime of liberty, must be carried out so that all are supplied with information and the judgements that will allow them a choice about what is happening.
>
> (quoted in Chiarenza, 2002, p. 172)

It is not too difficult to carry out a political reading of these two stands: the PCI emphasized constitutionality in order to benefit from its position as a part of the *arco costituzionale*, and thus implicitly to exclude extremist parties to its left and the right of the political spectrum (the MSI-DN). The Socialists wished to avoid "censorious" mechanisms because they could never aspire to a majority within Rai, but, as the second largest party in government, could control certain units within the broadcaster. More generally, the notion of objectivity received little support within the DC and the PCI because the notion that there could be a position which was outwith, and independent of, their respective normative and cognitive systems (the Catholic Church and Gramsciite Marxism respectively) was anathema.

The debate concerning objectivity did not operate at an exclusively party-political level (though the continued input of the parties is in itself revealing): journalists and editors in the print press had also debated the issue. Had they united around the concept of objectivity, the debate concerning objectivity in broadcasting might have turned out differently. Indeed, had the debate about the reform of Rai taken place a few years later, the concept might have stood in better stead, for the late 1970s was marked by greater rhetorical and actual moves towards objectivity. In January 1976, *la Repubblica* was born, and the new paper, whilst openly declaring itself to belong to the left, made "repeated references to the liberal political model: to judge the facts, for better or worse, even if they emerge from the area in which one has chosen to be politically active" (Castronovo et al., 1979, p. 8). It was the first post-war expression of C. P. Scott's famous dictum: "comment is free, but facts are sacred."

Equally, the newspaper which would within 20 years cede its primacy to *la Repubblica*, the *Corriere della Sera*, openly pursued objectivity during this period. The newspaper was bought by the Rizzoli group, a development which was welcomed by staff journalists who viewed the group as an *editore puro*, or an owner with no other economic interests which might lead to conflicts of interest or overt interference in output by the proprietors. The new editor, Piero Ottone, had long argued for more objective reporting (as we shall see below), and once again Enzo Biagi emerged as a high-profile new hire to signal a commitment to objectivity.

These commitments to objectivity, despite coming from what are now the two largest news dailies in Italy, were at the avant-garde then, and were even more so at the time of the reform of Rai. Within the profession, commitment to objectivity was limited; what support there was crossed party-political lines.

Moreover, opponents of objectivity had strong philosophical support on their side: Umberto Eco, writing in 1969, derided the concept of objectivity as a "myth" and, worse, a "manifestation of false consciousness". In Mazzanti's paraphrase,

> to believe in this myth ... is to believe, or, still worse, in bad faith have others believe, that it is possible to relate the news without interpreting it: more generally, to imply that a certain piece of news, an article in the newspaper, or a television bulletin, is in a position to offer an image of reality as it is, without manipulating or distorting the latter ... It is absolutely illegitimate to speak of this mirror-theory [*di specularità*]: the reality which appears in the media is a reality which is inevitably interpreted. For example, in the same moment in which one chooses to publish, rather than throw out, one news item, an interpretative act is carried out, deriving from the importance that the journalist judges that news should have.
>
> (1991, p. 193)

Eco's position was not uncontested; thus who did disagree with him generally argued that there were concrete steps that the Italian press could and ought to take in order to become more objective, and, thus, that the concept of objectivity was of use. Ottone himself admitted that

> It is true that absolute objectivity does not exist, but Umberto Eco is wrong, according to me, to place the problem on this level, because he ends up by saying things which are so obvious as to become irrelevant. It is as if, discovering a child stealing some jam, we were to begin a disquisition on the

impossibility of absolute honesty. Absolute honesty is a utopia, fine; but there's no need to steal the jam.

(Ottone, 1969)

Prescinding from debates on the possibility of absolute objectivity, these exchanges show that the myth of objectivity was not accepted in Italy as it was in other countries, and was instead interpreted by the majority of politicians and a plurality of journalists as, at best, a distraction; at worst, a philosophically mis-leading concept. Consequently, this myth could not play any role in defending the broadcaster. During the preparatory works for the 1975 reform,

> certain projects foresaw the institution of a watchdog committee, granted specific powers, and responsible for the objectivity of programs. According to others, however, objectivity could only grow from confrontation; it thus became necessary to ensure the right of access ... it is this second tendency which is found in law no. 103.

(quoted in Chiarenza, 2002, p. 172)

Yet, as we shall see, greater "access", and the concept of pluralism, through influencing the structure of the broadcaster, further accentuated its dependence on politics.

3.3 Concrete rules

During this period, the idea of rules concerning all Rai journalists – and in par-ticular, rules concerning the treatment of news – disappeared. In large part, this was a natural consequence of the changes in the structure of the company dis-cussed below (3.4). Anticipating that section, we may say that the idea of rules governing all of Rai's output fell away because there was no longer any co-ordination between the three television channels, and because the directors of the different *reti* (channel) and *testate* (division), despite being beneficiaries of the decentralization implemented by the 1975 reform, were themselves subject to centripetal pressures.

As far as co-ordination between the different directors was concerned, one director, Ugo Zatterin, lamented the fact that, whilst previously the directors had had regular meetings in order to co-ordinate their positions vis-à-vis the manage-ment, especially as far as hiring decisions were concerned, there were no such meetings between January 1982 and September 1984 (Brancati, 1984). Given that much power had been devolved from the central administration to the *reti* and *testate* directors, any co-ordination would have had to come from them, and yet this never happened.

The directors of the *reti* and *testate* were also, however, subject to pressures from below. Due to broader changes in Italian journalism which also took place in the late 1970s, the different *comitati di redazione* (editorial committees), com-posed of the journalists, had acquired substantial powers in relation to their directors, including the right to hear the "political-editorial line of the director" and vote on it, and subsequently to express their confidence (or lack thereof) in the director at any subsequent point. Directors who were not sufficiently agile to placate their subordinates were consequently subjected to no-confidence votes, not approved by the *comitati di redazione* at all, or made to sweat: Nuccio Fava and Nino Rizzo Nervo, both left-leaning former Christian Democrats, reportedly had a torrid time as successive directors of the third news bulletin, TG3, due to poor relations with their *comitati di redazione* which, implicitly, were of the secular left (Vespa, 2002, p. 313). Because the journalists in the different *reti* and *testate* were often selected on party-political grounds, with each channel nominally affiliated to a particular political area (see below), this had the effect of accentuating the partisan character of each *reti* or *testate*, and depriving Rai of the co-ordination which could mute these aspects.

The first stirrings of co-ordination only began when private competitors began to emerge and Rai needed to demonstrate its ability to cope with competition. "Awareness is growing that internal competition (a guarantee of pluralism at the time of the monopoly) must now be substituted with a team game in order to sustain competition with the private channels" (Manca, 1987). And yet Rai's first editorial plan was only approved in 1988 – after a previous struggle had given greater power to the director-general, Biagio Agnes (Marletti, 1988), and after some years of commercial competition.

> It is, roughly speaking, a political document in which this improper editor, a politically appointed board, explains what it expects from its executives. But, as Manca has explained, it is also a sort of self-regulation that the broadcaster has given itself.
>
> (Brancati, 1988b)

The logic behind this plan was to protect the company from attacks. Agnes was explicit about this in a later meeting, where he is reported to have argued that "We can't be continually attacked from the outside ... and have to go forward without even some cover from the editor [here, the board]. Give me a document I can hold on to, and from which I can give instructions" (Brancati, 1988a). Yet this strategy was only being tried 13 years after the original reform, and only five years before further radical reform – intended to be temporary – would change once more the powers of the director-general, further limiting his and the board's ability to impose rules governing content.

3.4 Structure, organization, recruitment in news

The absence of rules governing content can in large part be explained by the way the reform law of 1975 structured the broadcaster. The law established a 16-member administrative council, of which 10 were to be elected by parliament, and 6 by the major stakeholder (IRI, and thus indirectly the government). The council was formally entrusted with the management of the company; the legislative intent was clearly to avoid another powerful director-general like Bernabei. It was "perhaps in an excess of *garantismo*" which led to "the concentration of too many tasks in the hands of the council", many of whose members lacked business experience (Pini, 1978, p. 14):

> with the result of paralysing the company … In essence there were but two possible models for the council: that of the "guarantee" council … and that of the "governing" council (a collective managing director, as has been said numerous times). The ambiguity … [of the law was] to have fused these together in a manner which is not easy to disentangle.
>
> (Zaccaria, 1984, p. 19)

The power of the directly appointed level within the broadcaster (unusual in comparative terms) might have been an impediment to strong coherent management of the broadcaster irrespective of the other provisions of the law; but what was more important for the future development of the broadcaster was the power given to the channel directors. Article 13 of the 1975 law went into great detail concerning the organization of the reformed broadcaster, which was to have two television and three radio news bulletins, each with their own director reporting directly to the director-general. Additionally, each channel was to have "its own separate complement of organizational and administrative staff". Thus supplied with the necessary administrative resources, these *reti* and *testate* were in a position to draw up programme proposals which would be "co-ordinated" by the director-general, who emerged from the reform greatly weakened. The countervailing tendencies within the law, which envisaged co-ordination of time-slots and budgets, were never implemented (Pini, 1978, p. 163). The director-general thus appeared as more of a referee between competing factions than an executive in his own right: Scotto Lavina (1984, p. 165) goes so far as to claim that

> From that moment, from March 1976, the start date for the new telegiornali and the entry into force of the new bodies, it no longer makes sense to speak of Rai's TV schedule, but only of the offer (and thus the schedule) of the first and second channels … in essence the director-general's office was relegated to the position of a notary, so much were the major decisions taken by the networks under their own coordination.

The director-general's role was thus an unhappy one, and three appointees from different backgrounds succeeded one another in rapid succession (Scotto Lavina, 1984, p. 164).

This proliferation of posts and the subtraction of power from the office of the director-general was a direct consequence of the adoption of pluralism as the guiding principle for the broadcaster. Multiple networks and news desks were instituted "so as to pay the debt of pluralism contracted by the reform law" (Mauri, 1984, p. 268). This was made clear in the debate prior to passage of the law: DC deputy Frau described the principle of the reform as being that of "a plurality of voices within radio and television which may express themselves through different opinions, *through* two different structures which *allow* different opinions to be expressed" (debate of 12 March, col. no 20844; emphasis added). Manca (DC) expressed most fully the logic of this structural pluralism:

> *the plurality of rete and testate giornalistiche* do not follow the principles of *lottizzazione*,[10] but rather that of pluralism, which aims not at following the myth of objective information, but *to build, concretely, the conditions for the completeness that is to say, the impartiality – of the news. In other terms, it is from the pluralism of television networks and journalistic testate that the full expression of the professional capacity of our journalists and cultural workers flows, because the diversity and plurality of voices are in much better position to offer a more faithful and complete picture of a variegated, complex, and, indeed, pluralistic, reality, such as is found in Italian society.*
>
> (debate of 13 March, col. no 20935; emphasis added)

A plurality of *reti* and *testate* was therefore desirable, not in and of itself, but because such units, independently formed and independently managed, and thus in a position to compete, can offer a better, more truthful picture of reality. Although no legislator talked of it in such terms, the argument is similar to the one Milton made in his *Areopagitica* (1644): "there must be many schisms and many dissections made in the quarry and in the timber, ere the house of God can be built." Thus did the reform law create schisms and dissections in the quarry and timber of the public broadcaster. Of course, these dissections were also determined by less principled reasons.

Why did journalists and executives accept this system? In the same way that having more posts available made it easier for important posts to be subdivided between the parties, having more positions of responsibility meant that more journalists could aspire to executive positions; that fewer would lose out in the kind of hotly contested promotion fights that might take place in a more centralized broadcaster; and that any journalists or executives who fell out of favour could be given a promotion to a peripheral area should they become useful at a later time. That is, it

> also derived from the demand from the same bureaucracy and technocratic structures within the company to regulate in the quickest manner possible the unending questions of hierarchy, of division of labour, of major and minor management issues, which in any complex organization threaten daily the functioning of the machine itself.
>
> (Ortoleva, 1994, p. 92)

The division of posts was connected to the practice of *lottizzazione* – of the division of posts within the broadcaster between the parties. *Lottizzazione* had begun during the Bernabei period, as journalists and managers close to the Socialists and the Social Democrats were appointed, but the period after 1975 was the period of "classic" *lottizzazione* – which was gradually extended to encompass the PCI in 1986, when, after a meeting between Walter Veltroni, Biagio Agnes and Enrico Manca, the party was given the right to designate the channel director of the third channel, RaiTre and the editor of the associated news bulletin, TG3 (Balassone & Guglielmi, 1995, p. 11).

3.5 Political interference

Political interference during this period in large part consisted in the practice of *lottizzazione* – in the securing of posts for faithful journalists who would subsequently act in the interests of their sponsors. The system was so pervasive as to require regimentation: according to an unattributed formula, in every wave of appointments the DC was entitled to six seats, the PCI three, the Socialists two, and the Liberals, Republicans and Social Democrats one each (Mancini, 2009, p. 27).

The parties continued to ask in public for greater objectivity, but this did not lead them to endorse the natural concomitant of objectivity, namely, a news division organized in a way that did not reflect the strength of the parties, but rather a single, objective account of news, tailored, if need be, to different audiences. One polling company surveyed parliamentarians on whether they would prefer it if the current division of the *reti* and *testate* between political parties were abolished. A plurality (48%) said that they wished things to remain as they were; only 31% wished to see the current division between parties changed (Ricci, 1989).

That the parties were widely reported to be requesting, and obtaining, a division of posts based on party-political strength is not in itself sufficient to conclude that the broadcaster had low levels of independence – it is entirely possible, if improbable, that these journalists were faithless to their patrons. There are, and were, multiple responses to the issue of *lottizzazione*: many journalists have claimed that *lottizzazione* does not exist, that others might have been *lottizzatti* but that they themselves were not, and so on (Padovani, 2005, ch. 4, and *passim*); but there are instances of journalists who in debate admit that their work is conditioned by the party to whom their owe their position. This, for example, was the case of Bruno Vespa, who declared in one interview that he considered the DC his "reference point" (*editore di riferimento*): in any case, the admission did not hurt Vespa's career, and for the past 13 years he has hosted *Porta a Porta*, the most watched political debate show on Italian television, in addition to annually publishing books with Rai's publishing arm, Rai-Eri.

4 New hopes dashed (1993–2008)

4.1 The setting

Between 1992 and 1994, the Italian party system collapsed under the weight of multiple corruption scandals (*Tangentopoli*). In the wave of anti-party sentiment, the parliament elected in 1992 undertook a series of technocratic reforms, including reform of Rai. The law was intended to reduce party interference in Rai until a comprehensive television law could resolve the issue. To pursue these goals, the board was reduced from 16 to 5 members who would no longer be appointed by the government and the parliament, but rather by the presidents of the two chambers. Appointments, however, were to last for two years only, in a nod to the "provisory" nature of the reform bill. This choice was predicated on the belief that the presidents would continue to be drawn from the two principal opposing coalitions, yet instead this practice was discontinued in 1994 with the move to a more majoritarian political system. Yet despite this, the reform achieved its objective, and fewer partisan nominees were appointed.

More serious than appointments were Rai's finances, which were seriously threatened in 1992 by a deterioration in the real value of the licence fee and by a downturn in the advertising market as a result of the recession of 1991–1993. Rai's debts gave the government and parliament of the day extraordinary leverage over the company, as ad-hoc decrees were required in order to keep the company in business.

Rai's weakness came at an inopportune moment. If any pre-existing parties had benefited from *Tangentopoli*, it was those parties which had been most excluded from the practice of *lottizzazione*, the former PCI, now the Left Democrats (Democratici di Sinistra (DS)), and the post-Fascist MSI-DN, now the National Alliance (Alleanza Nazionale (AN)). These parties bore grudges in proportion to their past exclusion (see, for example, the introductions by Gianfranco Fini and Walter Veltroni in Mazza & Agnes, 2004, pp. ix–1). Yet the most important party for Rai was the new party, Forza Italia, founded by Silvio Berlusconi in order to compete in the 1994 elections. Berlusconi's position as both prime minister (May–December 1994; 2001–2006; 2008–) and owner of Rai's principal competitor Mediaset would be one of the most important structural problems facing Rai; Berlusconi's interference in Rai would become one of the most important contingent problems for Rai during the Second Republic.

These problems were only potential problems when the first board of the "new" Rai was appointed in July 1993. This board – nicknamed the "board of the Professors" – sought to remove employees appointed for their political sympathies rather than for their ability; and to recast Rai's journalism in a consciously "Anglo-Saxon" mould. It failed. The reasons why it failed illustrate some of the key claims of this book: that public service broadcaster chief executives must have security of tenure; that a history of self-regulation within the press aids self-regulation within the broadcaster; and that journalists will continue to be perceived as partisan where the potential recruitment pool is partisan.

4.2 Key rhetorical commitments

In 1993 Rai seemed to have turned back to the original values it was called upon to uphold, namely impartiality and objectivity. These, after all, remained the terms of the law on television, the *legge Mammì*, which defined the principles of broadcasting in its first article as involving "pluralism, objectivity, completeness and impartiality of information", though with no mention of how disputes between these various values might be resolved.

The call to impartiality and objectivity was acted upon by the new board, and motivated many of the changes to the organization of news which are discussed below. Yet, for reasons which will be discussed later, that experiment failed, and the ideas of impartiality and objectivity were once again interred. The concept of impartiality seemed to have been subsumed under that of pluralism, as outlined in an interview with Roberto Zaccaria. For Zaccaria,

ZACCARIA: My task was made up of two words. First, independence: to be, to the greatest extent possible, independent of parties, and of the government. Second, pluralism: to give light to the diversity present in the company and in the country.
QUESTION: But we've talked of 3 values here: independence, pluralism, and impartiality...
ZACCARIA: Yes, but pluralism and impartiality are concepts very close together. Certainly, one can be a sole person giving account of many varied points of view; this ideal is, however, a little theoretical [inaudible]; it's difficult for one to strip oneself [*spogliersi*] totally of one's subjectivity ... I'd say that the three – independence, impartiality, pluralism – can be subsumed under independence.[11]

With the end of the experiment initiated by the Professors, and with the entry into politics of Silvio Berlusconi and the consequent passage of the *par condicio* (law no. 515 of 10 December 1993; law no. 28 of 22 February 2000), the concept of pluralism returned as the dominant value in debates concerning Rai. The *par condicio* required not only that party-political broadcasts be made by the parties on an equal basis, but also that broadcasters divide their news coverage of the competing parties or blocs on an equal basis, or otherwise, as specified by the sectoral watchdog, Autorità per le garanzie nelle comunicazioni (AGCOM).

These laws have made necessary the collection of data on the amount of screen-time given to each competing subject. This monitoring is carried out not just by AGCOM (which has gone substantially beyond its mandate [as specified in Art. 1, §6b, ¶9 of law no. 249 of 31 July 1997], in collecting not merely information on political coverage during electoral periods, but also during normal politics, where no quantitative obligation is placed on broadcasters), but by a number of private organizations. Despite the fact that the *par condicio* only applies during electoral campaigns, data from these organizations were used by Rai, and by those outside it, to alternately defend or attack the broadcaster for a presumed lack of pluralism.

The most concerted attempt to reassert this kind of pluralism, and to put this conception on a sounder footing, was made by Roberto Zaccaria, president of Rai between 1998 and 2002. In the run-up to the 2001 elections, Zaccaria defended Rai from accusations of impartiality by citing data from two different monitoring companies which showed that Rai "had respected political pluralism

– the principle of the three thirds" (Caviglia, 2001), according to which screen time should be shared equally between the legislative majority ($\frac{1}{3}$), the legislative minority ($\frac{1}{3}$) and the governing institutions ($\frac{1}{3}$).

Zaccaria's use of this principle was sagacious. "Reliance on numbers and quantitative manipulation minimises the need for intimate knowledge and personal trust" – trust which certainly did not exist between the parties and Rai at that time. If "the drive to supplant personal judgement by quantitative rules reflects weakness and vulnerability" (Porter, 1995, pp. ix, xi), Zaccaria's move seems appropriate given the weakness and vulnerability of Rai in particular and the Italian journalistic corps in general. This principle also had the advantage of international precedent, having been previously employed by the French Conseil Supérieur de l'Audiovisuel. Had it won acceptance in Italy as it did in France, then this conception of pluralism might have become dominant. Unfortunately for Zaccaria, the criterion was not accepted by the legislative minority, who objected to over-representation of government ministers.

Francesco Storace (AN) claimed that

> those Italians who do not vote for [parties of the left] have been wiped-out by the public news. Between the 25th January and the 30th April ... the majority won with 60% against 40% for the opposition in news programmes; or as much as 70% in the news bulletins.
>
> (Fontanarosa, 1998)

This idea of pluralism had already been attacked in the 1980s. Whilst a global balance might be attained by Rai, it may either be a global balance because each individual programme is balanced, or it may be a global balance composed of well-distributed partial views. Yet "three twisted mirrors do not make a relatively objective mirror, three partial voices are not mutually correcting, and do not complement each other case-by-case" (Ronchey, 1988). Thinking in terms of the theory outlined in Chapter 2, the parties' reactions make sense – what matters is not that output globally be close to the point that a neutral observer would desire, but rather that each individual piece should be sufficiently balanced as to allow the observer to conclude that the journalist was not partisan, and that no better outcome could be achieved by replacing that partisan journalist with a non-partisan one, or vice versa. Indeed, the very reliance on screen-time data may have accentuated this problem, as the differences between the three Rai channels are now more apparent than ever. Consequently, it is perhaps unsurprising that the next president of Rai, Antonio Baldassare, decided not to follow Zaccaria's lead and discontinued the practice of regularly issuing information on screen-time.

4.3 Concrete rules

Because they saw their task as being more fundamental and involving organizational reform, the board of the Professors did not consider concrete rules governing output. Their reform is dealt with in the next section, but the boards which followed the "Professors" were, perforce, obliged to consider some rules dealing with the output of the agency. Successive boards continued writing editorial plans of the type first introduced by Biagio Agnes, but these documents had little weight given the limited tenure of their authors.

Trade magazine *Prima Comunicazione* noted that

> interest in what goes on at the top management rises only when there are nominations being made or when something affects the fabric of the company ... Little importance, for example, to the recently voted editorial plan ... four pages which speak of public service [and] pluralism.

It goes on to quote a "veteran of Viale Mazzini" (Rai's headquarters): "It's a rite that each management team feels they have to carry out ... It helps the *Vigilanza* [the parliamentary committee which supervises Rai]; it gives the politicians something to talk about."[12] Previous directors-general have recognized the problem. Gianfranco Iseppi (director-general, 1996–1998) devoted much of his book on public service broadcasting (Iseppi, 1998) to the need to develop clear "mission statements" for Rai. For Claudio Cappon (director-general, 2001–2002), "nobody really gives any importance to these written texts, but rather to the eternal negotiation of existence in a political environment ... people in Rai don't feel that these objectives ... are something that must be guaranteed by the community."[13]

Equally, Rai's ethics code – which, together with the editorial plans, forms the closest thing that Rai has to the BBC's Editorial Guidelines – commands scarce agreement. Although the code contained nothing new save pre-existing legal requirements,[14] it was immediately criticized by company trade union USIGRAI as "unacceptable", a document which "pretends to be constraining like a contract without ever having been discussed with employee representatives".[15] There was an internal publicity campaign dealing with the code, but employees were trusted to read the code themselves instead of formal training.

4.4 Structure, organization, recruitment in news

The most significant effort undertaken by the board was its attempt to reform Rai's news output. All board members were sensitive to the need for change, but Paolo Murialdi (Professor of Journalism at the University of Turin) was asked to write a report for the board on the issue (Murialdi, 1994, p. 31). The key problem was the structural duplication of effort in news, with three different news programmes covering very often the same stories. This structure undermined any belief that the news was in some way dictated by external events and objective, in a very limited sense: for if this were the case, what need would there be for three different news programmes which treated the same news events in different ways?

The solution eventually proposed by the board was to have four different news programmes differentiated by subject and by audience segment. The choice was a curious one for a company which was at the time facing severe financial difficulties. Instead of creating an additional, duplicate, set of fixed costs, the company might have reduced costs – and increased profits – by merging the three news programmes into one unit, reducing the total volume of news output, and filling the space with imported or otherwise low-cost programming which would likely have been more attractive to advertisers. Such a choice might have been rejected for several reasons: the board might not have thought potential replacement programming was of sufficiently high quality to be put on air without involving Rai in a "race to the bottom" with Mediaset. Yet the choice was not rejected for this reason, but rather for reasons which had to do with the belief that any single news programme is (willingly or otherwise) the inevitable expression of some political position. Murialdi, in discussing possible solutions to the problem of multiple news programmes, arrives at the figure of four news programmes by a process of elimination:

> We reject without discussion a single *telegiornale*. It would be the pawn of the government of the day. On the issue of two *telegiornali* there is the unknown factor of the majoritarian electoral system. With two political formations, the stronger *telegiornale* would go to the majority, the other to the opposition. To have three *telegiornali* smacks of the old tripartite division, because it won't be easy for some to reject the old generalist formula.
>
> (Murialdi, 1994, p. 32)

Why would a single news programme necessarily be a government appendage? We may construct a plausible chain of reasoning: there is no news outlet which is free of viewpoint; a single *telegiornale* would therefore have some viewpoint; the government's position is, politically speaking, the dominant one; the single *telegiornale* would therefore be likely to have the government's position rather than any other. And yet a single *telegiornale* could have been a central element in the claim that other PSBs have found so useful in defending their coverage: that the news is the news, and is dictated by events, not by the teams who produce it.

The board's efforts to change Rai's journalism were interpreted not as an attempt to impose impartiality, but rather to impose a carefully calibrated partiality marginally to the centre-left. This interpretation was strongest amongst those on RaiTre. Sandro Curzi and Corradino Mineo paraphrase the board president De Mattè as saying:

> "I want a Rai that doesn't scream", he said, "I want journalism in the English school [*giornalismo all'inglese*], a unitary Rai, which plays a team game". Which is to say: I want a neoinstitutional news, prudent and recherché, moderately progressive or prudently moderate according to the way the wind is blowing.
>
> (Curzi & Mineo, 1994, p. 125)

The element of novelty – the claim to wish impartiality (*giornalismo all'inglese*) – is essentially ignored or dismissed without any clear rationale. What, after all, is wrong with prudent journalism? In these quotes, we see the interpretation of notionally non-partisan aims in a partisan key.

The same interpretative key would be used when appointments were considered by the board. The board's desire to appoint experienced individuals who would be independent of politics was quixotic: the only individuals who were experienced were individuals who owed their experience to political ties.

> It's almost impossible to find a manager, however honest, talented and able, who is not now or ever has been connected to a political grouping. And for that reason it's equally impossible to escape polemics everytime that someone is nominated ... Neutrals can't be found; if they exist, no-one believes them to be such; if they genuinely are so, no-one trusts them.
>
> (Cardini & Riccio, 1995, p. 38)

One option would have been to dismiss large numbers of executives who had been particularly compromised by politics and promote from within to replace the dismissed executives. This option would have been plagued by multiple difficulties.

First, there was a risk that the dismissal of key individuals would in itself be perceived as a political act. If an individual was appointed thanks to the help of the PSI, anyone who seeks to remove him or her must perforce be an enemy of the PSI, either on the left or the right. Indeed, many individuals attempt to depict their removals as being motivated by political calculations instead of calculations of merit or suitability. The head of personnel, de Domenico, said to Murialdi, "'you're firing me because I'm a socialist'. [Murialdi] responded that he would be removed not because he was a socialist, but rather because he was responsible for *lottizzazione* under the aegis of Andreotti and, above all, Craxi" (Murialdi, 1994, p. 27).

Second, it was likely that widespread dismissals would have incurred such emnity on the part of the staff that any further reforms would have been blocked immediately. The board was given an early example of this potential when board president Demattè implied in an interview that the main editors should tender their resignations in order to give the board a clean hand, which ultimately led to accusations that the board wished the company ill (Murialdi, 1994, p. 165).

Third, it is likely that dismissals would have needed to have been so pervasive as to seriously threaten Rai's ability to continue operating. As Murialdi noted, "within Rai there are very few without some kind of label. What to do? Fire them? Is that possible? I don't think so" (Murialdi, 1994, entry 3 October).

Nor would making new appointments be any easier, given the tendency to interpret appointments in a political key. This was demonstrated by the negotiations leading up to the appointment of Gianni Locatelli as director-general. The board had searched for an external candidate, and had considered Paolo Glisenti (RCS Video) and Emanuele Milano (ex-Rai, now Telemontecarlo) (Murialdi,

1994, entry 19 July), but the former was blocked by Romano Prodi (at the time president of IRI, principal shareholder in Rai). Locatelli's eventual nomination was met with strong criticism by the employees' union USIGRAI, who viewed it as a sign that the reform was "dead", for Locatelli was a "known Catholic". Locatelli was thus considered "close" to the DC, despite not being a party member (Murialdi, 1994, p. 21).

Equally, the first round of appointments below director-general was met with criticism, particularly from the left. As Murialdi recalls:

> The reactions to the Demattè plan from the left and from journalists in Rai have been violent. The Rai editorial assembly has described the plan as inadequate and backwards. Last Thursday's nominations are the proof ... that Rai executives are taking up *lottizzazione* again. Mattucci is socialist, Fuscagni Christian Democratic ... Curzi said, "I see lots of familiar names still circulating."
>
> (Murialdi, 1994, entry 3 October)

Thus, the limited stock of journalists with no obvious partisan affiliation – and a willingness to attribute such where none were present – made the board's job extremely difficult. Any round of appointments would have been interpreted in a political light, and would have led those who were discomfited by the appointments to see them as part of a conspiracy, further impeding reform.

The dramatic changes to the Italian political system which took place between 1992 and 1994 could have led to an influx of new journalists free of partisan affiliations. This might have been possible given concentrated leadership from Rai and from the industry as a whole. Good intentions were present. Though she was forced to make considerable cutbacks, Letizia Moratti, who succeeded Demattè as President of Rai, did announce plans for a "Scuola Rai". Such an announcement was natural at that time: the first postgraduate courses in journalism had started just a few years earlier in Milan. Yet Italian journalism – and in particular broadcast journalism – still has few of the trappings of a professionalization project. The number of official journalism schools is limited, at 16;[16] the number of credible programmes more limited still, as can be seen by the number of failed journalism masters degrees. This compares poorly with the UK, an environment traditionally thought hostile to the conscious development of journalism as a profession, which numbers 25 NCTJ- or BJTC-accredited institutions offering postgraduate courses. The limited quantitative impact of formal journalism courses might be of little account if graduates of these courses held disproportionate power in shaping Italian journalism. Yet even Rai's own attempts at formal journalism training have had limited success in creating journalists capable of taking on leadership roles. Of the 29 alumni of the first programme offered by Rai's School of Journalism in Perugia, only one – Giovanni Floris – is well-known amongst the public,[17] and only one other – Antonio Preziosi – has held an executive position within Rai (as director of RadioUno and Rai's radio news). Many of the remainder work for Rai's regional news programmes, for radio news or for RaiNews24, which has acquired a reputation for nimble, relatively non-partisan journalism – but which has minimal audience share. None of the first group of students works for any of Rai's competitors, suggesting that this project has had no particular broader impact in the industry.

Progress for these individuals is blocked by continuous turnover involving a recurring cast of news and channel editors. Certain individuals with political connections have been able to maintain a holding pattern within Rai, occupying posts of lesser prestige whilst waiting for a more favourable political climate. This is the case for both individuals from the right, such as Antonio Marano, former Undersecretary of Posts and Telecoms and Director of Rai2 from 2002 to 2004, and subsequently again from 2006 to 2009, after having been demoted to head Rai's sporting rights department, and individuals from the left, such as Albino Longhi, director of *Tg1* in 1993, and again from 2000 to 2002, having acted as special adviser to Romano Prodi in the interim. Individuals such as these have prevented the formation of a new executive group capable of imparting direction to Rai; individuals who have formal qualifications, and are generally recognized as practising a relatively impartial form of journalism either leave for better offers elsewhere (Gianni Riotta, who has a masters degree in journalism from Columbia, and who left *Tg1* for *Il Sole 24 Ore*) or never arrive at Rai (Paolo Mieli, former editor of the *Corriere della Sera*, who turned down the post of president of Rai).

Even were Italian journalism characterized by a stronger emphasis on professional qualifications, and even if access to executive positions were not blocked by a cast of usual suspects, recruitment to Rai would still be problematic given the tremendous importance of media outlets owned by Berlusconi. The appointment of any individuals with prior experience working at Mondadori publications or Mediaset channels inevitably leads to protests by centre-left parties. The appointments of Augusto Minzolini and Clemente Mimun – former journalist for *Panorama* (Mondadori) and former vice-director of TG5 (Mediaset) respectively – were both subject to strong opposition from centre-left members of the board.

Executive appointments in general have provoked greater discord ever since the passage of the 2004 Gasparri law, which altered the system for appointing board members. The Gasparri law actually set out two distinct methods of appointment: one method to be used following the broadcaster's partial privatization, another to be used until that point. Since no shares in Rai have yet been sold, this second method has been used to appoint members of the board. The current board is composed of nine members, of whom seven are appointed by the Commissionare parlamentare per l'indirizzo generale e la vigilanza dei servizi radiotelevisivi (CPIV) by multi-member plurality, with the remaining two members, including the board president, nominated by the Treasury Minister. The appointment of the President must be ratified by a two-thirds majority of the CPIV. Appointments are for a once-renewable three-year term. Parliamentarians may be nominated but may not serve as board members.[18] The law refers to resignation and permanent incapacity of members of the board, but makes no provisions for their dismissal. This has not stopped the CPIV from arrogating that power to itself, passing a motion[19] calling upon Claudio Petruccioli to resign as president of Rai; this action led to two other councillors offering their resignations to the committee (Bruzzone, 2007). Boards appointed by this method have been the most politically active boards in Rai's history. Five of the nine members of the first board appointed by this method had been elected to parliament, and two (Nino Rizzo Nervo and Sandro Curzi) had edited party newspapers. Given such levels of prior political engagement, it is unsurprising that many of the key decisions regarding promotions and appointments are only decided by majority vote. Occasional attempts to nominate figures with non-partisan backgrounds – typically by parties of the left – have generally met with criticism from those parties themselves.[20]

4.5 Political interference

In the interim between the collapse of the old party system and the elections of 1994, interference in Rai's operations was rather limited. After the appointment of a new board, the pressure placed on the broadcaster grew. One new board member, medieval historian Franco Cardini, claimed that whilst he personally had not been subject to pressure, "I would be lying if I said that the Northern League, the Catholics, and AN never asked for anything" (Cardini & Riccio, 1995, pp. 31, 54).

The influence of the centre-left during its period in government was more muted, concentrated, as it was, on the structural aspects of the broadcaster, and the repeated reorganizations of the broadcaster which anticipated its part-privatization. It was only with Berlusconi's return to power in 2001 that the issue of the independence of Rai returned to salience.

Berlusconi's *behaviour* towards the media, and Rai in particular, has been just as controversial as his government's media legislation. There have been numerous episodes in which journalists or presenters judged to be hostile to Berlusconi have had their contracts cancelled or not renewed. Perhaps the most infamous of these episodes occurred on a state visit to Bulgaria in 2002. During a press conference, Berlusconi had declared that

> the use that Biagi [Enzo, noted journalist], Santoro [Michele, current affairs show host and subsequently MEP] and Luttazzi [Daniele, comedian] have made of public television – paid for with public money – is criminal. The new Rai administration must see that this does not happen again.

Following this incident – widely reported in the international press – Santoro's contract was not renewed and Biagi's show was discontinued.

Of course, there is no evidence, apart from this declaration, to suggest that Berlusconi asked Rai board members directly to dismiss Biagi or Santoro. It is possible that the statement itself was sufficient either to convince members of the board (appointed by members of Berlusconi's coalition) or the director-general Agostino Saccà (candidate for reappointment in two years' time) that not renewing the contracts would win political favour. At the very least, the fact that Rai dismissed these individuals after a statement of this nature shows the company was shockingly blasé about public perception of its independence from government.

Direct contact between Berlusconi and Rai employees has often been alleged. Former president of Rai Lucia Annunziata claimed to "know for a fact" that Berlusconi called television executives behind her back. Direct evidence, however, was not found until December 2007, when *Espresso* published a transcript of a phone call between Berlusconi and Saccà (by this time director of fiction) in which Berlusconi asked for two women to be given auditions for upcoming dramas. (The women were close to centre-left senators Berlusconi was allegedly trying to corrupt.) Following the publication of the transcripts Saccà was not dismissed, only transferred to a less important post; even this measure was met with opposition from the centre-right members of the board.

Yet the most constantly cited evidence of political interference in Rai is the extent to which Rai's coverage – and in particular the news coverage of the flagship news bulletin, *Tg1* – favours Berlusconi and his party. Under the current director, Augusto Minzolini, the main news bulletin *Tg1* has been repeatedly fined by the communications watchdog AGCOM for imbalances in coverage during electoral periods – imbalances which favoured Berlusconi's coalition. Minzolini has also made more frequent use than normal of direct-to-camera editorials, which have often criticized those who criticize Berlusconi.[21] Whilst editorial stances and imbalances in coverage may result from factors other than government interference, these choices have not commanded either respect amongst Minzolini's subordinates, or interest from viewers: editorial committees of all three news bulletins signed a protest against Minzolini's decision not to report details of Berlusconi's sex scandals,[22] and *Tg1* has lost considerable audience share since Minzolini's tenure began.

Whilst the Saccà case demonstrates that Berlusconi can ask for favours at the broadcaster and get them, and the Minzolini case potentially indicates that the effects on coverage are considerable, one can overstate Berlusconi's influence on public television. I have elsewhere (Hanretty, 2007) demonstrated that there was no big shift in Rai's coverage, measured in terms of the screen-time given to parties of the left and right respectively, before and after Berlusconi's coalition got the chance to nominate a new board; continued political fighting over the broadcaster is thus likely to be part of a longer, positional game aimed at cementing influence in the media.

5 Conclusion

Rai has, at a number of points in its history, come close to developing rules of conduct which are obeyed by its workforce and which affect the broadcast content produced by them. At no point has it come close to developing written codes which approach in length or sophistication the written codes developed by the BBC or even Sveriges Television; and at no point have these codes ever served as a basis for resolving politicians' complaints: the normal mode of recourse for aggrieved politicians remains to bring a defamation case against Rai journalists. Nor have these codes always aimed at producing content of the kind that might be produced by an impartial observer: the manuals produced under Filiberto Guala were principally concerned with reinforcing the hegemony of the Christian Democratic Party's view of society.

Yet at certain points these attempts at developing rules of conduct have given the company a modicum of independence. This was the case under Bernabei; it was somewhat the case under Agnes; and very recently it seems that the experiment has been taken on again by Claudio Cappon, who has dealt with issues like the Saccà case by referring them to internal complaints panels (n.a., 2008). Yet at each point, these reforms have been halted by ill-advised institutional reform, reform which has continually limited the legal independence afforded the broadcaster, which has never subtracted from the political influence bearing on the broadcaster, only divided it; and which has caused considerable turnover in the company.

Rai has therefore not just been plagued by structural factors such as the limited size of the market for news and the limited degree of legal protection: it has also been affected by bad decisions and bad timing. Indeed, Italy seems to have slipped behind Spain, where the reform efforts seem to have paid greater attention to objectivity and less concern with pluralism, and have in any case paid much greater attention to the term lengths of executives. This relative regression can be seen, for example, in Sabina Guzzanti's film, *Viva Zapatero!*; Guzzanti – another individual who left Rai in a storm of political protest – lauds the efforts of the Zapatero government to reform RTVE, seeing in it a model for Italy to follow. But whereas political influence over RTVE came from the government, and required only the government to forswear such influence, political influence over Rai is widely distributed, and reform would require a series of actors to give up influence voluntarily. It is for that reason that reform efforts have failed in the past;[23] for that reason that they remain likely to fail again in the future.

Nor are there any substantial incentives for reform, since efforts to deal with the conflict of interest and reform the broadcasting system lack a natural constituency in Italy. Whilst there has been a succession of extremely vocal popular protests against Berlusconi, the conflict of interests he embodies and political control over Rai, these movements, in particular the so-called *girotondisti*, have largely been confined to the educated middle classes, as already noted above (see p. 18).

The argument which leads to this rather pessimistic conclusion, and indeed the rest of the chapter itself, can be summed up thusly:

- First, pre-Fascist Italy, whilst it displayed some stirrings of professionalism in the North, was never able to develop either a market-reliant news agency or any professional association of journalists.
- Second, and consequently, Rai had to develop an autonomous newsgathering capacity without being able to import any professional norms to defend its output.

- Given this lack of professional norms concerning output, and given the limited legal protection vis-à-vis the Ministry of Posts and Telegraphs, Rai was born with limited independence.
- Third, calls for reform and the adoption of professional norms of objectivity and impartiality were ignored; instead, norms which derived from political compromise – such as the pursuit of pluralism – were adopted.
- Fourth, these norms, however, have failed to defend the company, and have instead legitimated further practices of *lottizzazione*.
- Fifth, and consequently, any new reform effort which aims at increasing the company's independence is likely to falter through offending entrenched political interests for whom the genuine independence of Rai from politics would mean the end of their career.

The outlook for Rai is thus bleaker than the outlook for the comparable case, the Spanish broadcaster RTVE, which is discussed in the next chapter. Whilst in Spain, the initial conditions – an extremely limited market for news – were equally poor, certain acts, such as the Franco regime's greater emphasis on journalistic training, were of paradoxical benefit to the broadcaster. In Italy, by contrast, poor initial conditions were compounded by badly thought-out reform efforts brokered through what was, in certain senses, an impeccably democratic compromise.

4   Spain

Huge steps forward?

1 From dictatorship to transition (1923–1977)

The first broadcaster in Spain began operations in autumn 1923 under the de Rivera dictatorship. Its position was retrospectively legitimated by a royal decree of the following year. The decree allowed the government to grant broadcasting concessions to multiple private entities, a considerable contrast with the legal position in most of the rest of Europe. During the short-lived Second Republic, proposals were made to establish a public service broadcaster (PSB), but the pressures of Civil War meant that these proposals were dead letters (Bustamante, 2007, pp. 19–20). The Francoist victory in the Civil War meant that only private operators with Fascist sympathies could continue to broadcast.

There were four principal broadcasters, each with strong links to the regime: two under the control of the Fascist Party; one a wing of the Francoist trade union; and the official broadcaster, Radio Nacional de España (RNE), which was a division within the Ministry of Popular Education (until 1951) and subsequently the Ministry of Information and Tourism (1951 onwards) (Bustamante, 2007, pp. 21, 24). In theory ministry and broadcaster were separate, but the head of the ministerial Servicio de Radiodifusión was at the same time the director-general of RNE. The fiction was, however, maintained: in 1957 a new, "autonomous" administrative organ was created to administer RNE, but it was never implemented. Instead, the ministry's control over broadcasting was extended in the following year when it was granted exclusive responsibility for television broadcasting, forming Television Española (TVE). In 1973 the two units (RNE and TVE) were merged to form RTVE, which again was theoretically independent from the ministry, but to which it remained inextricably linked (Bustamante, 2007, pp. 31, 47).

Nominal competition in the market for radio did not lead to the development of broadcast journalism. The market was hardly an open one: the directors of these stations were nominated by the regime, and, were this not enough to quash any possibility of dissonant messages being transmitted, the private emitters were prevented by law from broadcasting their own news bulletins, being instead forced to host 15-minute news bulletins from the state broadcaster RNE (the so-called *partes*), an imposition which was only removed in 1977. The later television news bulletins were slightly better, being sourced from two American news agencies, Columbia Broadcasting System and United Press International (Bustamante, 2007, p. 33). Nor, indeed, was the market for news in general open. The regime maintained rigid control over everything that was written and broadcast. The "war-time" press legislation of 1938 permitted preventative censure, and was not lifted until the passage of the new press law, the *ley Fraga*, in 1956, which formally banned the practice. Yet a more potent control was undoubtedly the power to limit entry into the profession: following the Francoist victory, only 1,800 of some 4,000 applications to practise journalism were accepted.

The regime's media policy was not purely restrictive. Although Bustamante (2007, p. 37) judges them to have been largely unsuccessful, a number of training institutions were set up by the regime: the Escuela Oficial de Radio y Televisión was founded in 1967, alongside the Escuela Oficial de Periodismo and the Istituto de la Opinion Publica. Although these three institutions were eventually merged into the newly minted Facultades de Ciencias de la Información in 1972, the formation of these department was in itself a comparatively early development compared to other Mediterranean countries.

In general, the official and actual aim of journalism during this period was the glorification of the regime and the moral views which supported it. In this, the regime was optimistic about the potential of the new medium.

> [There are] two fundamental principles which must be maintained, supported, and which must direct any future development of television in Spain: orthodoxy, and religious and moral rigour, in full respect for the norms that the Catholic Church may lay down, and the spirit of service and that selfsame service, which corresponds to the great ideals of the National Movement.
>
> (quoted in Bustamante 2007, p. 31)

Towards the end of the regime, pressure on the broadcaster became less ideational and subtle, and more blatant and manifest, as a number of television workers were accused of associating with illegal groups and disseminating propaganda. Nevertheless, in Spain's pacted transition, many of the leaders in RTVE present in these years would later play key roles in the first democratic ministries – including Adolfo Suárez, a future prime minister as well as director-general of RTVE between 1969 and 1973.

2 The early democratic years (1977–1996)

Spain's transition to democracy began with Franco's death in November 1975. The process of transition was long, and RTVE was no exception. It passed from the control of the Ministry of Information and Tourism to the Ministry of Culture, this time as an autonomous unit (*organismo autonomó*) of the ministry instead of a de facto sub-unit. Following this move, a provisional board of governors (*consejo rector*) was appointed, charged both with overseeing RTVE's performance and with drawing up a new statute to govern the broadcaster. Despite criticisms of the board's composition (the socialist party, the Partido Socialista Obrero Español (PSOE) withdrew its members in protest at the way the government, formed by the Unión de Centro Democrático (UCD), had appointed numerous co-partisans), the non-governing parties largely accepted the provisions of the statute as drafted.

> In an atmosphere of general satisfaction, the only voices of dissent came from the unions and the Communist group within RTVE, for whom the Statute marginalized workers, did not impose limits on the amount of advertising revenue the public broadcaster could raise and, above all, foresaw a non-democratic method of appointing the Director-General, pre-serving the power exercised by the Government.
>
> (Bustamante, 2007, p. 94)

Whilst the statute was formally approved in 1980, the climate introduced by the failed coup attempt of 23 February 1981 meant that links between the executive and the broadcaster remained tight, and genuine organizational reform within the broadcaster was not implemented until 1982. The choice of regulatory concepts during the transition period is particularly interesting. The concept of pluralism has been fruitfully deployed in the study of democratization; one might therefore have expected the concept of pluralism to be prevalent, if not dominant, in the legislative texts and declarations of this period. Instead, surprisingly, the concept of objectivity emerged as the key regulatory concept, both in legal documents and in the aspirations and declarations of the principal protagonists. One of the key tasks of the board of governors was to monitor "respect for the objectivity of information" (Bustamante, 2007, p. 67). Equally, Article 4 of the Statute, which details the principles to be followed by RTVE, lists the "objectivity, truthfulness, and impartiality of information" (clause (a)) and "the separation of information and opinion" (clause (b)) before "respect for political, religious, social, cultural and linguistic pluralism" (clause (c)); and even here, pluralism is depicted as a value which is to be respected, not attained or still less maximized. Critics of UCD interference used the same values in their criticism. When in the early 1980s letters from disgruntled employees started appearing in the specialist press, they complained that RTVE "not being pluralist, is not objective, nor truthful, nor impartial" (Bustamante, 2007, p. 101). Thus, whilst they are both Mediterranean-type media systems, the key regulatory concepts employed in Italian and Spanish broadcasting are importantly different in their emphasis. The affirmation of objectivity and impartiality preceded its implementation.

Government influence on the broadcaster was still present. In part this was a hang-over from the Fascist period: one journalist noted that

> the censors continue to operate at Prado del Rey [headquarters of RTVE], so much so that in the last two years the vetoes and the closedowns of

programmes have become more frequent … Whilst "moral" censorship has slowed up, political censorship remains strong, perhaps because the current executives hold the same management positions that they did during the sixties and seventies.

(quoted in Bustamante 2007, p. 86)

The emphasis on the role of executives is important, because – in another difference from Rai – the strong government pressure on the broadcaster does not seem to have implied that RTVE was politicized "all the way down". Government interference was largely restricted to overwhelming control of the choice of director-general and the director of information services; ordinary journalists within the broadcaster were opposed to continued government interference, and made their displeasure clear in letters to the press. The 1980 statute entrusts the choice of director-general to the executive, which is to make its choice "having heard the opinion of the Administrative Council". In reality, numerous directors-general have been appointed without an opinion from the Administrative Council, in certain cases because representatives of the governing majority, fearing an adverse vote, abandoned the meeting in order to prevent it from reaching quorum (Bustamante, 2007, p. 100). Equally, whilst the statute required any government move to dismiss the director-general to have either the support of the Administrative Council, in practice directors-general during this period held office only whilst they enjoyed the government's confidence. The first director-general to hold office under the 1980 statute, Fernando Castedo, was effectively dismissed by the government following a formal request by the prime minister and the UCD party president on 23 October 1981. He had been previously forced to remove his director of information services, Iñaki Gabilondo. Bustamante writes of Castedo that "it was probably Castedo himself … who ratified these political choices, choosing to sign, even before his nomination, a letter of resignation, leaving all decisions over his mandate to the Government" (2007, p. 99). In general, Bustamante argues that the key determinant of RTVE's limited independence of government was the government's power of appointment. "It is evident that the original sin, the prime cause of the malfunctioning of the office of Director-General, lay in assigning the power to name the Director-General to the government", with the consequence that

> post of Director-General assumed such an explicitly political connotation as to characterise, without exception, the corresponding executive group, which was fired at the first opportunity should a particular program be badly managed, or should there be a simple shift in the balance of power within the governing coalition.

(Bustamante, 2007, pp. 109, 70)

The Socialists in government

The electoral disaster which befell the UCD in 1982, and the consequent formation of a PSOE government, did not lead to greater independence for RTVE.

Frequent changes of director-general and, through this appointment, the director of information services, continued. Squabbles continued between the broadcaster and the government, occasionally involving questions of principle, such as whether the parties could decide which party members they wished to represent them, and, in extremis, whether they could prevent dissident party members from appearing. These questions of principle were, however, usually answered with detriment to the position of RTVE: the programme *La Clave* invited a dissident socialist to participate in a debate on local government, and the PSOE's displeasure with the decision led to the resignation of the director of information services, José Luis Balbín (Bustamante, 2007, p. 126). When the government was not pressuring directors-general, it was choosing them with an eye to their political affiliation. This was certainly the case with Luis Solana, brother of the noted socialist exponent Javier Solana, who was accused by the opposition of a "lack of impartiality", particularly during the 1989 elections. So strong was the opposition's rancour that they signed a joint accord to "protect political pluralism and the objectivity of the information broadcast by RTVE", depositing the accord with the Central Electoral Office (Bustamante, 2007, p. 128). Indeed, objectivity, and, secondarily, pluralism, remained the key concepts employed in the debate. When private television was agreed in 1988, the key regulatory concepts which were used by RTVE were ported across to the private broadcasters. That is, the private operators were to be "guided by the same criteria of objectivity and pluralism present in the January 1980 Statute on Radio and Television" (Bustamante, 2007, p. 155). Equally, greater soft regulation emphasizing such values was pursued as a potential solution to the problem of independence. A self-regulatory code was agreed between the Ministry of Education and the television companies in April 1993; this did not prevent a special Senado committee in 1993 calling for a *Consejo Audiovisual*, similar to that existing at the time in France, to "oversee the pluralism and objectivity of information" (Bustamante, 2007, pp. 136–137).

The emphasis in these proposals upon the key regulatory concept of objectivity was shared by journalists at the time – and, in particular, by those younger journalists who had less experience of the period of transition. Survey results reported by Canel and Piqué (1998) show journalists were typically non-ideological, extremely well educated and largely unaffiliated with parties. A "definition of good journalism as avoiding personal ideological preferences from biasing their work [was] quoted by a high rate of the sample, especially among the younger journalists". Almost all of the sample claimed "to have studied at university level, [with] 87% claiming to major in communications" (Canel & Piqué, 1998, p. 303). A majority of respondents did not identify with a party at all. Although the PSOE governments passed various important laws in other important fields – on regional television, private television, state support for cinema, reform of state support for newspapers and intellectual property law – they did not make any significant reforms to the public broadcaster.[1] The legislative framework was thus unaltered when the Partido Popular (PP) gained power in 1996.

3 From Aznar to Zapatero

Despite having strongly criticized the PSOE's behaviour towards RTVE, the PP was equally, if not more, domineering in its dealings with RTVE. The first sign of its reversal of course with respect to RTVE came when it nominated its first director-general, Fernando Lopez Amor. Not only was Amor a PP parliamentarian, but his nomination was also communicated to the Administrative Council of RTVE by fax, undermining the legal requirement that the council should have a voice in the nomination. (Although Amor benefited from this approach in his selection, it was to be to his disadvantage just 20 months later when the government dismissed him whilst abroad, without his knowledge.) Again, the key players in interpreting the wishes of the government were the director-general and the director of information services. Of particular note during the later period of PP government is Alfredo Urdaci, who adopted an extremely visible profile – much more similar to the profile enjoyed by directors of the *telegiornali* in Italy – exposing him to severe criticism.

Urdaci's profile was hardly helped by a highly significant judgment of the High Court (Audiencía Nacional) in 2003. A trial had been brought by the national trade union which argued that RTVE had deliberately minimized the amount of coverage given to the nationwide strike it had organized, and furthermore distorted its coverage to imply that the union was less representative than it in fact was. The Court agreed with the claimant, arguing in particular that RTVE had cherry-picked the results of a poll carried out by the Centro di Investigaciones Sociologicas (CIS), and finding that RTVE had thereby damaged workers' right to strike (though it stepped back from invoking a judicially evaluable standard of impartiality or truthfulness), and ordering the broadcaster to issue a correction and apology on all its news services.

The treatment of the national strike of 2000 was just one of a number of high-profile events which were widely judged to have been covered badly or partially, and which led to protests outside and within the broadcaster. The latter led to the formation of a Consejo provisional de informativos, which proposed the drafting of an ethical code for broadcast journalists. In the run-up to the 2004 elections, this work intensified, and many of the same journalists involved in the Consejo Provisional formed a Comité Anti-Manipulacion, chaired by a seven-member executive committee (Montano, 2006, p. 182). Whether these efforts would have eventually led to an increase in the broadcaster's independence, or whether they would have created greater pressure for legislative reform increasing independence, is not known. The most powerful – and certainly the most emotive – factor in producing reform was the attempt by the PP to have RTVE blame Basque terrorists for the explosion in Madrid on 11 March, the eve of the election. The person in charge of news coverage that day, Urdaci, denied that the PP was involved, yet the perception that it was fuelled the movement for reform of the 1980 statute. Whilst opposition parties had promised in the past to reform the broadcaster when in power, such promises had been disregarded. The new government therefore pre-committed itself to the reform path by pledging to accept the recommendations of an independent committee set up to draft a new statute and suggest new legislation.

This committee, which included numerous media experts, and no directly political nominees, produced a report which called for substantive changes to the broadcaster, particularly concerning methods of appointment. Yet even this pre-commitment was not immune to steps backward. The report proposed that an administrative council of eight members be nominated by a two-thirds majority in each branch of parliament, with each branch electing its four nominees separately. The duration of their mandate was to be six years, without the possibility of re-election. The director-general was subsequently to be appointed by the Administrative Council after a public recruitment exercise. The general structure of the broadcaster would thus have been similar to most European PSBs, with a dual board system. Yet when the proposals came to be transposed into law, the parliament rejected this proposal, choosing instead to have a single board with an executive president, chosen by the parliament. Bustamante notes that whilst this retrograde step was regrettable, "parliamentary election with a strengthened majority nevertheless represents a huge step forward for RTVE's autonomy compared to previous periods", though he notes that there is an extremely risky clause which provides for election by simple majority in the event that no candidate is elected within two months of the nomination of the council as a whole.

4 Conclusion

Any comprehensive judgement on RTVE must wait until the effects of the Zapatero reform have been demonstrated. Nevertheless, we may place this reform effort in its proper context by briefly repeating the principal steps in this chapter, namely, that

- although the Spanish market for news was not open in any sense, efforts at journalistic education and professionalization were advanced relative to other Mediterranean countries;
- second, because of this, journalists within RTVE have occasionally united to promote efforts aimed at adopting rules for content;
- third, no official efforts at producing rules for content have been made, because of the frequent replacement of directors-general and directors of the news service;
- fourth, RTVE has consequently been unable to defend itself in the face of political criticism of its output, not just in normal political clashes, but also in front of the court system;
- fifth, that the frequent replacement of directors-general has been due to the limited legal protection afforded the broadcaster;
- sixth, when politicians and academics sought to increase the independence of the broadcaster, it was legal protections against dismissal of the chief executive that they modified. Consequently, although the low levels of independence shown by RTVE are entirely in line with our expectations of a

broadcaster in the Polarized-Pluralist/Mediterranean model, these low levels of independence result more from extremely limited legal protection, which is relatively tractable, and result less from the levels of professionalization, which are high compared, for example, to Italy.

The prospects for future independence are thus positive.

5 The United Kingdom

"Treading delicately like Agag"

The British Broadcasting Corporation (BBC) is the largest public service broadcaster (PSB) in the world. By accident of language and dint of graft, it is also the most important and influential. Over 80 years, it has won a deserved reputation for independence. In the statistical analysis of Chapter 2, the BBC counted as but one case amongst others; it no more determined the validity of the theory than did the public broadcasters of Slovakia or New Zealand. Yet any theory of PSB independence which does not hold when applied to the BBC will ultimately be unconvincing even if valid.

In this chapter I apply my theory of PSB independence to the BBC. My analysis is divided chronologically into three sections, which cover the period from the company's founding until the advent of competition, from then until the beginning of the Thatcher government, and from Thatcher until the present day. Within each section I briefly consider the history of the period, including developments in the media market (*.1), the key rhetorical commitments of the BBC (*.2), its concrete rules as they developed (*.3), the structure, organization and recruitment of news staff (*.4) and alleged cases of interference during that period (*.5). I find that the BBC's independence has derived from its willingness to develop rules which constrain its output, permitting it both to wrest control from politicians who would enforce much less malleable rules and to defease potential intervention. This reasoning has been recognized since the BBC's foundation. Although these rules have not always been popular, they have been politic, and as Reith himself wrote in the *Radio Times*, "it is well to be politic and like Agag to tread delicately" (Scannell & Cardiff, 1991, p. 27).[1]

1 From foundation to competition (1922–1955)

1.1 The setting

The market for news in the United Kingdom in the early 20th century was large both in absolute terms and relative to population. For a time, the world's best-selling newspapers were British. The historical reach of the British Empire had contributed to the growth of expansive networks of several press agencies, including Reuters, Press Association, Exchange Telegraph and Central News, all

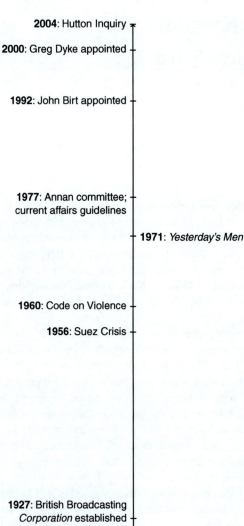

Figure 5.1 BBC timeline.

founded prior to the 1880s. There were journalists of note: Charles Dickens was one of their number. Yet British journalists had rejected the professional model of journalism represented by the 1884 founding of the National Association of Journalists (later the Chartered Institute of Journalists), preferring instead to adopt the trade union model with the 1910 establishment of the National Union of Journalists.

As a rich country, the potential market for radio sets in Britain was also large. Manufacturers knew this, but needed to make the purchase of a set attractive. To that end, the six largest British manufacturers of radio receivers formed the British Broadcasting Company in October 1922. The companies had been encouraged to merge by the Post Office, who much preferred "co-operation to competition" (Briggs, 1995, pp. 105–106).[2] John Reith was appointed managing director of the new company, and served both the British Broadcasting Company, and its successor the British Broadcasting Corporation (a public corporation chartered under royal warrant), until 1938. He was responsible for the development of the concept of public service broadcasting as it applies in Britain today, and it is difficult to over-state his influence over the BBC's development. Yet at the time, he had no experience of radio, nor of journalism. It was thus necessary to quickly acquire expertise and set precedent. There were, wrote Reith (1924, p. 100), "no precedents to cite; no stores of wisdom to be tapped; no experienced staff to hand. The iron had to be made hot by the striking, and better so". Setting values was important, and some were crucial: controversy (valued negatively), impartiality and expertness.

1.2 Key rhetorical commitments

1.2.1 The avoidance of controversy

Controversy was both something which was (negatively) valued by the BBC and a rule which it was obliged to follow. Precisely whether this obligation followed from the BBC's own desire to avoid controversy or whether it was a rule imposed by others is unclear. The Post Office claimed that "a general veto was imposed by the Cabinet from the beginning of broadcasting on all subjects of political and religious controversy".[3] Had this been the case, the avoidance of such material could hardly have been part of a BBC strategy to tread delicately and thereby win independence. However, the BBC disagreed with this interpretation, arguing that the avoidance of controversial matters was a self-imposed limitation. Reith wrote to the Assistant Secretary of the Post Office, F. W. Phillips, in May 1924, challenging him on this interpretation of events:[4]

> on the question of broadcasting speeches and controversial matters, you say at the beginning that the Post Office had requested us to avoid these speeches. This may be a small point, but I do not remember anything like this having been done; we avoided them of our own volition from the start.

Irrespective of the origin of the rule, the BBC was formally requested to avoid discussing controversial matters in a letter from the Postmaster-General sent on 11 January 1927. Reith, however, was opposed to a formal ban. His intent was not to broadcast discussion of controversial matters; instead, he intended to substitute an internal rule for an external one. In a 1926 letter, Reith argued that the broadcaster was sufficiently responsible to be allowed to discuss controversial issues, for

> it appears from universal experience that *the broadcaster himself is the most important censor* of the form and extent of controversial matter ... even where government control is so remote and loose as to be negligible, the self-interest or sense of responsibility of the broadcaster requires that controversy should be prudently and tactfully introduced.
>
> (Scannell & Cardiff, 1991, p. 42; emphasis added)

As Scannell and Cardiff dryly note, "this letter succeeded where all previous ones failed". The Post Office decided in March 1928 that, in "appreciation of the loyal and punctilious manner in which [the Governors] have conformed to the obligations ... imposed" on them, "the bar upon the broadcast of matters of controversy shall for the present be entirely withdrawn".[5] Following the withdrawal of the ban, the Corporation implemented its own controls on controversy, discussed below. But non-controversy, as a value to be aimed at and not as a constraint, also expressed itself through the choice of programming in the early years of the Corporation. "The early BBC gave political discussion and analysis a low priority in its main concerns. And correspondingly the politicians left it alone in the other areas where it rapidly built up a national reputation and standing" (Kumar, 1975, p. 71). Even when Reith was writing in a personal capacity, he displayed "a critical absence [of] ... any concern with the political role of broadcasting or sense of its importance" (Scannell & Cardiff, 1991, p. 5).

Even had the BBC not sought to develop rules to contain controversy, its output might not have attracted attention. One can exaggerate the "avoidance of politics" argument. Some programmes were challenging, controversial and concerned with current issues of public policy. One example was *Time to Spare*, a documentary on unemployment, cited in the Commons by one Labour MP in order to demonstrate the paucity of benefits payments. George Daggar claimed that individual stories featured on the programme "could be accepted as reliable because they were broadcast by the BBC and hence were free from political theory or bias" (Scannell & Cardiff, 1991, p. 65). The government, naturally, contested the figures given by those featured in the documentary, and Reith was summoned by Prime Minister Ramsay MacDonald and told that the series had to stop. Reith, whilst acknowledging the government's residual power to order the BBC not to broadcast any programme, noted that if such an order were given,

> he would, at that time in the schedule when the talks should be given, instruct the announcer to declare that the next twenty minutes would be silent because the Government had refused to allow the unemployed to express their views. Macdonald backed off, and the series continued.
>
> (Scannell & Cardiff, 1991, p. 66)

This was a very high-stakes example of a work-to-rule practice.

1.2.2 Impartiality

The concept of impartiality first arose in connection with the avoidance of controversy. Reith wrote to the Post Office in late 1924 to "represent again our desire for permission to handle outstanding controversial subjects, providing we can guarantee absolute impartiality in the act" (Scannell & Cardiff, 1991, p. 27), and the phrase was repeated at various times in the Corporation's early history. Since the Corporation was initially prevented from gathering and broadcasting its own news (see below), the need for such a regulatory concept was initially limited. The first systematic exegesis of the concept, in a form which could subsequently be cited so as to justify particular decisions, came in 1935, when the General Advisory Council (GAC) was asked, as one of its very first tasks, to formulate a paper on the concept of impartiality and what it entailed.

The document – GAC(9) – is noteworthy insofar as it is a relatively sophisticated analysis of the concept at a very early stage in the Corporation's life. At the same time, it is most clear upon what impartiality is not, or what impartiality may not be applied to. Many of these negative injunctions have been repeated at later stages in the Corporation's life. Thus, the first paragraph of the report argues that the BBC's general attitude, *qua* public monopoly, ought to be that of impartiality, "except so far as it is proper that, in a free country, the state itself should interfere with the free expression of opinion – e.g., in the case of actual incitement to rebellion, etc.". Second, impartiality was not to be equated with "expressing or encouraging a 'middle' view between two extremes", which would itself represent a departure from impartiality. The positive injunctions required by impartiality were limited. By adopting impartiality, the BBC committed itself to the task "of giving adequate attention to all public events in proportion to their real interest and importance" – where real interest and importance were interpreted by the BBC itself. Impartiality also implied constraints on the activity of the staff, who could not "be seen to be expressing a view or showing any preference, even for a middle opinion or a compromise". Later on, this ban on expressing opinions on public affairs grew to include all outside appearances where the expression of an opinion "might call the Corporation's impartiality into question".

Before the war the concepts of impartiality and objectivity were often used interchangeably: the same GAC paper spoke of the obligation of impartiality being discharged by the "objective presentation of all the alternative points of view". If a distinction was drawn, it concerned the sphere of application of the concept: as one internal memo from 1957 put it, "the word 'impartiality' is usually applied to the broadcasting of controversial issues. The word 'objectivity' is usually applied to the broadcasting of news, where the application of the policy of impartiality necessarily takes a somewhat different form".[6] Gradually, however, the references to objectivity became fewer. It is important to note that any and all statutory references to impartiality during this period were "borrowed" from BBC usage. The Ullswater committee, which reported in 1936 – a year after the aforementioned GAC paper – employed the concept to define the BBC's obligations in news, namely, to offer "a fair selection of items impartially presented". The term itself did not find its way into statute, but the policy was endorsed by the government in its "Prescribing Memorandum", attached to the Royal Charter and Agreement, in which the Postmaster-General stated that he relies upon the Corporation to carry on *its existing policy* of treating controversial subjects with complete impartiality.[7] The BBC's policy finally found statutory vindication in 1954, where the Act of Parliament that created the independent television companies (ITV) laid an obligation on the same to be "impartial" in their presentation of news and current affairs.

The link between impartiality and independence was, by that time, clear and readily assented to. Hugh Greene – who, rarely amongst BBC directors-generals, was on friendly terms with Reith – thought that Reith "saw that impartiality and independence went hand in hand" (Greene, 1969, p. 130). Greene himself stated the connection quite clearly:

> Without true independence, therefore, it is difficult for any broadcaster to maintain the highest standards of truth, accuracy, and impartiality. Conversely, of course, without a reputation for these things – truth, accuracy, and impartiality – it is difficult for any broadcasting organisation to be recognised as truly independent and to be generally trusted.
>
> (Greene, 1969, p. 106)

The clearest statement of the link between the adoption of a self-imposed requirement of impartiality, and the independence of the BBC comes from a note of 1957:

1. The policy of impartiality was conceived and initiated by the British Broadcasting Company
2. It was seen as a positive ideal, valued in itself and appropriate to a body based fundamentally on a motive of public service and providing information available to all.
3. It was seen also as an indispensable condition of a necessary advance, on the basis of public confidence, towards the freedom of the broadcasting service to deal independently with news, events and opinion, as to which broadcasting was at the beginning subject to many restrictions. This view proved to be correct. The present freedom of the broadcasting service results largely from it. None other would have served.
4. ...
5. The BBC has never been required or directed in any Charter or Licence to observe impartiality.
6. The PMG's references to impartiality in his prescribing memorandum issued to the BBC in terms of Licence 15(4) takes [*sic*] the form of an endorsement of the BBC's own policy, and a reliance upon it, not of a direction.

7. Charges of bias have been brought against the BBC on innumerable occasions but successive independent committees of inquiry have invariably approved the record. The BBC's basic impartiality has been widely recognised. It has seldom, if ever, been seriously challenged, and never successfully, in Parliament or elsewhere.[8]

1.2.3 Expertness

"Expertness" was one of Reith's essential requirements for public service broadcasting, as described in his 1924 "manifesto". Expertness in technical matters was already assured; "the concept of expertness in programme matters took longer to establish ... certainly by 1939 a professional ethos was already apparent, though it was by no means universally shared or approved" (Briggs, 1995, vol. II, p. 424). However, certain programmes can be identified precisely because they did not demonstrate high "expertness". The example given above of a controversial programme (*Time to Spare*) was unusual because it was more immediate than typical BBC programming. That is, it allowed normal citizens to come to the microphone and express themselves, and it did so in a way which was not mediated by experts who interpreted those expressions. This was in contrast to the typical BBC talk, often given by speakers drawn from Oxford or Cambridge, whose background gave their talks the disinterested air of expertness. As Scannell and Cardiff (1991, p. 166) note, "the impersonal style became the rule for expert speakers precisely because the BBC wished to avoid the accusation that it allowed them to use radio to promote their personal views".

This impersonal style meant that any expressions of personal opinion – any "I think"s, or "my view is" – had to be excised from the prepared scripts. In this, speakers were "aided" by the talks producers, who, thanks to their knowledge of the special demands of radio, were able to exact changes in speeches on the grounds of "what worked best". Impersonality was also the hallmark of BBC announcers. With the exception of the period of war, where the ability to recognize a trusted voice was at a premium, all BBC announcers were anonymous. The reason for anonymity was, again, to avoid the impression that the BBC could ever broadcast clashing voices:

> The BBC is one Corporation, and can only be thought of by the listener as individual. It has many voices but one mouth. It can speak in many styles, but the variety is due to the difference of subject matter and must not betray any inconsistency of treatment. It is a commonplace that "announcers sound all alike". That is a tribute to their training.
>
> (Briggs, 1995, vol. II, p. 123)

The commonplace that "announcers sound all alike" should not be taken as implied criticism for, at least according to listener research, the "dispassionate style of announcing" was appreciated by "virtually everyone" (Briggs, 1995, vol. V, p. 71).

1.3 Concrete rules

In addition to its commitment to expertness and impersonality, the BBC had a series of rules designed to minimize controversy. Three examples will suffice: the creation of a Controversy Committee; the adoption of the "14-day rule", and the development of the Maconachie file. All three rules, or structures, served to constrain output; all three had a tactical use; and all three were abandoned as soon as the threat to the BBC's independence was over.

The Controversy Committee was established following the lifting of the formal prohibition on the discussion of controversial issues. The committee was to meet weekly and issue "recommendations upon the various proposals which were obviously, or likely to prove, controversial in character" (BP5). Whether because checks at lower levels prevented much business from reaching the agenda of the Controversy Committee, or because the need to demonstrate caution to the government had already passed, the Controversy Committee was eventually abolished 20 months later in late 1929 (BP5). It had, however, served its purpose: by 1929 the nation was more likely to concentrate on the effects of the Great Depression than the selection of speakers on the BBC.

The second rule arrived much later in the BBC's history and was much more consequential. The "14-day rule" was a commitment by the BBC not to broadcast debate or discussion programmes concerning issues which were to be discussed in either house of parliament over the coming fortnight. The policy had initially been adopted by the Corporation during war-time,[9] and had been set on a more formal basis when, in 1946, the BBC met with the main political parties in order to reach a written agreement on how to handle political programming. The rule was agreed to in order that parliament would not be unduly influenced by any discussion outside of parliament. Both Churchill and Attlee judged it would be "shocking to have debates in this house forestalled, time after time, by expressions of opinion by persons who had not the status or responsibility of MPs" (Briggs, 1995, vol. IV, p. 607). The rule obviously served to constrain output, but by reducing the topicality of discussion programmes, it also reduced the risk that politicians would see programmes as partisan merely due to the heat of the moment.

Yet by 1953 the rule had begun to chafe, and over the next three years the BBC attempted to revise their initial agreement with the parties. The BBC's first move in the argument was to assure the parties that if such discussions were to be allowed, they would be handled with the Corporation's customary tact: its representatives argued "that the matter was the responsibility of the BBC, which had a duty to be impartial, and not for the parties",[10] and that the public (and occasionally members of parliament who had not been informed by the leaders of their parties who had imposed it) falsely attributed the rule to the BBC, accusing it of timidity. As Asa Briggs has noted, "the BBC was claiming the right for the first time in its history to decide how to present current issues to the public without external constraint" (Briggs, 1995, vol. IV, p. 606).

When this line of argument was rebuffed, director-general Ian Jacob tried a more obvious appeal on the basis of internal control:

> A possible solution would be to say to the party leaders that the Corporation recognises the force of the opinions expressed, and in general will proceed so as to avoid the possibility of broadcasts taking place of a character that might swing opinion just before a debate. We will not however subscribe any longer to a written rule on a subject which lies entirely within the responsibility of the Governors ... If we can in this way substitute *an internal rule, which we can interpret sensibly and freely, for an external agreement which has to be rigidly enforced* no matter what the merits of any particular insistence may be, I suggest that we shall have won our point without doing violence to our relations with the Party leaders.[11]

The Corporation was eventually forced to call the government's bluff, and insist that it would no longer be bound by its agreement with the parties. In response, the Postmaster-General[12] issued an order, permitted under the Charter, formally enshrining the 14-day rule. This provoked "furore" on the part of the public and commentariat, with *The Economist* urging the director-general to go to the Tower of London sooner than comply with the rule. Eventually, the enormity of the Suez Crisis, and the eventual resignation of Anthony Eden from the premiership, first made the rule untenable and, second, made it politically possible for the government to reverse its course.

I turn finally to the "Maconachie rules". Sir Richard Maconachie was appointed Director of Talks in 1935 after having served as a civil servant in India and Afghanistan. His appointment, which came after a period of interregnum, was designed to increase control over the Talks Department, which had been seen as too "progressive" under its previous head Hilda Matheson. Consequently his appointment was seen with trepidation by many of the staff. Yet over the next 10 years, he managed to codify much of what the BBC was doing, and also win over the affection of those who worked for him (Briggs, 1995, vol. II, p. 149). The result of his labours was the Maconachie file,[13] a compendium of several papers on different aspects of the BBC's existence, continuously updated until shortly after the end of the war. Although many of the entries in the Maconachie file concern institutional aspects of the BBC and not its output, Maconachie's work meant that the BBC was able to record its decisions on different topics, and thus have a better basis for justifying its decisions to cover those topics in that way.

1.4 Structure, organization, recruitment in news

1.4.1 The press agencies

The manufacturing companies who had formed the British Broadcasting Company had asked for permission to broadcast their own news, but had been turned down by the Post Office. Instead, the four main press agencies – Reuters, Press Association, Exchange Telegraph and Central News – agreed to supply to the BBC a "daily summary of the world's news", "solely for the purpose of distribution within the British Isles" between 6 and 11 in the evening. In return, "the BBC promised that it would make use of this news only in its broadcast programmes, and that BBC news bulletins would always begin with the acknowledgement, 'Copyright News from Reuter, Press Association, Exchange Telegraph & Central News'" (Briggs, 1995, p. 132).

These terms were written into the Company's broadcasting licence, issued in January 1923 by the Post Office. Three principal reasons motivated the Post Office's decision to prevent the BBC from gathering its own news. The first reason was purely financial: the Post Office derived revenue from the press agencies' use of telegraph and telegram services. A competitor to the press agencies capable of employing a new technology, wireless telegraphy, from which the Post Office derived no revenue, was thus an indirect threat to Post Office revenue. A second reason was security. In their negotiations with the Post Office, the press agencies were represented by Roderick Jones, the managing director of Reuters. During the First World War, Reuters had come under suspicion for its links with the German press agency Wolff and its perceived friendliness to the German cause. As a partial result of the outbreak of war, Reuters' financial results suffered, and other companies had indicated their desire to acquire the company. The government wished to avoid acquisition of Reuters by outside companies (including the Marconi company, which had expressed interest). In a bid to resolve these issues, the government proposed injecting capital into a refounded Reuters in which the government enjoyed special share-holder rights. Roderick Jones was influential in securing Reuters' consent to the deal. Reuters could therefore be trusted not to disseminate information prejudicial to national security interests. The same was probably true of the other press agencies, who knew of Reuters' difficulties, and who knew that the government had stepped in to some degree both to help Reuters and to secure its own interests (Putnis, 2008). In this respect the situation in Britain was similar to that in Sweden with Tidningarnas Telegrambyrån.

A third reason, however, was the need for impartiality. The Post Office was aware of the potential political influence of broadcasting, particularly with a monopoly provider of radio news. Consequently, the Post Office needed to "concern itself with the question of relations between the BBC and the press" and, "by insisting that the BBC should secure its news from news agencies ... [secure] 'some sort of assurance that the news was of the general type of uncoloured news'" (Briggs, 1995, p. 168).

The press agencies also made a similar argument. Jones argued that the BBC should not only be prevented from collecting news, it should also be prevented from arranging news, lest amateur or (still worse!) partisan opinion manifest itself in this arrangement:

> News values must always be to some extent a matter of opinion. But it is better to have trained, expert and dispassionate opinion rather than the

reverse, and this is secured by the agreement of the News Agencies, endorsed by the newspapers and the Post Office, to work together as far as broadcasting is concerned.

(Briggs, 1995, vol. I, p. 172)

Thus the restrictions on the licence granted to the BBC reflected the desire of the government in part to constrain the broadcaster, and prevent it from offering partisan output.

1.4.2 Own news

From 1927 onwards, the BBC was permitted to broadcast a limited number of eye-witness descriptions, provided that they did not obscure the press agencies' work. The BBC's News Department, however, was only founded in 1934 under the leadership of John Coatman, a Professor of Imperial Economics at LSE. Coatman's intent was fully in line with the BBC's aspirations: he "made it abundantly clear to all the newcomers to the News Department that his intention was to create a service on new professional lines which would be responsible through the chief news editor to [Alan] Dawnay [Controller of Programmes]" (Briggs, 1995, vol. II, p. 156). In order to establish such a service, however, Coatman was obliged to borrow from existing experience accumulated by the press agencies and by the newspapers. The press agencies helped by providing rules on content which were subsequently employed by the BBC's own editors.

> One of the very first letters from Arthur Burrows, Director of Programmes in London, to the Broadcasting Editor of Reuters, established some general principles, and an embryo definition for broadcast news, which subsequently were consolidated as guidelines for BBC News for many years.
> (Scannell & Cardiff, 1991, p. 106)

With the formation of the News Department, the general principles which had served in the assembly of Reuters- and PA-provided news also helped in the formation of own-sourced news.

By the 1950s, there were three sources of potential guidance: "Standing Instructions for Duty Editors and Chief Sub-editors"; "Standing Instructions for Sub-editors", and the News Department's "Guidance Index". These documents were not paper tigers: when, in the 1950s, D. H. Clarke attempted to compile the first BBC's Producers' Guidelines, a regional executive replied rather sniffily that, although his region

> has never prepared and issued a privately printed policy book as has apparently been done by certain of the large London establishments ... I would not like you to think that staff are not informed of Corporation policy. Here we keep a private policy file made up of various instructions ... All newly joining members of the staff are informed of this file and are particularly

asked to look through it and make any necessary notes at the earliest possible moment they can after joining us.[14]

Whilst the press agencies contributed to the development of rules for news, the
newspapers contributed by furnishing a reference model for the BBC's output
and by providing the journalists necessary to implement it. The BBC's reference
model was always the quality press, and indeed the comparison was explicitly
used by the BBC, as well as invoked by others. In its evidence to the Beveridge
Report, the BBC argued that its own news values "probably came closest to
those used by the *Daily Telegraph*". Similarly, Scannell and Cardiff (1991,
p. 112) have argued that the role of BBC news was to be a "popular and nationwide analogue of the *Times*". In one respect at least the BBC followed this
paper's lead: West (1987, pp. 40–41) claims that the BBC defused complaints
about its parliamentary service by

> analysing the number of minutes given to each contribution [which] was
> then compared with the number of column inches given to the same speak-
> ers in the reports in the Times. Even over a brief period the comparison
> showed that the BBC had been as unprejudiced as the press; what more
> could be asked of it than that?, was then the query raised.

Even if it begged the question of whether the press was unprejudiced in absolute
terms, the Corporation was able to defend itself by invoking this example.

When the example of the press was not explicitly invoked, its values spread
to the Corporation through recruitment of journalists from the quality newspapers. Two newspapers then known for their separation of fact and comment –
the *Manchester Guardian* (as it was then) and the *Daily Telegraph* – provided
the mainstay of the BBC's journalistic staff. When the BBC's own news desk
was formed in 1935 under John Coatman, the *Guardian* supplied both the
domestic and foreign news editors, R. T. Clark and Kenneth Adam; that paper
also supplied the domestic editor some years later, Patrick Ryan. The *Telegraph*
supplied one future director-general (Hugh Greene, who joined the BBC in
1940), and one future editor of news (Donald Edwards, who also joined the BBC
in 1940). There were no major recruitments from the *Times*, perhaps because the
BBC at this early point in its history was not a sufficiently attractive option for
job-seekers: before Reith was appointed Managing Director of the Company, the
position had reputedly been offered to one "prominent journalist" who had
turned the job down (Briggs, 1995, vol. I, p. 137). The *Times*, however, did vindicate the Corporation's choice of journalists, choosing Patrick Ryan as its
assistant editor and William Haley, the BBC's director-general between 1943
and 1952, as its editor. The newspaper also helped in less obvious ways, such as
advising on possible candidates "with a good knowledge of politics and public
affairs, coupled with a non-partisan outlook" (Scannell & Cardiff, 1991, p. 113).

These recruits were organized on fairly rigid lines. Whether by design or by
accident, News was governed by a succession of autocratic department heads,

who espoused puritanical views about the future direction of the service. Coatman was the first of this type; he was followed eventually by heavy-handed control of a different type during the war, with the government closely involved in the production of news bulletins. Seaton and Curran (2003, p. 123) argue that this was responsible for a change in the outlook of the BBC journalist:

> With unhealthy links with the Foreign Office and the civil service ... "journalists stopped being passionate advocates and saw themselves rather as independent professionals, and their writing as a negotiated product of conflict between partisan views ... politics was an activity which only happened between major political parties".

Yet even if the experience of war reinforced the image of the journalist as an independent professional, the BBC had already selected for this trait before the war. What the wartime experience certainly did was accustom journalists to the experience of strong hierarchy which could rule certain expressions as out-of-bounds. Strong hierarchy in News continued after the war with the appointment of Tahu Hole as head of News. Hole – a New Zealand journalist who had joined the BBC in 1943 – was loathed by the majority of his subordinates. Miall (1994, p. 125) thought that he had been promoted into a post that was "well beyond his capabilities":

> BBC News at that time was respected throughout the world. Hole thought he could maintain that reputation by following a line of extreme caution. Insecure, and uncertain in his news judgement, he ran the News Division on a policy of safety first. There must never be a mistake, no matter how slow and pedestrian the news bulletins were, and all items broadcast must be supported by at least two sources.

Hole's policy had a stultifying effect on BBC News. This was made obvious when ITV's television news appeared. The effect was disastrous for staff morale and retention. Hole's policy was, however, important in establishing the unity of BBC news. "[Hole] believed strongly not only in 'objectivity,' but in consistency: the BBC's news services must not speak with different voices" (Briggs, 1995, vol. IV, p. 577). Hole's News department served all of the BBC, even after the post-war reorganization of the existing channels into the Home, Light and Third Programmes. While within the structure the "individuality" of each programme was emphasized, all three programmes would draw on three "supply divisions – Entertainment ... Talks ... News" (Briggs, 1995, vol. IV, p. 78). This News department itself would become more unified, as the existing news units – spread out throughout London due to space constraints – were concentrated in Egton House (Briggs, 1995, p. 575): one editorial meeting at 11 a.m. set the BBC's news agenda for the day. Although there were differences in the selection of news between domestic and foreign services, the "theory" behind all BBC News – in the regions as in Egton House and in Bush House – was that "in all versions the basic facts must remain the same"; and indeed the BBC boasted as much to the Beveridge Report on broadcasting (Briggs, 1995, vol. IV, p. 577).

The unity pursued by Hole did have some defenders. "There was an 'old guard' that shared [Hole's] outlook" (Briggs, 1995, vol. V, p. 68), and the service did get recognition from the director-general, Ian Jacob, as a "central service" with a "special quality", which justified its placement directly beneath the director-general (Briggs, 1995, vol. IV, p. 578). Undoubtedly, such recognition would have come about anyway after the war with the massively increased appetite for news from the public. Yet observers did seem to rate the service passably. US TV network NBC claimed that the BBC's television *Newsreel* was "strikingly consistent in its excellence" (Briggs, 1995, vol. V, p. 69), though perhaps greater emphasis should be laid on "consistency" rather than "excellence". Sveriges Radio director-general Olof Rydbeck, upon visiting the BBC, found its news service distinctly unappealing, with the same news on each channel. "Consistency" did insulate the BBC from criticism: Asa Briggs reports that when the GAC decided to discuss the issue of news in 1949, the resulting debate was slight. "Sir George Gater said he had tried to collect criticisms of the news service but had failed to find any" (Briggs, 1995, vol. IV, p. 578).

1.5 Political interference

There are two main cases of interference in the BBC's news output which bookend this period: the BBC's handling of the General Strike of 1926, and its treatment of the Suez Crisis.

The General Strike came at an awkward time for the BBC. The Crawford Committee had, to Reith's satisfaction, recommended that the Company be transformed into a Corporation established by Royal Charter; yet the government had not yet acted upon this recommendation at the time the strike began; the threat of non-renewal of the Company's licence was thus ever-present. Since the General Strike also affected newspapers, the BBC was the sole source of news for many citizens, or at least those who did not read either of the two partisan newspapers, the *British Worker*, produced by the Trades Union Congress, or the *British Gazette*, produced by the government and edited by Winston Churchill. The government was split on its approach to this newly relevant medium. One wing, led by Churchill, wished to take over the BBC and turn it into an instrument of propaganda much as the *British Gazette* was. Another wing, led by Leslie Hoare, thought that "it would be wiser to leave the BBC a measure of independence or at least of 'semi-independence'" (Briggs, 1995, vol. I, p. 361). Whether independence was valued intrinsically or whether the government thought it had a tactical value, the prime minister, Baldwin, was inclined to follow this second group.

The BBC and Reith were aware of this threat. They responded by treading a narrow line between preserving impartiality and supporting the government. Reith, in a note to the prime minister, wrote that the BBC "must maintain with discretion its essential news service ... [and preserve its] reputation for sincerity and impartiality [but] would emphasise and initiate statements likely to counter-act a spirit of selfishness and hostility" (Reith, 1949, p. 109). In news, editors were instructed to include statements from trade union leaders if they were known to be true; outside of news, the BBC strayed ever further into editorializ-ing. Thus, the BBC neither broadcast falsehood, nor censored true news from uncomfortable quarters; and yet, Reith himself admitted that it did not display "complete impartiality", but that this could hardly be expected in the situation (Reith, 1949, p. 112). Preserving a "tradition of accuracy and fair play" (Reith, 1949, p. 112) did matter: the BBC's output was sharply differentiated from that of the government-run *British Gazette* (Briggs, 1995, vol. I, p. 362). Interest-ingly, the reaction from the Labour Party – which would return to power on its own only in 1945 – was not hostile to the BBC, even though it was clear from its output that it thought the TUC should end its strike sooner rather than later. Reith met with Charles Trevelyan and William Graham from the Labour Party, neither of whom seemed upset.

> Reith wrote to both Graham and MacDonald ... explaining how his hands had been tied during the strike and hoping they would not attribute BBC actions entirely to him. What he had been able to do, he said, was to make news bulletins as authentic and reliable as they could have been in the cir-cumstances and to include a considerable amount of TUC news.
>
> (Briggs, 1995, p. 377)

It was only gradually afterwards, when newspapers began to circulate again, that listeners re-evaluated the BBC's news output unfavourably, leading some to dub it the BFC, or "British Falsehood Corporation". These viewers were not, of course, in a position to sanction the Corporation, which had effectively avoided sanctioning or external compromising of its independence by tilting its output to favour the party in power.

The heart of the Suez controversy concerned the right of the government to request broadcasts to the nation, and the right of the opposition to request a response. Under the 1946 aide-memoire between the parties and the BBC dis-cussed above, the government had the right to request a broadcast to the nation, but the BBC had the right to grant, upon request, a rebuttal from the opposition party if the government's broadcast was considered partisan. When British troops invaded Egypt in 1956, the prime minister, Anthony Eden, broadcast to the nation; but the Labour Party, under Hugh Gaitskell, requested a response. Gaitskell's response – and the BBC's initial refusal to let visiting Australian prime minister Robert Menzies to broadcast a response to the response – infuri-ated Eden. Eden and his advisers drew up a list of options for sanctioning the BBC, including a cut in funding for the World Service – which in the meantime had continued to broadcast the full range of British opinion on Suez to the Arab world. In the end, the World Service's increase in direct funding was a derisory one, far less than the BBC deemed urgently necessary, but still far from a sanc-tion (Briggs, 1995, vol. IV, p. 135).

Although the crisis was a serious one, the BBC escaped relatively unharmed. The government attacked the weakest part of the BBC, that part which relied on direct funding. The intention behind cutting funds to the World Service was made clear: this was a punitive action. "Contrary views" had been broadcast to the world, "to the confusion of people in certain parts of the world", who did "not understand our political system" (Briggs, 1995, vol. IV, p. 124). The government attempted to link this to domestic output (Briggs, 1995, vol. IV, p. 121), but a sanction applied to the whole of the BBC via funding would have been much more difficult.

The BBC's response was at times fairly calm because it believed its rules would defend it. Director of Spoken Word, Harman Grisewood,

> had left his post [to go into hospital] confident that whatever course events took in the Middle East ... there was no cause for alarm that he could foresee "from the standpoint of the BBC". "The programmes which would deal with these events were well manned and the system of control was by now in good order. Relations with Parliament were better and closer than they had been."

For Briggs (1995, vol. IV, p. 85), Grisewood "was over confident about the values of his Rules, or at least about the willingness of politicians to follow them in periods of crisis". Yet Grisewood was right in one respect: Eden had no problems with the ministerial broadcasts and the opposition's right to reply, both of which were covered by the rules. "Clark [press adviser to Eden] had been told before Eden broadcast that if Gaitskell were to request a right to reply, the Board would probably concede it, and he acknowledged that this was understood, was indeed expected, by the PM" (Briggs, 1995, vol. IV, p. 97). What Eden did object to was the subsequent coverage of Gaitskell's speech in the World Service: Clark, on Eden's behalf, asked that "too much prominence should not be given in that Service to describing domestic opposition to the PM's policy" (Briggs, 1995, vol. IV, pp. 99–100).

Sticking close to impartiality was also useful for the other broadcaster at the time – the network of independent television companies set up by the Television Act 1954. During the conflict, Eden asked Sir Kenneth Clark, Chairman of the Independent Television Authority

> into No 10 for a talk. Could not Clark slant the news about Suez? was the question. Clark replied that had he been inclined to do so and he was not – he would not have been able to do it. "We were working under an Act of Parliament which called for impartiality."
>
> (Briggs, 1995, vol. IV, p. 109)

Thus, the ITA was able to defend itself by citing its conformity with a rule which had previously been accepted by politicians.

2 The years of Butskellism (1954–1979)

2.1 The setting

The period beginning with the Suez Crisis and the ending with the appointment of Margaret Thatcher as prime minister is often viewed as a time of political consensus: these were the years of "Butskellism" – *The Economist*'s portmanteau term to indicate the similar Keynesian economic policies of Chancellors Rab Butler (Conservative) and Hugh Gaitskell (Labour). They were also years of active interest in politics, and of a high demand for news. With the BBC relatively secure after the government's failure to sanction it over Suez, the Corporation's news offer expanded to meet greater demand. It was joined by its competitors, the new Independent Television (ITV) companies, introduced by the 1954 Television Act. In this context, the BBC's key value – for internal as well as external consumption – was the value of professionalism, which to some extent absorbed the previous requirements of impartiality and expertness, since an impartial presentation was a professional one.

This commitment to professionalism, however, did breed concern amongst politicians that broadcast journalists, though they might not be partisan, might be heavily critical of politicians and condescending towards them. The BBC was able to develop more rules – rules which prevented employees from political activity, which covered content in news and current affairs and in drama, and which introduced proper complaints procedures – which mitigated these concerns. News operated within the context of these rules and of increasing two-way traffic in personnel with ITV. What complaints there were motivated more by perceived condescension rather than perceived partisanship.

2.2 Key rhetorical commitments

During the 1950s BBC staff came to see themselves as "professionals". This is one of the principal claims of Tom Burns' (1977) book on the BBC, *Public Institution and Private World*. Burns dated the emergence of a "professional ethos" to the early 1950s, at precisely the time the BBC began its first training courses. From the 1950s onwards the proportion of BBC broadcasters who had come to the BBC from the press decreased as the numbers of BBC-recruited and -trained broadcasters increased. This increased investment in training was, in one sense, a natural consequence of the BBC's considerable growth during and since the war. In another sense, it was a competitive necessity: the independent television companies had started operating in the mid-1950s, and needed experienced programme staff.

Many of those trained in the 1950s became leading figures in the BBC, particularly those on the BBC's Graduate Trainee Scheme, introduced in 1954. Other more specific training courses also ran: David Attenborough (future Controller of Programmes) was an early graduate of the BBC's first television training course. Training was also included for secretaries, "who played the major part in linking the formal and informal structures of the BBC" (Briggs, 1995, vol. V, p. 383).

More important than the empirical claim about the use of this term is Burns' analysis of the way this term became used to evaluate and thereby moderate or encourage/discourage conduct within the broadcaster. Bluntly: everything good was professional, everything bad was unprofessional. Consequently, talk of impartiality was subsumed under professionalism. Impartiality was good, and therefore professional; and what was professional was therefore impartial. Professionalism "was used in relation both to news broadcasting and to light entertainment. It was also applied to both producers and performers" (Briggs, 1995, vol. V, p. 24). BBC employees (ab)used this term for the same reasons discussed in Chapter 2 – to assert that one is a member of a "profession" is to assert a claim that one uses specialized and/or technical knowledge in one's job. That specialized knowledge can then be employed to subdue or disarm criticism.

The advance and conquest of the professionalization project within the BBC is more remarkable when set against traditional scepticism towards the concept of professionalization in British journalism. Delano (2002, pp. 136–137) has more recently found that only a bare majority of journalists would describe what they do as a profession, with others preferring to describe it as a "trade", "craft" or "vocation" – although broadcast journalists are more likely to describe it as a profession.

Burns, in truth, regards impartiality not as something which was subsumed under professionalism, but as something separate. The connection between professionalism, impartiality and thereby independence is made much clearer by Krishnan Kumar (1975), in an argument in part based on his own experience as a BBC producer. Kumar makes two separate arguments. First, he argues that the technical demands of broadcasting led to the accretion of power around the producer and the consequent subtraction of power from the politician who appears on television. Despite the

> general power of the technical apparatus of the broadcasting organization, to which the professional broadcaster is directly and at every moment linked ... [h]e is in any case relaxed and at home in the often very complex and bewildering environment of the studio, an environment in which even regular contributors can easily lose their way and become the prisoners of technical constraints ... the requirement of professional orchestration can seem so over-riding as to submerge the contributors and their contribution under the general onward flow of the programme, as directed by a virtuoso presenter.
>
> (Kumar, 1975, p. 74)

Upon arriving at the studio, the politician to be interviewed is thus placed under pressure; consequently, any infelicities of expression that he or she may commit cannot be so easily blamed on the broadcaster or partisan animus, but merely on his or her own lack of knowledge or familiarity with the technical requirements of broadcasting. Second, Kumar argues that the BBC during this period adopted a new "survival strategy", involving "the careful selection and promotion of a small group of professional broadcasters-announcers, news-readers, presenters" (Kumar, 1975, p. 67). This survival strategy was needed because the BBC's previous survival strategy – the use of anonymous presenters – was no longer viable on television, and because of greater politicization of previously uncontroversial issues.

The reasons behind the BBC's original preference for anonymity were clear: what is personal may be idiosyncratic; one idiosyncracy may be attitude towards political issues or personalities; these attitudes may manifest themselves in the presentation of news or current affairs; such manifestation damages our claim to provide news which would not be more favourable to a particular party if the current presenter or broadcaster were replaced by another. And indeed, if the attitudes of presenters were very idiosyncratic or out of tune with the BBC's ethos, the selection and promotion of this group would indeed risk the BBC's independence. Yet, these presenters "have been selected and promoted precisely because they have shown the capacity to internalize the BBC's dilemmas and problems, and to resolve them in some sense by the style and manner of their presentation" (Kumar, 1975, p. 81). Their capacity to do so allows the BBC to use as presenters even those who, like Robin Day and Ludovic Kennedy, have previously been politically active. This survival strategy is not a purely negative one, for

> it is this context of professional presentation that allows the BBC to exhibit a range of contributors that is far wider than its critics usually acknowledge. The problem, strictly speaking, of whether or not a particular individual should be allowed to appear on the air is not one that exercises the BBC to the extent often thought. Most sorts of opinions and attitudes get some sort of hearing. Everyone from the most extreme Marxist group to the most extreme right-wing group will at some time or the other have appeared ... if you challenge the higher management of the BBC on the grounds of unfair neglect or omission of particular groups and opinions, any one of them will smoothly run you off a list of people and groups that have appeared ... The important point, of course, is that such individuals and groups are almost never allowed to appear on their own. Their views are refracted through the prism of technical and professional presentation, shaped subtly, and sometimes far from subtly, by the professionally defined canons of balance, lively but controlled debating, and licensed controversy.
>
> (Kumar, 1975, p. 75)

Kumar was writing at the end of the 1970s, but the phenomenon he observes dates back at least to the 1950s. In particular, the establishment of ITV as a competing broadcaster was partly helpful for the BBC's professionalization project, since "there was a profession in common" (Born, 2005, p. 40). ITV was able to be more daring in the recruitment of political journalists, and thus provided a proving ground for journalists who might not have initially found favour with the BBC. Robin Day and Ludovic Kennedy, for example, were both recruited from Independent Television News (ITN); both had stood as candidates in the 1959 General Election, both for the Liberal Party. Leonard Miall had been aware of their work, and, when they were forced to resign from ITN in order to contest the election, phoned them and asked if they would be interested in working for the BBC's new *Panorama* programme should they not be elected to parliament.

The professionalization project was also boosted by the BBC's director-general during much of the intervening period, Hugh Greene, who was well aware of necessity of professionalizing as a path to independence. Greene had worked as the director of Nordwest Deutsche Radio (NWDR) during the Allied occupation; in discussing the broadcaster, he notes "the need, in the interest of the political parties, to get their spokesmen to accept some training in broadcasting" even before moving on to discuss "the functioning of the new NWDR training school and all sorts of other things including the personnel policy of NWDR" (Greene, 1969, p. 49). The point here is not to suggest that Greene gave training broadcasters secondary importance – on the contrary, Greene was entirely supportive of the professionalization project: "We are all professionals", he stated in a speech in New York (Greene, 1969, pp. 65–66). Rather, it is to note that offering training to politicians is, in itself, a claim to superior knowledge of how politicians can best present their argument in a particular medium; and that this claim is itself important in understanding relationships between the two. The price of professionalization was the acceptance of certain rules which constrained employees' actions, particularly in relation to political activity.

Greene was forced to explain this point to European broadcasters who were considering or who employed systems of *proporz* or *lottizzazione*:

> We have a strict rule that neither outside candidates nor staff members considered for any post may be questioned as to their political views or party political allegiance. Although I am the director-general, there is no reason why anyone should know how I cast my vote at the last general election, and it would never occur to anyone to ask. And the same is true of the whole of our staff. Sweeping statements are sometimes made to the effect that our whole staff inclines too much to the Left or too much to the Right. Statements of this kind are not heard from responsible quarters, and we can afford to ignore them.
>
> (Greene, 1969, p. 80)

A similar statement was made a decade later, in a lecture on "Editorial Responsibilities", by one BBC editor: "I cannot recall having made, in the 21 years I have worked for the BBC, a single overtly political statement in public ... most BBC journalists are equally careful" (Taylor, 1975, p. 4). This orientation to politics was preserved not only by informal rules of politesse, but by formal rules on staff members' political engagements. Such rules applied to the BBC at all levels – the BBC Governors, for example, have a standing agreement not to speak on broadcasting issues without informing one another, and those Governors who also sit in the House of Lords are prevented by custom from speaking on broadcasting due to the Lords' "Addison rules".[15]

An example of the seriousness and thoroughness with which the BBC applied these rules on political activity can be found in local Bristol politics. One BBC reporter for BBC Bristol had attended a protest meeting outside an electoral meeting for the National Front, for which action he received a warning. The story appeared in the Bristol newspapers, and Tony Benn – at the time the member of parliament for the area – wrote to the BBC to complain and register his "absolute shock". Michael Swann, replying for the BBC, defended the action:

> this [participation] must damage his credibility as an impartial BBC producer not only in the minds of listeners ... but in any negotiations that he may have to conduct with the National Front or, for that matter, with any other political party ... nor can I accept [the] excuse that because Mr. Dunne was only protesting against racism, we had no right to warn him ... this was a pre-election meeting which totally alters the situation ... We have every intention of maintaining our constitutional corporate neutrality in such matters.

If the BBC was minded to defend this rule even when doing so implied respectability for a virulently racist party which at the time was polling less than 0.75% nationwide, it seems that the rule was fairly entrenched. The consequence of these rules was that politicians were often unable to ascertain whether journalists were partisan or not – or if they did believe that journalists were partisan, they were often wrong. The case of Grace Wyndham Goldie is illustrative in this regard. Goldie started off as a radio talks producer, and became a leading figure in television current affairs and electoral coverage. As Miall (1994, p. 138) put it, "Grace's own political instincts were conservative. [Her husband] used to work part-time for the Conservative Central Office, and she was a close friend of Earl Woolton, the chairman of the Tory party"; and yet Anthony Eden thought she was a "well-known socialist", and those she chose for her programmes were typically "right-wing socialists".

2.3 Concrete rules

These personnel rules went alongside the development of written and codified rules concerning content. The tendency during this period was for existing BBC policy, found in myriad notes collected in reference works such as the Maconachie file, to be collected, edited and published in slim volumes that could be circulated both internally to journalists and producers, on the expectation that they might read the whole document, and also externally, to politicians, in the hope that they might refer to it or be impressed by it.

One aspect of the development of these rules is the creation of a formal BBC complaints handling procedure, which pre-empted criticism of the BBC's dismissive attitude towards politics (see pp. 111–112). An earlier example of the use of rules to assuage political (and popular) criticism is the BBC's development of codes on the presentation of violence. The BBC's "Code of Practice on the Use of Violence in Television Programmes" was originally drawn up in 1960 by Kenneth Adam, then Controller of Programmes (Television), partly in response to Hilde Himmelweit's research on the effect of television on children. The initial development of the code does not seem to have stemmed from any cases of political or popular criticism, but rather as an independent initiative: the codes were, however, periodically reiterated when criticism resurfaced, as it did towards the end of the 1960s when more violent depictions of criminality began to appear on screens. The Code was thus recirculated in 1965, with additional notes on the portrayal of sex and blasphemy, with the following comment:

> The reason I am doing this is because, as you can see from the Press, the anti-BBC hounds are baying these days even more shrilly than before … I think we must avoid as much as possible anything which will needlessly "rock the boat". In short, we must guard against any thoughtless or inadvertent mistakes. So, read on and commit to heart.[16]

Five years later, the issue resurfaced again, with Home Secretary James Callaghan promising ill-defined action on the issue. In response to this pressure, the BBC created an advisory group ("Advisory Group on the Social Effects of Television") to look at the issue, and consider possible revisions of the Code of Practice. The terms of reference of this group were set so as to maximize the external value of the announcement and minimize the internal imposition: in a Board of Management meeting of April 1970,

> there was further consideration … given to the possible powers and functions of the proposed body to consider violence on television. DG [Director-General] stressed that the BBC's proposals must be effective *enough to get the Home Secretary "off the hook"*, but, considered from a political angle, should be *no more than enough to relieve the BBC from the possible imposition of an external supervisory body*. The BBC and the ITA were agreed in opposition to any kind of external "Viewers' Council".[17]

Even the former author of the Code, Kenneth Adam, was by this time somewhat jaded with the cynical use of the Code: in an article for the *Evening News* on 28 April 1970, he wrote that

> The last thing I want to do is jump on Jim Callaghan's bandwagon. But if he is worried about the new violence of our native TV product then I am with him all the way. Four series … are currently driving a coach and horses through the codes of violence. I have a right to interpret the BBC's rules because I set them up ten years ago, and they are still on the book, to be smugly trotted out on inquiry from earnest American researchers … Neither

[code] is perfect, by any means, but both are understandable and workable ... producers are flaunting their intention, and managers are turning a cynical eye on standards to which they are officially committed up to the hilt.[18]

To earnest American researchers one might well add members of parliament – a further revision of the Code in 1978 was circulated to a list of 62 MPs. The same was also done for the BBC's nascent code on News and Current Affairs – and it is to news that I now turn.

2.4 Structure, organization, recruitment in news

Recognition of the special role News played within the BBC came in 1949, with director-general Ian Jacob's speech of that year to the News Division. Jacob recognized that many other BBC employees looked upon News with some distrust, but justified the "special nature" of the service. According to Harman Grisewood, the Director of Spoken Word (thus ultimately responsible for news broadcasting), "the BBC had followed no 'news policy' before Jacob's direct intervention".

If Grisewood meant that there were no policies in news, he contradicts himself, for he noted that "a mass of tradition – has grown up around news and the BBC's handling of news" (Briggs, 1995, vol. V, p. 65). We must therefore understand that the BBC, until that time, had no policy for news – no views about how large or important a part of the BBC's output it should be, and how it should relate to the rest of the organization. Policies in news did exist, and, as with policies on violence, they were regularly trotted out upon receipt of foreign enquiries. In response to a request from Radiotjänst concerning the reporting of court cases, the BBC was able to enclose "a copy of the Guidance Index, which is kept up to date from time to time for the use of our News Room", though the BBC's liaison officer did not add that it was unlikely to be of "great interest since the Guidance notes are mainly applicable to our situation here in the UK".[19]

The Guidance Index was primarily for internal use. It was superseded by the BBC's guidelines on News and Current Affairs, which from the outset were designed to be quoted and read outside of the broadcaster. Work on guidelines in News and Current Affairs began in spring 1979, alongside the development of revised codes on the portrayal of violence. MPs were kept informed of these developments, and a circular, which included a "detailed statement on news and current affairs future plans on BBC1 and 2, and [the] Sims Report [on violence] with associated revised guidelines", was sent to 62 MPs in that same year.

2.5 Political interference

The BBC's main problems of this period, however, did not concern violence, nor news and current affairs in its purest form. Rather, the BBC was attacked for displaying a lack of respect for politics. Two programmes were emblematic: *That Was The Week That Was* (TW3), a comic revue, and *Yesterday's Men*, a documentary on the activities of Labour leaders after the party's defeat in the 1970 general election. Politicians' negative response to both programmes fed proposals to "democratize" the BBC – to change its institutional structure so as to afford it less legal protection. The BBC's response to this was typical: it promised to set up new structures which would either provide new rules on content, or better adjudicate existing rules.

TW3, which began in 1962, was an example of a programme which was both cynical towards politicians and a major ratings success. Its cynicism was mild by today's standards, yet it implied that politicians lied and were grasping and/or out of touch. Reaction to TW3 from politicians was, understandably, typically negative, but it was rarely sufficiently concentrated, and rarely concentrated amongst those who could cause any strong official reaction. Macmillan was sanguine about the programme: better to be laughed at than ignored, he said. He wrote to his Postmaster-General, Reginald Bevins, explicitly telling him not to take any action against the programme (Briggs, 1995, vol. V, p. 360).

The programme-makers justified this approach by claiming to be "on the side of the audience", in rhetorical contraposition to the "Establishment". Of course, during a period of Conservative government, "to be anti-Establishment ... meant being anti-Conservative" (Briggs, 1995, vol. V, p. 360). After Greene had heard from "Westminster circles" that that the programme "was wearing thin", the programme was put on hiatus for the summer, but with the promise that it would return. Eventually, Greene

> came to the conclusion that it was "in the general interest" and "in the interests of the BBC" that TW3 "should not go on" ... It had now become, he complained "a gigantic red herring, diverting attention from the real achievements of the BBC and prejudicing judgement of broadcasts on important but difficult social themes" ... While he realized that there would be protests over what would be seen as BBC cowardice, there were "political considerations" that most people would find convincing. A general election could not be far away.
>
> (Briggs, 1995, vol. V, p. 372)

TW3 allowed the BBC to push boundaries; it did not exceed them. Paradoxically the more damaging programme was a straight documentary which, however, retained the cynical attitude which had developed during the 1960s. *Yesterday's Men* was a 1971 documentary which followed a number of former Labour cabinet ministers as they went about their post-ministerial lives. The most controversial part of the documentary was an interview with former prime minister Harold Wilson, in which Wilson was asked about the amount of money he had received for his memoirs, and whether he had thus profited from his access to state papers in writing them. Wilson's press adviser (Joe Haines) thought that he had secured an agreement with the interview team that questions pertaining to the memoirs would not be included, but, somewhat predictably, interpretations about the scope of this agreement differed. The programme's final tenor was unfortunate: the title had not been disclosed to interviewees, who found it insulting. *Yesterday's Men* fed one school of criticism of the BBC, namely, that it was contributing to a deterioration in public confidence in politics by making programmes which started from the presumption that politicians were concealing something and/or acted from base motives; in such a context, the task of the programme-maker or interviewer was thus to unmask the politician's lie and produce a "gotcha" moment. This in itself was not a violation of impartiality or indication of any bias (though the effect may have been harder on government politicians), and so it was initially difficult to reconcile complaints of this manner to the traditional manner of complaint handling. This school of criticism included Labour ministers who might otherwise have been thought to be friends of the BBC, such as Dick Crossman:

> Time and time we [Hill, Curran, Crossman] came back to the problem of bias and whether I thought the BBC was biased against the government. I said I didn't, but that I thought great trouble was caused by the instructions that staff were given. I reminded him of the time when the supposedly impartial Chairman of my roundtable discussion on trivialization popped in an absolutely unexpected question at the end and joining in the attack. I also emphasised the difference between BBC and ITN interviewers. The ITN people just come to get your news and to get you to put it over objectively in your own way. The BBC comes to argue with you, to keep something in reserve and then pounce on you, and this makes you wary of them and produces a worse broadcast.
>
> (Crossman, 1977, p. 912)

Crossman had been due to give a speech on the relationship between the press and politics, "showing that there is one member of the Government who understands the problems of the press, radio and TV, is sympathetic about them, and is expounding fairly objectively the problems of co-operation between the Government and the TV authorities" (Crossman, 1977, p. 229). Unfortunately, Crossman's analysis was rather pre-empted by a much less sympathetic critic of the BBC, Tony Benn. Benn – who had worked briefly for the BBC, and who thought it "wildly right wing" (Briggs, 1995, vol. V, p. 518) – had given a speech to around 30 members of his constituency in which he declared that broadcasting was "really too important to be left to the broadcasters" (Briggs, 1995, p. 787). Benn's views were shared by much of the left of the Labour Party at this time, and an impressive roster of academic opinion in the '76 group ("a pressure group composed mainly of programme makers and academics": Freedman, 2001, p. 196) and the Standing Committee on Broadcasting (SCoB), another mainly academic group. The call for greater "democratization" of broadcasting was to be met by abolishing the BBC and IBA and creating a Public Broadcasting Commission supervised by a Communications Council (Freedman, 2001, p. 202).

Whilst a concern about broadcaster-led erosion of trust in politics could easily be shared by those across the political spectrum, the demand for democratization of the media was more partisan. In part, it derived from suspicion that the BBC treated Labour poorly, probably due to Labour's being in government, since government initiatives are always scrutinized more carefully. In part, though, it derived from dissatisfaction with particular areas which were difficult to portray concisely and fairly. One of these was industrial relations. Some years later the Glasgow University Media Group would show (Glasgow University Media Group, 1976, 1980) that the BBC was both more likely to feature employers than employees in industrial disputes, and also to ignore the root causes of the industrial dispute. This diagnosis would have been favourably received by the left of the Labour Party, which sought "for broadcasting [not] to be at the service of profit and bureaucracy, but to be at the service of our Movement and the people as a whole" (trade unionist Alan Sapper, quoted in Freedman, 2001, p. 202). Wilson did not share Benn's policy proposals, but did share his suspicion of the BBC. He thought Radio 1 disc-jockeys "brought in news items with an anti-Labour slant". Dick Crossman thought Wilson's attitude to be "absolutely lunatic" and his "outstanding weakness as a leader" (Crossman, 1977, p. 388). Yet Wilson, as prime minister, was able to act on such feelings whilst Crossman was not. In 1970 he announced to Cabinet that there would be an inquiry into the BBC, with Lord (Noel) Annan as Chair. Crossman derided the move as "another instance of a major decision being privately taken by Harold and a few others" (Crossman, 1977, p. 921).

The inquiry would not take place – at least, not that year. In the election of June 1970, Labour lost office, thus setting the stage for *Yesterday's Men*. Although the BBC would go through the usual steps – internal report partially exonerating the Corporation but acknowledging that some misunderstandings had arisen – there was a sense in which the Governors, because of their own involvement in the process, could no longer arbitrate at the interface between politics and the BBC. "The notion of seeking redress solely from the BBC Governors ... no longer commanded public support" (Sparks, 1981, p. 469). This, equally, was a key element in the Annan Report when it was brought back to life by the Wilson government which returned to power in 1974.

The formation of a new complaints-handling mechanism and revised rules on current affairs would partially assuage critics. The first move, which followed directly from the farrago over *Yesterday's Men*, was the establishment of a complaints commission:

> [Board chairman Charles Hill] who genuinely liked asking questions, now asked himself whose duty it was to protect those who believed that they had been unfairly treated by the BBC. The Governors had vetted the programme and some had seen it ... The upshot was the setting up in October 1971 of a BBC Programmes Complaints Commission, which issued its first report in May 1973. Lord Parker, a former Lord Chief Justice, was its first Chairman, and the other two members were Lord Maybray-King, a former Speaker of

the House of Commons, and Sir Edmund Compton [former Parliamentary ombudsman].

(Briggs, 1995, p. 900)

The establishment of the commission subsequently became a pre-emptive defence in the BBC's evidence to the Annan committee, where it claimed "that the case for a Complaints Commission was said to have already been recognised" (Sparks, 1981, p. 470), and that the committee's proposal for an independent complaints commission for both broadcasters was not necessary.

Greater editorial control was also implemented. Jean Seaton has written that "one benefit [of *Yesterday's Men*] was the emergence of new guidelines" (Seaton, 1997, p. 88). Whilst the Annan committee was taking evidence,

> [t]he BBC set up advisory bodies on the Social Effects of Television and on Industrial and Business Affairs. The two authorities have updated and jointly published their codes on the portrayal of violence; guidelines to policy and practice in the News and Current Affairs field have been codified and made public; and public meetings have blossomed ... *These moves reduced the pressure for new structures of public control.*
>
> (Sparks, 1981, p. 471; emphasis added)

3 From Thatcher to Blair (1979–2005)

British politics changed after 1979. The advent of Thatcherism brought the end of easy alternation between different flavours of Keynesianism, and the beginning of conviction politics – a type of politics that survived the Conservative Party's fall from power in 1997 and the beginning of a period of electoral dominance for the Labour Party under Tony Blair. This period also saw particularly marked conflict between the BBC and the government during each period of party rule: conflict between 1984 and 1986, culminating in the sacking of director-general Alasdair Milne; and conflict between 2003 and 2004, ending with the resignation of Greg Dyke and Gavyn Davies, director-general and Chairman of the Board of Governors respectively. Following each episode, the BBC attempted to rebuild its independence from government by toughening its rules on content. This development was particularly associated with the period in office of John Birt, memorably described by playwright Dennis Potter as a "croak-voiced Dalek", but nonetheless a manager whose policies pre-empted attacks from both Labour and Conservative governments.

Given the importance of periods of conflict since 1979, this section is structured slightly differently in three parts, dealing with the BBC under Alasdair Milne (3.1), the restoration of the BBC under John Birt (3.2), and the Hutton affair (3.3). My analysis – insofar as it credits Birt with restoring the BBC's position – is not novel, but nor is it uncontroversial: the debate between Birtists and anti-Birtists is a virulent one. The analysis of the Hutton Inquiry is perhaps more unusual: I argue that prior to the death of David Kelly, and the subsequent appointment of a judicial investigation, the BBC had successfully bogged down in the government in a series of increasingly sterile exchanges about when the BBC was and was not allowed to use single-sourced stories. Consequently, had David Kelly not died, and had no other extraordinary event occurred to widen the conflict, relations between the government and the BBC would likely have ended in stalemate, and the BBC would probably have retained its director-general and chairman.

3.1 Milne

The Thatcher era began auspiciously for the BBC. The Conservative Party did not feel poorly treated by the Corporation; and most of the criticism launched at the Corporation both on the structural level (with the Annan report) and on the programme level (with controversies over single incidents such as *Yesterday's Men* or the allegedly pro-business coverage of industrial affairs) came from the left of the Labour Party. The director-general, Ian Trethowan (1977–1982), was widely suspected amongst BBC staff to be a Conservative, though there was no official confirmation of this (nor could there be) (Wyatt, 2003, p. 16).

Given, on one hand, "widespread distrust" amongst all political parties towards the BBC towards the end of the 1970s, and, on the other hand, "alleged contempt for the whole parliamentary process" on the part of BBC staff, Trethowan had been "careful to build bridges between the BBC and the Government" (O'Malley, 1994, p. 3). Whether due to this strategy or not, the BBC was fortunate enough to secure the first multi-year licence fee settlement, particularly important in a period where inflation rapidly exhausted the real value of fees with fixed face value. The fee increase was granted by Willie Whitelaw, Home Secretary, who had always been friendly to the Corporation. One BBC producer dated the decline in government–BBC relations to Whitelaw's move from the Home Office in 1983; up until that point – and the contemporaneous row over *Maggie's Militant Tendency* – none of the major government–BBC crises, including Suez and TW3, "had much long-term effect on the BBC" (John Grist, quoted in Seaton & Hennessy, 1997, p. 116).Certainly, those Governors who were appointed by Whitelaw were not overly critical of the Corporation, nor were they as a rule Conservative. Those who were appointed later, by contrast, tended to be much more critical, and much more likely to view faults with the BBC's management.

Faults, however, were present. In particular, under Alasdair Milne (director-general, 1982–1986) relationships between the director-general and the Board of Governors broke down, and the flow of information to the director-general from programme-making units deteriorated. Why this should have occurred is not quite clear: most commentators place the blame on Milne's personality: whilst ferociously intelligent, Milne was perhaps too socially maladroit to be a good director-general, or had too limited an appreciation for how others might misunderstand issues, programmes or policies (O'Malley, 1994, p. 146). An internal report in 1985 was thus able to conclude that the governors felt "inadequately informed and insufficiently forewarned" (O'Malley, 1994, p. 46). O'Malley

(1994, p. 138) concludes that "there is no doubt that the relationship between the BBC Board of Governors and its senior managers deteriorated seriously in the years 1982–6".

Milne, in his defence, argued that the Governors had grown too powerful and too involved in day-to-day decision-making: if they felt ill-informed about certain matters, it was because they had no right to involve themselves in those matters (Horrie & Clarke, 1994, p. 208). Milne was perhaps too courteous to add what O'Malley (1994, p. 138) went on to claim:

> the deterioration was a result of the range of policies pursued at government level against the BBC [including placing] on the BBC Board of Governors people deemed to be politically acceptable to Mrs Thatcher, breaking with the convention of bipartisan appointments.

Yet these appointments were not party-political; those board members who were party-political and close to the Conservatives felt inhibited by their affiliation – as Brian Wenham put it (in O'Malley, 1994, p. 138):

> a sizeable faction of the board wanted rid of Milne and his chief editorial associates but could not bring themselves to strike. So they merely wounded, damagingly for the BBC, whose wounds were then further exposed to the turning of the Tory knife.

Party-political board members close to Labour ultimately came to share their colleagues' concerns. The deterioration therefore seems to have been at least partly motivated, and more specifically motivated, by a general breakdown in referral procedures which meant that the Governors were often uninformed because Milne was often unaware himself.

In part, this was structural. Before Milne, there had been a director of News and Current Affairs who had ultimate authority, but Milne rejected this arrangement; responsibility for News and Current Affairs was now given to the different networks (Barnett, Curry & Chalmers, 1994, p. 74). This structural arrangement meant that Alan Protheroe, who acted as Milne's "flak-catcher", was outside of the production system and thus was forever playing catch-up, unable to monitor and/or intervene at early stages of programme development. A number of commentators concur in concluding that Protheroe "was not sufficiently plugged in" (Barnett et al., 1994, p. 73; Horrie & Clarke, 1994, p. 14; Leapmann, 1986, p. 292). In addition to his structurally weak position, Protheroe was by this time nearing the end of his career and reportedly worn-out by repeated Conservative attacks aimed at "softening-up" the BBC in preparation for the election. The Governors subsequently expressed no confidence in his work when he had retransmitted a TV-AM interview with Princess Margaret without attribution and covering over TV-AM's on-screen ident (Barnett et al., 1994, p. 25).

The Governors felt insufficiently informed about three cases in particular: *Maggie's Militant Tendency* (1984), *Real Lives* (1985) and *Secret Society*

(1986). The first of these was a documentary in which it was alleged that members of the Conservative Party[20] had links with neo-Nazi organizations, and which led to a libel trial; the second, part of a series featuring Northern Irish politicians, one of whom (Martin McGuiness) was alleged to be part of the IRA; and the third was a documentary made by BBC Scotland which revealed the existence of the Zircon spy satellite. This last documentary was banned by Milne on national security grounds, but the film-maker subsequently organized screenings of the film which made it a cause célèbre. *Maggie's Militant Tendency* had been "meticulously checked and rechecked" and approved by the BBC's political and legal advisers. Milne had gone through the issues with the Board led by Stuart Young; however, the libel trial that resulted from the broadcast only arrived in court after Young's resignation and the subsequent appointment of Duke Hussey as Chair and Joel Barnett as deputy.

The libel trial became more difficult for the BBC as it seemed more and more witnesses had been pressured by the Conservative Party; the Board – or more accurately, Barnett – forced Milne to settle out of court at the most damaging moment possible, namely, after the two Conservative MPs' lawyers had given their opening statements savaging the BBC (Horrie & Clarke, 1994, pp. 58–59). The collapse of the case led to an Early Day Motion calling for Milne's resignation signed by 100 Conservative MPs. *Real Lives* was "cleared by BBC management using its special vetting procedures for programmes on Ireland" (O'Malley, 1994, p. 57). Home Secretary Leon Brittan asked the Board of Governors to ban the programme; they agreed whilst Milne was on a boating holiday in Sweden (Horrie & Clarke, 1994, p. 47). The decision provoked the first-ever strike of BBC journalists.

Secret Society was, of the three, the only instance in which management was clearly unaware of the true political import of a BBC programme. "Protheroe was alerted late", write Horrie and Clarke (1994, p. 94):

> [Protheroe] was worried that information about the satellite might break the Official Secrets Act. He took his concerns to a regular meeting of the D-Notice Committee, the self-regulatory body set up by the Ministry of Defence to prevent journalists inadvertently printing military secrets. Protheroe did not mention Zircon during the meeting, but asked the committee's chairman, Clive Whitmore, if he could stay behind for a little chat ... At the mention of the word Zircon, Whitmore's jaw dropped. "Oh my God!", he yelped. He locked the door. Protheroe spent an hour telling him about the proposed programme. Whitmore listened intently before saying: "Alan, you are really on dodgy ground here. Very difficult ground indeed".

Indeed, Protheroe "believed Zircon, along with Real Lives and Maggie's Militant Tendency, was one of the reasons [the Board] had demanded Milne's head" (Horrie & Clarke, 1994, p. 95). Milne's decision to ban the programme was taken in December 1986; he was dismissed in January the following year.

The (perceived) failure of editorial control can be seen in the Board's interviews for Milne's successor. Those candidates which supported the merger of

News and Current Affairs into "a single journalistic unit" – Michael Checkland, deputy director general since 1985, and Michael Grade – were received favourably by the Governors; those who were opposed – Brian Wenham – were not (Horrie & Clarke, 1994, pp. 74–75).

3.2 Birt

It was not, however, to be Checkland, the winning candidate, who would be responsible for merging News and Current Affairs and restoring the government's confidence in the BBC's editorial control, but rather the man who Checkland was obliged to choose as his deputy, John Birt.

Birt was at the time programme controller at LWT. He was known for having distinct views on news and current affairs and for developing the bureaucratic structures necessary to implement those views. The influence of the printed press on the BBC had been slight from the time of the Beveridge committee onwards; yet under Birt it enjoyed a modest resurgence: for Birt's views on journalism were shared by a circle of journalists close to the *Financial Times*. Whilst the *Times* and the *Telegraph* could still be cited in the 1950s and 1960s as examples of "uncoloured news", their position had changed by the 1980s as their coverage became more subject to the whims of Rupert Murdoch (1981 onwards) and Conrad Black (*Telegraph* owner from 1985). The *Financial Times*, however, continued to provide non-partisan, analytic journalism, shorn of trivia – for Birt's critics, hardly mass-market enough to provide a model for the BBC. Birt, however, persisted: he admired John Lloyd, the *Financial Times* journalist, who would much later publish a book with arguments which overlapped with those of Birt (Lloyd, 2005), and later appointed Ian Hargreaves, *FT* correspondent, as the managing editor of the (merged) News and Current Affairs section.

Birt's preferences were long-standing. Whilst at LWT, Birt had co-authored with Peter Jay a series of articles for the *Times* arguing that television had a "bias against understanding": since television news privileged events which could be captured on film, it omitted causes which could not; consequently, in order to counteract this bias, news and current affairs had to be given a "mission to explain". Concretely, each piece was to have a finding, or a thesis: footage and raw material would then be collected to elucidate this analysis, instead of vice versa. This approach to news was criticized on its merits (since it was believed to lead to sterile journalism) and also occasioned *ad hominem* attacks: "'Birtism', a set of idiosyncratic theories about television journalism Birt had been working on since the 1970s ... [has been explained] as an endlessly flexible doctrine that amounts to whatever will further the career of John Birt" (Horrie & Clarke, 1994, p. xiv), or straightforward "political subordination" (Born, 2005).

Yet Birt was not just an "ideas man": he also had great use for structures. Birt had previously established a "substantial bureaucratic structure" at LWT for a programme, *Nice Time*, in order to pursue safely(!) the youth-orientated anarchy the show's producers wanted (Horrie & Clarke, 1994, p. 88). The Birt-implemented merger of News and Current Affairs was one element of a new bureaucratic structure which suited Birt's ends. A further element was the development of new written codes for News and Current Affairs. It was during this period that the first collected edition of the BBC Producers' Guidelines was assembled. The original publication in 1987 was followed by several subsequent editions, before being renamed as the BBC Editorial Guidelines in 2005.

The initial development of the guidelines was not welcomed by many within the Corporation. "Everyone thought this was the most sinister thing that had ever happened."[21] Staff had equally negative views about other changes affecting News and Current Affairs. Yet Birt's system of editorial control may only have appeared so intrusive because previous systems had been forgotten. Horrie and Clarke (1994, p. 166) write that Birt felt sure that "with his referral procedure in place he would be in a position to prevent or tone down anything too provocative before it reached the screen". Yet, of course, the referral procedure was not Birt's invention, and any suggestion that it was must surely indicate that referral prior to Birt had fallen into disuse.

Certainly, it was far from the situation depicted by Huw Wheldon when, in a mid-1970s lecture, he noted that "the wrath of the Corporation in its varied human manifestations … is particularly reserved for those who fail to refer" (quoted in Burns, 1977, p. 195). The imposition of the new guidelines and organizational changes was justified by repeated reference to impartiality, which "was what individual journalists chose to make of it in the mid-eighties".[22] Yet within one to three years, writers and producers came to accept the Guidelines as authoritative. They did so because "they began to see that the guidelines were protection for them, not control".[23]

If Birt succeeded (ultimately) in placating staff, he also managed to placate the government of the time; certainly if the intent of the reforms was to reassure the government that the BBC's editorial control was adequate, they succeeded. Certain members of the government thought they had already noticed an improvement in the BBC's output after Milne's departure (O'Malley, 1994, p. 156); Thatcher concurred:

> The appointment of Duke Hussey as Chairman of the BBC in 1986 and later of John Birt as Deputy Director-General represented an improvement in every respect. When I met Duke Hussey and Joel Barnett – his deputy – in September 1988 I told them how much I supported the new approach being taken.
>
> (Thatcher, 1993, p. 637)

3.3 *Dyke, Gilligan, Kelly and Hutton*

Birt left the BBC in 2000, and shortly afterwards was appointed a special adviser to Tony Blair. Birt was replaced by Greg Dyke, a television executive who had, in the past, made public his support for the Labour Party. Some within the Corporation thought that this made him ineligible for the post, lest the BBC seem too close to the government of the day (Wyatt, 2003, pp. 20–21). Dyke's eventual fate is thus ironic. In the spring of 2003, the BBC came under strong private pressure from the Labour government over its coverage of the war in Iraq.

Government pressure became highly public and controversial following a broadcast on the *Today* programme by reporter Andrew Gilligan, which alleged that the government probably knew that certain parts of its original case for war were wrong, and that the dossier making the case for war had been "sexed up" by Downing Street. David Kelly, the source for Gilligan's story, was eventually named; he subsequently committed suicide on 17 July 2003. The government asked Lord Hutton to carry out an inquiry into the circumstances surrounding Dr Kelly's death. Hutton's report largely exonerated the government, but criticized the BBC's editorial system ("defective"), management ("at fault ... in failing to investigate properly the Government's complaints"), and Governors ("should have made more detailed investigations") (Hutton, 2004, pp. 213–214). Following the Hutton Report, BBC Chair Gavyn Davies stepped down, and director-general Greg Dyke was forced to resign.

The incident is often depicted as proof that the BBC is less independent from government than it would like to believe. I would argue that the government was able to achieve its desired objective – the resignation of Dyke and Davies and the consequent re-evaluation of the BBC's journalism – only because the Hutton Inquiry intervened. Prior to the inquiry, and Lord Hutton's interpretation of the BBC's journalism (which most commentators have described as overly exacting), the BBC's natural defence of citing its own guidelines had dragged different members of the government into a futile debate about the exact meaning of those guidelines.

The BBC's guidelines were frequently cited in government letters to the BBC from the very beginning of the government's tussle with the BBC. Gerald Kaufman, Labour MP and then-Chair of the Commons Select Committee on Culture, Media and Sport, wrote privately to Gavyn Davies concerning "violations of the BBC's war guidelines"[24] on the day after combat operations began in Iraq. The BBC's written procedure aided the BBC in its initial stage of confrontation with the government. Publicly available correspondence from the BBC repeatedly cited the Producers' Guidelines; government correspondence subsequently focused on narrower areas of disagreement with the BBC – in particular, the Gilligan broadcast's use of an anonymous single source, and was drawn into debating the finer points of its case.

There are two points to be made about the use of the Producers' Guidelines. First, the Producers' Guidelines were employed as a valuable resource in the BBC's public campaign against government interference. Between March and May, when the BBC's relations with the government were fraught but remained private, there was little mention of the guidelines, either by Alastair Campbell or Richard Sambrook, BBC Director of News. Only after the Gilligan broadcast on 29 May was much mention made of them. Alastair Campbell cites them in letters of 6 and 26 June, making essentially the same criticisms; Richard Sambrook, dealing with the same parts of the Producers' Guidelines, makes essentially the same responses in letters of 11 and 27 June. It is important to note that the correspondence of 26–27 June was made publicly available by both sides. Similarly, subsequent correspondence between Ben Bradshaw, Richard Sambrook and Stephen Whittle, was made public, with the BBC making the first move, on 29 June and 1 July.

Second, the effect of concentration on the Producers' Guidelines was systematically to narrow the range of disagreement between BBC and government. Until the publication of a report by the Commons Foreign Affairs Committee on 7 July, Alastair Campbell had maintained both that the BBC's general coverage of the war was biased and that Gilligan's 6.07 a.m. broadcast was false; the former charge was withdrawn. On the specific issue of the Gilligan broadcast, Campbell and Bradshaw had initially argued about the appropriateness of Gilligan's use of a single source, given that the Producers' Guidelines counsel against doing so; but by 1 July Bradshaw, employing the form of words used in the Producers' Guidelines, is writing to ask Whittle whether procedure followed by the *Today* team "shows any reluctance on behalf of the BBC to rely on one source".[25] The issue is narrowed further: given that reluctance to rely on a single source might be shown by BBC efforts to contact the MoD prior to broadcast of the allegations, the key issue is redefined by Bradshaw and Geoff Hoon as whether the specifics of Gilligan's broadcast were adequately discussed on the evening of 27 May with the MoD press office.[26]

Former BBC correspondent and current MP for Exeter, Ben Bradshaw had quickly become involved in the tussle. Bradshaw had been a BBC reporter and presenter between 1986 and 1997, featuring on *World At One* and *World This Weekend*, both for Radio 4 (Dod's, 2006). He appeared on the *Today* programme on 28 June to make the government's case. Bradshaw used his experience of the BBC to attempt to shame the BBC into admitting its mistakes:[27]

> the BBC guidelines are very clear, when I worked for the BBC we were taught not to report something without three reliable sources, I know the World Service has and still has higher standards than the domestic service, but the allegation…
>
> I know from talking to people in the BBC John [Humphrys, *Today* presenter], and I'm sure you do too, that there are many, many senior journalists in the BBC who are deeply unhappy at the way the BBC has handled this.

Humphrys was sceptical of the reasons for Bradshaw's appearance:

JOHN HUMPHRYS: Ben Bradshaw, Minister of State now at the Department of the Environment, good morning to you … And of course formerly of this programme, a journalist yourself.
BB: That's right.
JH: Is that why you were put up to do this interview?

The same tactic of using insider knowledge to try to shame the BBC into admitting it had not followed procedure was used by another former BBC employee–

turned-MP, Chris Bryant, who wrote to Gavyn Davies "as a former head of European Affairs at the BBC" to ask whether each Governor believes the BBC's allegations to be true or false.[28] Those inside the BBC were concerned that Bradshaw's attempts might succeed. Editor of *Today* Kevin Marsh emailed Mark Damazer, Deputy Director of BBC News, about the need to present a single front about the evidence used in the *Today* broadcast to stop "what Bradshaw tried to do last week – and run BBC v. BBC red herring",[29] or the argument that Bradshaw has the ear of the disaffected within the BBC.

It is impossible to know how relations between the BBC and the government would have continued had David Kelly not died. However, the internal BBC correspondence released by the Hutton Inquiry gives no indication that the BBC was ready to back down, and it was unlikely that the government would have chosen to escalate the situation: Alastair Campbell had already had to scale back his involvement in the incident after a disastrous interview on *Channel 4 News*: given the general low esteem with which Campbell was held by the general public, his further involvement in the government's fight with the BBC threatened to damage the government's case by association; in general the public perceived the BBC more favourably than the government (YouGov, 2004).

4 Conclusion

Just as individuals, organizations can display virtues, and the BBC is known for displaying the virtue of independence vis-à-vis the government. This perception is enhanced by the BBC's willingness to dispense advice to other broadcasters in democratizing countries. Even in established democracies, the BBC is often held up as an example of the virtuous broadcaster. In Italy, acts of interference within Rai, or acts of perceived censure by the broadcaster, are often either dismissed or explained away by invoking the familiar formula, "*non è la BBC*" (it's not the BBC). Yet there is a tendency to think that since the BBC displays this virtue, it will be virtuous in all aspects of its existence – that it, as an organization, will demonstrate the unity of the virtues.

Yet this is clearly not the case: as this chapter has shown, the management of the BBC regularly acts in an overbearing manner to impose structures on its own journalists that perhaps in other countries would be viewed as contrary to free expression or overly censorious. Journalists accept these impositions ultimately because they know that they provide protection: if assurances can be given that a journalist has followed the Editorial Guidelines, then they will be defended by management against political interference – even when, in the case of Andrew Gilligan, such assurances were dubious.

Although incidents like the Gilligan–Kelly–Hutton affair call into question the degree of the BBC's independence, we should not let this overshadow the realization that the BBC is amongst the more independent PSBs in this study – certainly more independent than the Spanish or Italian broadcasters, and likely more independent than DR. That this independence should have been called into question recently is unsurprising given the dramatic tail-off in the size of the market for news in the UK. The BBC has been forced to work harder at maintaining its distinct news culture, and avoid the danger noted by the Governors of "mov[ing] in line with tabloid and Sunday newspaper journalism where contacting people who might deny a story were avoided", where the culture is one of "creating rather than reporting news".[30] That hard work, however, is reflected in the body of rules concerning content, not just as currently exemplified by the Editorial Guidelines, but throughout the BBC's history. These rules can be expressed as a function of the initial state of the market for news in Britain.

To summarize this chapter in line with the theory presented in Chapter 2, I have shown that

- the market for news in Britain was large, especially when considered in absolute terms;
- second, this market permitted four competing news agencies, all of which lobbied furiously to limit the BBC's independent news-gathering ability;
- consequently, the BBC was forced to rely on these companies, and sought their advice even when this was not necessary;
- third, thanks to policy imported from such agencies, and to an independent drive on the part of long-tenured BBC executives like Reith and Maconachie, the BBC developed extensive codes governing output, and strong public commitments to impartiality;
- fourth, these commitments have been repeatedly cited by the BBC itself as the bulwark of its impartiality;
- fifth, codes implementing these commitments – particularly developed as far as politics was concerned – are revised and distributed to politicians when the need arises (as, for example, in the 1970s), pre-empting the concerns of politicians;
- sixth, when these codes are followed, and when their adequacy is a matter only for politicians and journalists, the BBC can deal with concerns; where communication breaks down (Milne) or where BBC codes are held to be quasi-judiciable, the BBC loses out, and its independence vis-à-vis government is diminished.

6 Ireland

Importing experience

In the previous chapter, I demonstrated certain patterns in the BBC's history which were connected to the pursuit, attainment and defence of its independence. To the extent that the UK and the Republic of Ireland have similar media systems, we can employ Ireland as a check on our theory: to extent that the theoretically derived patterns found in the history of the BBC are also found in the history of Irish public broadcasting, our theory is strengthened; to the extent that they are not found, or do not work in the expected direction, our theory is weakened.

Despite numerous other mooted comparisons,[1] comparison of the British and Irish experiences is warranted for a number of reasons. First, as Pine (2002, p. xii) notes, "up to 1922, Ireland and Britain shared a legal and administrative structure, and therefore in the mid-1920s the evolution of radio in each country, however different their societies may have been, followed cognate paths". Second, Ireland benefited from its proximity to a much larger media market, which had a positive influence on the professionalization of journalism. The first Irish association of journalists was a local chapter of the British National Union of Journalists (NUJ) (Horgan, 2002, p. 53); Irish journalists continue to be represented by the NUJ. Irish journalists were cognizant of the requirements of British journalism, since many of them had to produce it: many of the editors of Irish dailies moonlighted as Dublin correspondents for the major British newspapers (Horgan, 2002, p. 38). London-based journalists who returned to Ireland were able to stand up to the parties even in party-owned newspapers (Horgan, 2002, p. 37). And, as we shall see, ideas and personnel imported from Britain played a key role in the development of what was then called 2RN and later known as Radio Éireann.

1 From 2RN to television (1926–1960)

The first broadcasting organization in the Irish Free State was "2RN", a broadcaster based in the Ministry of Posts and Telegraphs which began operating in January 1926 after permission from the Ministry of Finance arrived in June the preceding year (Pine, 2002, p. 114). The Ministry of Finance's approval was necessary because of the (erroneous) belief that the broadcaster – funded by licence fees and by import duties on radio receivers – would be a drain on the Exchequer. (In fact, 2RN made more than IR£331,567 for the Exchequer between 1926 and 1936: Pine, 2002, p. 136.)

The choice to establish the broadcaster as a unit within the ministry was anomalous. Indeed, it had been opposed by the then-Postmaster General, J. J. Walsh, who noted that the "only other country in the world which was tempted to choose the path of total state control was Russia" (Horgan, 2002, p. 17). Walsh's White Paper had envisaged an Irish Broadcasting Company built on similar lines to the British Broadcasting Company, with an exclusive concession from the state to supply broadcasting services. The proposal, however, was not accepted, as scandal engulfed one of the proposed concessionaires, attacked as being an "agent of British interests in Ireland" (Savage, 1996, p. 3).

Against the objections of the Finance Ministry, 2RN was established as a state organ. Despite the failure to imitate the form of the BBC, 2RN drew heavily on British experience. The BBC director-general John Reith sat on the station's first interview board; BBC representatives were also involved when the first station director, Séamus Clandillon, was chosen and approved by the minister (Pine, 2002, pp. 138–139), and Clandillon was subsequently sent to the BBC to "acclimatise" to radio (Pine, 2002, p. 70).

The BBC also supplied 2RN with much of its news. "Early news broadcasts were for the most part re-broadcasts of material taken (with permission) from the BBC, and from other stations" (Horgan, 2004, p. 4). When 2RN chose to broadcast its own news, the BBC acted as a check on the selection made: Cumann na nGaedheal leader W. T. Cosgrave "on one occasion expressed his wonderment at the fact that on one particular day, the BBC news had reported two speeches from the Dáil in its 6pm news while [2RN], 40 minutes later, had reported only one" – that of the minister (Horgan, 2004, p. 9).

Reporting was, however, a limited part of what 2RN did. Pine (2002, p. 8), paraphrasing Lasswell, notes that 2RN "was not so much concerned with who *said* what as with who *sang* what, since its early programming was predominantly musical". News programming was minimal and current affairs programming almost non-existent. As Ireland had no indigenous press agency, any domestic news would either have to come from 2RN stringers or from material re-broadcast from newspaper copy; and yet agreements similar to those in place in the UK prevented 2RN from carrying items from the morning and evening newspapers. This meant that much news was international, and consequently less controversial. Despite the station being a part of the government, the political branding of the station's output was "marginal" (Pine, 2002, p. 145) and non-ideological. "Controversy was conspicuous by its absence." Ministerial statements were few in number; any excess of enthusiasm – such as an unconfirmed leak about coalition negotiations suspected to have been planted by the minister in charge – was balanced by a compensatory broadcast for the opposition.

Whether this avoidance of controversy was the design of the station or of the ministry is not clear: Horgan (2004, p. 7) sees it as benefiting the government of the time:

if controversial political statements by or on behalf of government spokes-men had to be balanced by statements from the Opposition, the absence of controversial statements by the Government would have the beneficial effect of keeping the opposition away from the microphone. And this, for quite some time, seems to have been part of the rationale for the editorial decision, conscious or otherwise, to afford news a generally low priority.

The Fianna Fáil government of 1932 employed the station more than its Cumann na nGaedheal predecessor: Éamon de Valera began a habit of biannual radio addresses (McLoone, 1991, p. 13), directed as much to Irish abroad as to the domestic market. Fianna Fáil did remove some figures felt to be opposed to the party, such as C. E. Kelly (Director of Broadcasting between 1948 and 1951 and erstwhile editor of satirical review *Dublin Opinion*), but others with more objec-tionable views were left in place or promoted: former Cumann na nGaedheal General Secretary Séamus Hughes was even made Acting Station Director under Fianna Fáil (Pine, 2002, p. 141).

2RN during this time was thus more a state broadcaster than a public broad-caster. It was so in two senses. First, it participated in the state's mission of making good Irish men and women, wherever they might be. Thus, the govern-ment made ambitious plans for a shortwave service to broadcast to the Irish diaspora; the funds which had been allocated to this project were subsequently redirected, allowing 2RN to develop its first internal news service (Fisher, 1978, p. 22; Horgan, 2004, p. 14). Second, for structural reasons connected to its place-ment within the ministry, it enjoyed less independence than the public service broadcaster *par excellence*, the BBC (McLoone, 1991, 13).

Greater independence came in 1951 when Erskine Childers took over as Minis-ter for Posts and Telegraphs. Childers was committed in principle to greater inde-pendence for Radio Éireann (as it was latterly known), but was forever tempted to interfere in day-to-day matters. Nevertheless, aided by his department's private secretary Leon Ó Broin (Horgan, 2004, p. 16), Childers instituted a series of changes, resurrecting the five-member Comhairle (Council) which had lapsed in 1933, and which was to act as an executive body sandwiched between the manage-ment of the broadcaster and the minister himself. Childers also persuaded TDs not to place detailed questions about Radio Éireann's operation in the Dáil (Ó Broin, 1976, p. 14), and permitted the first unscripted political discussions.

The increased standing of Radio Éireann was shown when one minister, Neil Blaney, was moved from the Ministry of Posts and Telegraphs after having expressed no confidence in Radio Éireann without having first expressed his views either to the Comhairle or the to management. When Maurice Gorham, station director (and former director of the BBC's television service) threatened resignation, de Valera moved Blaney to Local Government, judging him more expendable than Gorham and the members of the Comhairle, who were at that time participating in anguished discussions concerning the introduction of televi-sion (Savage, 1996, p. 95). That is was finally approved in 1960 with the passage of the Broadcasting Authority Act.

2 Refoundation, confrontation (1960–1976)

The 1960 Act re-established Radio Éireann, now Radio Telefís Éireann (RTÉ), as an independent entity responsible to the Minister of Posts and Telegraphs. The decision to give Radio Éireann additional responsibility for television was not expected: plans for commercial television were well developed and looked to have the cabinet's favour before Taoiseach Sean Lémass abruptly changed his mind. Indeed, the name of the broadcaster's board – the RTÉ Authority – is a relic from earlier legislative plans which would have seen a regulatory not executive authority oversee commercial television.

The new Authority members were appointed for three-year terms, and could appoint the director-general of RTÉ given ministerial consent. Maurice Gorham was succeeded by American Edward J. Roth; he was aided by another international import, Gunnar Rugheimer, "a Swedish national [who] had acquired much of his broadcasting experience in Canada" (Horgan, 2004, p. 22). The 1960 Act required RTÉ to present areas of controversy "objectively and impartially". It is worth quoting John Horgan's discussion of this term at length (Horgan, 2004, pp. 24–25):

> The phrase "objectively and impartially" bespeaks a cultural, political and ideological worldview firmly rooted in the 1950s. The drafters of this phrase, the politicians who introduced it, and the audience to which is was addressed, would have been in little doubt about what they thought it actually meant. Impartiality and objectivity were the Holy Grail of Journalism; the idea that they might be difficult of attainment, or even problematic in themselves, was a hot topic only in the dim and distant recesses of the Frankfurt school ... *Fair representation of the views of those you were reporting did not present much of a problem: journalists had been doing this one way or another since the partisan press of the nineteenth century had to some extent been over-taken by the mass circulation media of the twentieth* ... Most of the legislators who debated the 1960 Broadcasting Act would have understood [impartiality] as primarily related to the permanent struggle between government and opposition. Some more sophisticated commentators might have interpreted it as having a relevance to the amount of coverage given to different political parties whether in government or not. Nobody, it is safe to say, would have interpreted it as having a relevance to – for instance – a conflict of wills as between the Dáil and elements in civil society.

The italicized section of the extract is consequential. The overtaking of the partisan press is a phenomenon which arose in Ireland thanks to contamination by Britain, and which did not arise in our other cases. As far as the "amount of coverage given to different political parties" was concerned, most of the clashes between the government and the broadcaster did not concern the distribution of time between the parties – which RTÉ regularly dealt with by furnishing break-downs on screen-time (Horgan, 2004, p. 20) – but rather with *raisons d'état* and the presence of civil society. With the former, the government was able to convince RTÉ to pull programmes: one programme on the government's civil defence initiatives, for example, was cancelled by the broadcaster after the minister forcefully intimated to executives that its broadcast would not be welcome (Horgan, 2004, p. 20). With the latter, however, new boundaries were being set. The most celebrated incident of this period was a programme concerning the government's agriculture policy, which is notable not so much for the incident itself (which involved a government minister phoning the broadcaster to reproach it for the "excessive" space given to farmers' representatives in the National Farmers' Association (NFA)) but for the statement made by Taoiseach Sean Lémass in response to criticism that arose (quoted in Horgan 2002, pp. 85–86, emphasis added):

> RTÉ was set up by legislation as an instrument of public policy and as such is responsible to the government. The government has overall responsibility for its conduct and especially the obligation to ensure that its programmes do not offend against the public interest or conflict with national policy as defined in legislation. To this extent the Government *reject the view that RTÉ should be, either generally or in regard to its current affairs and news programmes, completely independent of Government supervision.* As a public institution supported by public funds and operating under statute, it has the duty, while maintaining impartiality between political parties, to present programmes which inform the public regarding current affairs, to sustain public respect for the institutions of Government and, where appropriate, to assist public understanding of the policies enshrined in legislation enacted by the Oireachtas.

Lémass's statement is certainly not as crude as some who later deployed it made it out to be, but it is nonetheless indicative of the somewhat Gaullist attitude referred to earlier. It should certainly not be depicted as a power-play by Fianna Fáil to take over RTÉ: as John Horgan notes, "on the part of some of the politicians involved, the primary emotion being expressed was less hostility than bafflement" (Horgan, 2004, p. 27).

Despite Lémass's statement, RTÉ had the upper hand in negotiations with politicians that followed the NFA dispute. This is shown by the meeting between RTÉ executives and politicians following the NFA dispute: the account given in Dowling, Doolan and Quinn (1969, pp. 89–90) shows how RTÉ executives were able to out-interpret the agreements they had previously concluded with the politicians:

> Jack White and Gunnar Rugheimer [Director of Television] went to Leinster House to discuss *Division* with the Party Whips. This was on foot of a telephone call from the Fianna Fáil Chief Whip, Mr. Michael Carty, who said that RTÉ had broken the agreement about *Division* (presumably because Mr. Deasy [NFA] was not a politician). His real purpose, it was felt at the time, was to ensure that Mr. Deasy be withdrawn from the programme – in which

case Mr. Haughey would go on. This was a political foxtrot. Rugheimer knew that there was no such agreement. He suggested that since Mr. Carty believed that RTÉ had broken the agreement it must be a very serious matter. Why did Deputy Carty not call a meeting of the whips? [At the meeting, White and Rugheimer] produced the memorandum from the meeting which had agreed the procedures for *Division*. It simply stated that politicians would be invited through the Whips. They read this aloud and then enquired what Mr. Carty's complaints were? If the other two Whips did not know what was going on at the beginning of the meeting, it slowly began to dawn on them. Mr Carty was trying to make it appear that the Whips had understood *Division* to be a programme for politicians only. His co-whips weren't having any of this nonsense. They said there was no such agreement. Things rested so. The broadcast was to go ahead without Mr. Haughey.

RTÉ executives were therefore able to use agreements struck with the political parties in exactly the same way that the BBC had done, and in exactly the same way as outlined in Chapter 2: Mr Carty objected to particular content; and was rebuffed by RTÉ's demonstration that this content was precisely in accordance with rules that Mr Carty himself had agreed to.

Bafflement from politicians resulted not only from the novelty of the medium but also from the less deferential approach adopted by television and radio journalists, many of whom were not traditional journalists but were instead drawn from academia. Noted political scientist Brian Farrell was also an RTÉ reporter. So was Mary McAleese, at the time still a lecturer in law. These

> younger producers and directors, and some presenters, were effectively broadcast journalists even though their job descriptions did not include the word. Many of them, in the programme division, were not members of the journalists' trade union, the NUJ, but of equity or the Workers' Union of Ireland. They found themselves in many respects rejecting the political consensus that had been established under older media systems and challenging its basic tenets.
>
> (Horgan, 2004, p. 48)

One such basic tenet was impartiality, which, during the 1960s, was not openly attacked but certainly was paid less heed. Much later, Eoghan Harris, a producer, wrote training documents which openly challenged

> traditional notions of "impartiality" and "objectivity" ... and argued that such antediluvian notions had been banished from RTÉ's Programmes Division by Lelia Doolan and himself, "which is why Today Tonight is so good and why the public trust it". Television, he argued, was not about thought but about emotion, not about facts but about truth – and "professionalism" ideologically excluded both.
>
> (Horgan, 2004, p. 187)

Though it would be tempting to conclude so, it was not covert or overt disregard for impartiality which led to the dismissal of the RTÉ Authority in 1972 and the subsequent adoption of a Broadcasting Act in 1976 which granted RTÉ greater statutory independence in exchange for an explicit commitment to objectivity and impartiality in all of its output, not just in news and current affairs. Rather, it was coverage of Northern Ireland. The "Troubles" in that province began in the late 1960s and posed serious problems not only for the British and Northern Irish governments, but also for the government of the Republic which needed to demonstrate to the Heath government that it too was "tough" on the IRA. To that end, it issued a directive under Section 31 of the 1960 Act, which empowered the minister to prevent broadcasting on any subject or class of subjects in language, and which was analogous to a provision in the BBC's Royal Charter. That directive required RTÉ to "refrain from broadcasting any matter that could be calculated to promote the aims or activities of any organization which engages in, promotes, encourages or advocates the attaining of any political objective by violent means" (Horgan, 2002, p. 91).

The directive was, of course, entirely unhelpful, and the ministry refused to make it clear that the target of the directive was Sinn Féin, the IRA's political wing. Nor was the government entirely or equally vigilant: a number of interviews with Sinn Féin members were inadvertently broadcast before one such interview, in 1973, came to the government's attention. Having ascertained that the directive had been breached, being unsatisfied with the Authority's response (essentially a plea in mitigation), in need of a token to show to the Heath government, and having no other possible sanctions to employ, the government dismissed the Authority and appointed a new one. This power would shortly be taken away from the government when Fine Gael and Labour returned to power in 1973 – but they too imposed a similar directive, and were critical of RTÉ's impartiality and objectivity, or lack thereof.

3 1976 until the present day

Following the 1973 election which brought a Fine Gael–Labour coalition back to government, a Broadcasting Review Committee was established. The committee's judgement on RTÉ was largely negative, accusing the broadcaster of exercising inadequate care in the "recruitment, appointment, training and supervision of staff", as well as that the station was "falling short of required standards in relation to impartiality and objectivity". The negative judgements were confirmed by an internal News Division report, which said that "there was lack of discipline, rehearsal, and pride" in the News Department's work (Horgan, 2004, pp. 127, 126).

The government's response was to tighten the relevant provisions of the Broadcasting Authority Act pertaining to objectivity and impartiality. These two terms would now be requirements across all of RTÉ's output, not just in the treatment of controversial affairs. This extra requirement was balanced in the new legislation by the drastic curtailment of ministerial powers to dismiss the board: whilst the minister retained the power to initiate dismissal, any such dismissal (of a single member of the board or of the entire board) would have to be confirmed by a two-thirds vote of the Oireachtas.

The Section 31 restrictions continued to be a bone of contention between broadcaster and government, but did not provoke further recriminations as serious as those seen in 1973. On certain instances, RTÉ was able, thanks to the force of its arguments, to break the rules: in the late 1970s the company judged that Sinn Féin, despite being the political wing of the IRA, was nonetheless entitled to party political broadcasts as a party registered in and competing in the Republic. As Horgan notes,

> The government then – as RTÉ more or less anticipated it would – moved to add party political broadcasts by or on behalf of Sinn Féin to the matters proscribed ... the fact that the government amended the directive rather than charge RTÉ with being in breach of it demonstrated the objectivity validity of RTÉ's decision.
>
> (Horgan, 2004, p. 173)

Finally, though, it was RTÉ which was able to convince the minister that self-regulation would be a more astute course than the maintenance of a ban. In this it was aided by the presence of a telecommunications minister (Michael D. Higgins) who, far from being dyspeptic, had a "sense of humour" in his dealings with RTÉ (Quinn, 2001, p. 13). The Authority sent Higgins a series of guidelines which it promised to follow should the Section 31 ban be lifted. The guidelines "may have strengthened [the minister's] hand. When the directive was finally allowed to lapse on 19 January 1994, Higgins having secured Cabinet approval ... the revised guidelines were issued within 24 hours" (Horgan, 2004, p. 201). In this respect, RTÉ was able to do a favour for the BBC: the continuance of the British policy became anachronistic in the light of RTÉ's successful lobbying, and a "somewhat annoyed" Mrs Thatcher was forced to rescind the similar directive which bound the British broadcaster.

Despite their maintenance of power, Fianna Fáil continued to be suspicious of RTÉ. (This suspicion can perhaps be interpreted as an oblique compliment to RTÉ's independence from government.) In part, this was because they suspected the station of having been infiltrated by sympathizers for, if not militants in, Sinn Féin/the Workers' Party. Fianna Fáil's response was varied. There was a squeeze on finances: Ray Burke, who was, exceptionally, both Foreign Minister and Communications Minister, had imposed a cap on the amount of revenue RTÉ could raise and had mandated RTÉ to provide transmission services for a new commercial competitor, Century Radio, at a rate which RTÉ believed was not only below commercial rates, but below cost. These moves undoubtedly derived from Burke's animus towards RTÉ, which was also manifested in outbursts towards RTÉ staff: in the early 1990s, he warned one current affairs producer (Peter Feeney, later to become RTÉ's head of Public Affairs) that his "career would go no further" (Quinn, 2001, p. 109). It did not help, however, that commercial competitors to RTÉ were bribing Burke to further their case (McNally, 2002).

A second response was to set up another public channel which, it was hoped, would be more sympathetic to Fianna Fáil. "When Charles J Haughey, then Taoiseach, was emerging from the RTÉ studies in the late eighties after a not too friendly interview, he turned to his companions and said, 'Never mind, we'll soon have our own fucking station.'"

That station became Telefís na Gaeilge, set up with much (government-mandated) help from RTÉ.

Towards the end of the 1990s, however, with the issue of the treatment of terrorist groups in Northern Ireland less salient, and with Fianna Fáil seemingly sated, the cases of interference became limited, at least at top levels. Bob Quinn, a former RTÉ producer who had resigned in the 1960s over what he saw as the commercialization of RTÉ, and who had written a book on the topic with two other producers (Dowling et al., 1969), was appointed to the RTÉ Authority in 1995 thanks, again, to Michael D. Higgins' good sense of humour. And whilst Quinn from his works seems sensitive to political interference, the example that he cites – and indeed, the example that led him to resign from the broadcaster in 1999 – is not a clear case of political interference in the sense I understand it, but rather an uneasy collusion between the politicians' view of politics-in-the-Dáil as all-important, and the broadcasters' view of political views as represented in the Dáil as the all-important metric for representing public opinion. The issue concerned RTÉ's treatment of referendums in those cases where party opinion in the Dáil was overwhelmingly in favour of one option, but where public opinion was more evenly divided. In defending its position, RTÉ took the case to the Supreme Court, incurring significant legal fees on the way.

Quinn thought that the case offered RTÉ the best of both worlds – it could cut down on the party-political broadcasts it offered (which were in any case little appreciated by the viewer) and thereby mitigate questions of bias in this most formal allocation of broadcast time. He therefore viewed the actions of the management of the broadcaster with suspicion, intimating that RTÉ's continued defence of its position was a result of political pressure:

> If RTÉ is an instrument of public policy and the body politic legislates for this policy, then RTÉ must at least minimally conform to government wishes. Hence, when informal contacts suggest a political unhappiness with a situation – particularly a threat to politicians' unfettered and free access to the airwaves – it must be inevitable that there will be certain, perhaps inarticulated, pressures on RTÉ to act in the interests of its paymasters. The political establishment could certainly not be seen to challenge Coughlan [the initiator of the complaint] directly. My perhaps naïve deduction was that that was the reason why the attorney general, on behalf of the government, "associated" himself with RTÉ's appeal against the Coughlan judgement.
>
> (Quinn, 2001, p. 247)

Yet even here, there is only the suspicion of governmental influence. Whilst the inference is weak – Quinn would certainly not have known of much going on at lower levels of RTÉ, which indeed was one of his complaints – it seems that at the highest levels RTÉ by the end of the 1990s was not subject to overt attempts to interfere in its work. RTÉ is, therefore, like its neighbour and initial inspiration the BBC, relatively politically independent.

It is clear that RTÉ does not owe this independence to the size of its market for news. Rather, it has benefited from importing certain views about impartiality, and certain approaches to politics – for example, inter-party agreements on coverage of politics – from the BBC. Thus, the negative effects of a small market for news in particular may be circumvented where the broadcaster in that country learns from a larger homolingual neighbour. As far as legal protection is concerned, it is clear that the (limited) degree of independence RTÉ enjoyed from its foundation until the 1960s cannot be explained by the degree of legal protection it enjoyed. Only after the reforms of 1960 and 1976 did RTÉ gain a modicum of legal protection. This too, however, was accompanied by demands for impartiality and objectivity, demands which were convenient both to politicians and to the broadcaster.

4 Conclusion

This chapter has, in part, attempted to act as a check on the findings of the previous chapter concerning the BBC. In part, however, the conclusions of this chapter demonstrate the great influence of the BBC upon Irish broadcasting. Although this undermines the usefulness of RTÉ as a control case, it does vindicate the usefulness of precisely the techniques and strategies identified by the BBC to minimize political interference – after all, these practices were not forced on RTÉ, but adopted in view of their usefulness. The extent of diffusion can be seen in recapitulating the main findings of this chapter, namely that

- the market for news in Ireland was extremely limited, so much so that Irish journalists had to moonlight as Irish correspondents for London newspapers;
- second, despite the limited market, or perhaps because of it, Irish journalists understood the requirements of journalism as practised in Britain; in particular, the concept of impartiality was readily understood and accepted at the time Irish public broadcasting started;
- third, the notion of impartiality within the first Irish public broadcaster, 2RN, was further bolstered by the re-broadcasting of content from the BBC, which often became a comparison for the station's output;
- fourth, over time 2RN and Radio Éireann actively worked to import experienced individuals and practices – such as agreements with party whips – from the BBC;
- fifth, these agreements, and commitments to impartiality, were used by Radio Éireann and later by RTÉ, in order to defuse government objections and to win greater legal protection respectively;

- sixth, where RTÉ has fallen short of required standards of impartiality, the government has stepped in to impose greater impartiality.

Consequently, although the genesis of rules concerning broadcast output does not conform to the theory outlined in Chapter 2, the more recent history of RTÉ does show that, once impartiality and rules surrounding its attainment had been imported from the neighbouring BBC, they were used in just the way I have suggested – to dampen government interference in the public broadcaster.

7 Sweden

"Disturbing neither God nor Hitler"

In a debate organized by the Swedish public broadcasting company Radiotjänst, Olof Forsén, head of the talks section, admitted that radio had hardly challenged listeners during its first three decades. Forsén attributed this to the "considerable extenuating circumstances" surrounding the new medium, and explained Radiotjänst's approach thusly:

> At the time we used to say that one should "disturb neither God nor Hitler", and obviously no swear words could crop up. In radio, we stuck to the view that we could hope to remain free so long as we kept ourselves neutral and didn't touch upon exciting issues. Otherwise we would become state radio, and lose the freedom that we appreciated so highly.
>
> (quoted in Hadenius 1998, p. 119)

This chapter is devoted to justifying Forsén's claim: that Radiotjänst and its successor companies Sveriges Radio (SR) and Sveriges Television (SVT) have historically maintained their independence from politics by binding themselves to certain rules governing their conduct, rules which were at times criticized for their excessive rigidity, but which nevertheless aided the company in maintaining its independence.

This strategy was partly a result of external circumstances over which Radiotjänst had no control – the company was, for example, required to take all of its hard news from the largest wire agency, Tidningarnas Telegrambyrån (TT), until 1943. Yet as Forsén's quotation demonstrates, the adoption of certain self-binding strictures was also a conscious strategy to preserve the broadcaster's room for manoeuvre. These rules were moulded over time to fit the circumstances: certain strictures came to be seen as unnecessary or old-fashioned, whilst certain other rules were required by the possibilities opening up. The apogee of this strategy came under the directorship of Olof Rydbeck, an outsider to Radiotjänst, who centralized and systematized news coverage to a considerable degree, winning the broadcaster continued latitude despite difficulties arising from, variously, Communist Party representation in parliament, Swedish foreign relations and increased permissiveness in Swedish society. The importance of this strategy is seen in the consequences of its non-application at the beginning of the 1970s. Massive expansion of the broadcaster, combined with parliament-imposed limits on Rydbeck's influence in recruitment, meant an influx of journalists with radical left views. Their main target, however, was often as not the Social Democratic Party. Paradoxically, the backlash prompted by this radicalization only came with the return of the bourgeois parties[1] to government in the late 1970s, and organizational reforms which brought politically connected journalists and chief executives to positions of power within the broadcaster.

This chapter is divided into three broad parts, each of which deals with a particular period in Swedish public broadcasting. The first period runs from 1922 to 1955, a period in which Radiotjänst's output was heavily conditioned by its reliance on the press agency TT and by its limited news-gathering resources. The second period, from 1955 to 1969, corresponds roughly to Olof Rydbeck's time

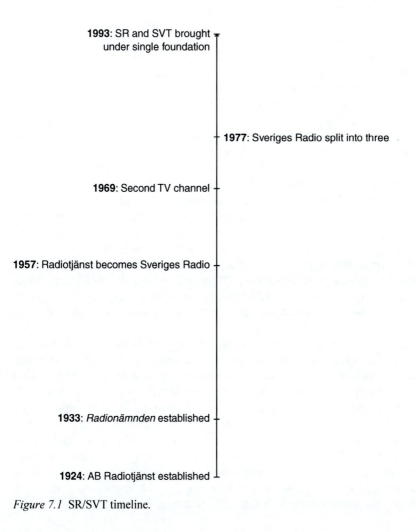

Figure 7.1 SR/SVT timeline.

in charge of the broadcaster, as SR had to deal with the difficulties of presenting its own news and current affairs. The third period, from 1969 to the current day, is dealt with more briefly, and recounts the backlash against a perceived radicalization of SR and SVT.

1 An abundance of caution (1922–1955)

1.1 The setting

Despite Sweden's relatively small population, the Swedish market for news was boisterously competitive. After all, the potential market, in relation to the total population, was extremely large. Near-universal rates of literacy were reached by 1850, when literacy amongst rural males was around 85% and about 93% in the prison population (Nilsson, Pettersson & Svensson, 1999, fig. 1; Cipolla, 1969, p. 77: statistics for the general population are not available). These figures – astonishingly high in comparative context – meant not only that the vast majority of the adult population were potential newspaper-buyers, but also that the potential stock of journalists was much greater, and much less likely to be drawn from Establishment circles.

Given such potential, newspaper sales at the beginning of the 20th century were also high. The largest newspaper at the turn of the century, *Stockholms-Tidningen*, had a circulation of around 100,000 – more than the *Times* and the *Manchester Guardian* combined (Wadsworth, 1954, p. 3), on a metropolitan population of approximately a quarter of a million. Total newspaper circulation in Stockholm was roughly 300,000 (Lundström, Rydén & Sandlund, 2001, p. 27). Sales had also become more concentrated. "Small companies with an editor and one or two co-workers became fewer in number" (Petersson, 2006, p. 35). With growing circulation came growing wages. Editors began to be increasingly well-rewarded for their work, with wages of between 10,000 to 12,000 kronor per year, roughly 10 times the wage of a skilled municipal worker (carpenter, plumber) in Stockholm (Bagge, Lundberg & Svennilson, 1935, p. 55). By 1920, an estimated 1,000 journalists were earning roughly two-thirds as much as doctors, with editors faring better still (Lindahl, Dahlgren & Kock, 1937, Appendix H, p. 521).

Questions concerning pay were, however, only part of the explanation for the growth of organized interest representation amongst journalists. Status also mattered. The first attempts to unionize journalists began in the late 1860s, with a series of meetings held around the country. Whilst these meetings – which would eventually lead to the formation of the Publicistklubben in 1874 – discussed a variety of issues, "the theme which was most often debated during those first years was raising the reputation of the press" (Petersson, 2006, 40). Indeed, the Publicistklubben's predominant concern with increasing the reputation of the press at the cost of neglecting other objectives led to the breakaway, in 1901, of a minority of the club which left to form the Swedish Journalists' Union, the Svensk Journalistföreningen (SJF). This yearning for better reputation was necessitated by the disparate social background of journalists. Even before the word "journalist" came into popular use, Swedes had already begun to use a term for "hack journalist": *murvel*, "a person lacking both in character and in competence", according to one 19th-century dictionary (Petersson, 2006, p. 43). Even the very name of the Publicistklubben tells us something about the strategies employed by journalists. The term publicist

> denoted a writer in general. Through its origin in the Roman concept of the public space, it had a promising ring to it, and was associated with public discussion. It therefore became natural for the press to annexe it in its battle for legitimacy in society.
>
> (Nordmark, Johanesson & Petersson, 2001, p. 225)

The term publicist – soon supplanted by the more specific "journalist" – served as a replacement for another term, *litteratör*, another import – this time from French – which, denoting those who occupied themselves with literature in general, did indeed connote distinction, but which could hardly be maintained as the market for news in Sweden grew beyond the intelligentsia and became a non-literary mass product.

These changes of nomenclature would not aid the project of improving journalists' social standing if both access to the profession and its output were not carefully overseen. The SJF, in its first wages campaign, asked for a minimum salary for journalists, provided they had a minimum of two years' education, lest "individuals who had failed in other areas or whose personal characteristics in certain respects made them unsuitable for intellectual activity" be recruited (Petersson, 2006, p. 69). For its part, the Publicistklubben concentrated on journalistic ethics, drafting the first moves towards a journalistic code of ethics in 1900, and publishing the first rules in 1923 (Sterzel, 1971, p. 12). These rules were, for a time, toothless, as there was no organization in place to sanction any infringement of the rules. The Publicistklubben's first congress in 1916 had agreed unanimously that a press ombudsman should be set up, but economic difficulties meant that the post was only established in 1928, and even then on a part-time basis only (Petersson, 2006, 161). Nevertheless, the formation of the rules – the so-called *publiceringsregler* – played an important symbolic role in defending the journalistic profession, just as similar rules would defend later SR: the Publicistklubben was able to revise its rules in 1933 in response to a Riksdag motion on smut and violence in the newspapers, thereby pre-empting legislative action (Petersson, 2006, p. 365).

Despite the predominant position of civil society organizations in the organization of journalism, it was the state which took a lead role in the development of radio. The key player was the state Telegrafstyrelse, or Telegraph Board. This board had represented Sweden at various international conferences on the assignation of frequencies through its active radio unit, headed by Seth Ljungqvist. When, between spring 1922 and spring 1923, various companies began to submit applications for radio broadcasting licences, the Telegrafstyrelse submitted a proposal to the cabinet, recognizing that radio technology was a positive development, and arguing three main points: first, that a single programme company should be given a concession, since this was the most rational, not to mention the cheapest, solution; second, that any programme company which received the concession should include both radio manufacturers and TT; and third, that the government should delegate authority to the Telegrafstyrelse to negotiate the concession (Hadenius, 1998, pp. 21–22).

The Telegrafstyrelse's degree of involvement in early planning for radio was not unusual. Bureaucratic bodies in other countries had moved aggressively to "manage" radio – the Post Office in the UK also encouraged the formation of a single programme company (see p. 91). What was unusual was the Telegrafstyrelse's insistence that TT be involved in the concession bid. I argue that this insistence is a result of the particular emphasis placed by TT on impartiality, or *opartiskhet*.

1.2 Key rhetorical commitments

There is no reason why the concept of impartiality should have taken hold in Swedish broadcast journalism. In their typology of media systems, Hallin and Mancini (2004) group Sweden with other Central European Democratic Corporatist countries as countries with moderate to high levels of political parallelism. Many of the numerous regional newspapers published in Sweden had a party-political affiliation. Consequently, there was, on the part of newspaper proprietors at least, an expectation, not of impartiality, but rather of partiality.

Nevertheless, the concept of impartiality did take hold in Sweden due to journalists' own efforts, and due to co-operation between different news outlets. Journalists had long understood and lobbied for clear statements of the need to separate fact and opinion: the inclusion of this principle in the SJF's *publiceringsregler* of 1953 was a very belated recognition of this fact (and, as we shall see later, a recognition which was challenged barely a dozen years after its inclusion). Consequently, one might have expected impartiality to emerge as the result of journalists' own demands.

More important, however, in establishing impartiality as a governing principle of the new broadcast media was the press agency TT. Whilst the Swedish market for news enjoyed rude health on a per capita basis, the limited absolute size of the market, and the strong regional basis of media competition, meant that newspapers typically faced unaffordable fixed costs in certain areas – including coverage of foreign affairs. As a result, newspapers throughout Sweden relied on agency copy for up to 90% of their foreign coverage (Lundström et al., 2001, p. 285). This reliance had proved to be an issue during the First World War. The dominant news agency, FGT Eklund's Svenska Telegrambyrån (Swedish Telegram Bureau), was thought to be pro-German, insofar as it favoured the copy it received from Germany's Wolff over Reuters- or Havas-supplied copy. Reuters and Havas eventually broke with the agency in the summer of 1918, choosing instead to supply the main competitor Nordiska

Presscentralen – initially founded with support from Allied powers (Lundström et al., 2001, p. 126). The marked division between these two news agencies was an embarrassment for neutral Sweden. After the war, neither of the two companies was financially viable, deprived as they were of financial support from foreign powers. Both companies were eventually bought out by a consortium of provincial newspapers. The new company – Tidningarnas Telegrambyrån (TT), literally, the Newspapers' Telegram Bureau – placed great store on the impartiality of its information. This emphasis made a virtue of necessity. Given the diversity in the partisan affiliations of many of the provincial newspapers who part-owned TT, the press agency could scarcely pursue a partisan line in domestic politics. Additionally, an emphasis on impartiality in both domestic and foreign news served to differentiate the company from its predecessors, and thus ensure that strong divisions between pro-German and pro-Allied newspapers would, in future, be muted. This emphasis was seized upon by the Telegrafstyrelse, which had already foreseen the dangers of partisan broadcasting. In a meeting of Nordic regulatory authorities in Copenhagen in 1922, members had agreed that broadcasting, "should it fall into the wrong hands, could be exploited in a politically-biased fashion", a conclusion which was repeated in the proposal to the Cabinet (Thurén, 1997, p. 28). For the Telegrafstyrelse, including TT would avoid this danger: the company would be "a guarantee against misuse" (Hadenius, 1998, p. 22).

Hadenius (1998, p. 25) implies that TT had an additional advantage, in that, through its ownership structure (it was owned by a consortium of local newspapers), it represented the entire political spectrum. Yet we should not take this to mean that politicians, still less broadcasters, sought to achieve impartiality or balance by the presentation of opposing partial interests. TT's news ideal, that of *opartiskhet* (impartiality), infused radio. "The news ideal which TT represented was also radio's: there was confidence in TT's capacity to disseminate the day's most important bulletins in an impartial fashion" (Djerf-Pierre & Weibull, 2001, p. 31). There was, it must be said, an expectation that TT would represent the interests of the state: the company had signed a secret agreement with the Foreign Ministry according to which TT agreed to refer potentially damaging news bulletins to the Ministry for their decision (Djerf-Pierre & Weibull, 2001, p. 25). But it was unlikely that any politicians personally expected to be in a position to exploit radio: they largely adopted "a restrained and cautious attitude. There was no-one in any party who distinguished himself as a specialist in radio" (Hadenius, 1998, p. 32).

That TT's inclusion was essential can be seen from the quality of the bids which were turned down in order to make way for TT. A large joint application made by AEG, Svenska Radiobolaget, ASEA, Ericsson, NK and Åhlén & Holm was frozen out after having ignored press and TT interests (Hadenius, 1998, p. 24). When industry realized it was being outmanoeuvred by the warm ties between TT and the Telegrafstyrelsen, they became less haughty, and after its initial formation as an entirely press-owned enterprise, AB Radiotjänst was reformed as a joint-stock company with a capitalization of between 100,000 and

300,000 kronor, with a total of 47 groups owning shares in the company. Groups representing the press owned two-thirds of the shares; groups representing industry one-third (Sävström et al., 1946, p. 8). The return on capital, at around 6% a year, meant that the investment was pursued primarily as a way of influencing the company, rather than obtaining profit. Nevertheless, thanks to the terms of the agreement with the Telegrafstyrelse, "the press failed to get a board majority on a company in which it owned more than two-thirds of the shares" (Hadenius, 1998, p. 29). The agreement between the Telegrafstyrelse and AB Radiotjänst was approved by the king on 3 October 1924; Radiotjänst started broadcasting on 1 January the following year. Under the agreement, Radiotjänst would be a monopoly supplier of radio broadcast material, with the radio network owned and maintained by the Telegrafstyrelse.

1.3 Concrete rules

The initial concession granted by the state to Radiotjänst was limited to just one year, but following a request from the board of the new company, that period was increased to two years from 1927, and later to three years. The text of the concession agreement required Radiotjänst to source all of its news from TT (§9 of the agreement between the company and the Telegrafstyrelse, reprinted in Olsson, Wagnsson, Nyblom, Ljungqvist & Reuterswärd, 1935), though draft versions of the agreement had been even harsher, requiring all messages "with political overtones" to be supplied by TT (Djerf-Pierre & Weibull, 2001, p. 26). The concession agreement also specified that Radiotjänst was to act "on a high intellectual, cultural, and artistic level, and to be distinguished by reliability, truthfulness, and impartiality" (§7).

Two bodies were set up to oversee the broadcaster and its pursuit of truthfulness and impartiality. The board of the company was made up of seven members: the King-in-Council was appoint the chairman of the board as well as one additional member (§16), with the remaining five members to be appointed by the shareholders, which in practice meant three representatives of the press and two from the radio industry (Hadenius, 1998, p. 33). (This balance was reversed 10 years later, however, with the King now appointing four of the seven members, including the chairman: Hadenius, 1998, p. 50.) Board members' terms were left unspecified, except that the company's annual AGM had as a recurring agenda item the appointment of shareholders' representatives to the board. The company was to be run on a day-to-day basis by the managing director appointed by the board, who would refer important decisions to the board's three-member executive committee. Yet in addition to the board of the company, management also had to deal with a radio board (*radiorådet*) of five members charged with "establishing and overseeing program work" (Hadenius, 1998, p. 50). The idea of such a board had been dismissed in earlier negotiations, but was revived on the suggestion of Sven Lübeck, the new right-wing communications minister in Ernst Trygger's government. The board was (rightly) perceived by the management of Radiotjänst as a potential source of interference in the broadcasters' operation. Radiotjänst viewed the programme council as an "authority standing between the government and radio" (Hadenius, 1998, p. 52), and indeed the council's remit was broad: it was to be "at the side of the board", of "an advisory nature, schooling the board and assisting in certain respects with the establishment and oversight of radio programs" (Olsson et al., 1935, p. 28) – an impossibly vague objective. Had this board grown unchecked, it could have ended up enfeebling management, just as the *programudvalg* in DR (see next chapter) ended up enfeebling management there. Extreme caution seemed to be the broadcasters' method of depriving the *radioråd* of much work, and, eventually, suborning this partly external control and turning it into an internal aid. This cautiousness in programme output also forestalled attempts to involve the parliament in the work of the broadcaster: a 1930 motion asking about what measures the Riksdag could take concerning Radiotjänst was sent to the first chamber's first committee, which dismissed the motion, motivating its decision by saying that there were no grounds for complaints about the objective conduct of Radiotjänst's management. Had the proposer of the motion, John Sandén, cited grounds, then perhaps the motion would have had a better chance of being referred on. But, absent any further background to the motion, the committee was able to cite the proposer's own judgement on Radiotjänst, namely, that "the management responsible for the choice of programs and for broadcasting has, to a considerable degree, handled its burdensome task in an objective and considerate fashion" (Olsson et al., 1935, pp. 105–106).

This judgement was also shared by the 1933 committee which investigated Swedish broadcasting. The committee's principal remit was to explore issues relating to the organization of broadcasting, and in particular, nationalization of the broadcasting company. Nevertheless, the committee also touched on issues of programme standards, noting that "the work carried out within Radiotjänst had become so stable that there was no need for the kind of complaints division" the *radioråd* represented (Hadenius, 1998, p. 51). In so finding, the committee was aided by Radiotjänst itself, which provided the committee with a less drastic alternative to abolition of the *radioråd*. It drew on existing experience from the world of journalism, and suggested that the programme council should concern itself solely with complaints, without also being an intermediary with the communications department – in other words, "a type of press ombudsman" – a body of the same kind as the Publicistklubben had set up to deal with reader complaints (Elgemyr, 2005, p. 45). This was agreed to in a 1927 revision of the agreement; the board was thereby weakened, and the conclusion of the 1933 committee led to its abolition and replacement by the *radionämnden* (lit., "radio committee"), which continued as a complaints body in the same manner as the press ombudsman.

1.4 Structure, organization, recruitment in news

That the 1933 committee felt able to abolish the *radioråd* because of the "regularity" of Radiotjänst's output must in no small part be due to TT. TT supplied

Radiotjänst with up to three news bulletins a day. Each consisted of up to 20 different news items – telegrams, really – which tended not to be repeated between the different editions. As noted above, the style of these bulletins was extremely formulaic and cautious. The very regularity and automaticity of the broadcasts was elevated above its true importance, so much so that Radiotjänst criticized TT for delivering an extra, unscheduled bulletin on the occasion of the Lindberg flight across the Atlantic (Djerf-Pierre & Weibull, 2001, p. 31)! Even outside of the news broadcast by TT, the TT style permeated Radiotjänst's work. The company had ceded to TT the monopoly on news, but was nonetheless permitted to broadcast reportage and accounts of happenings in the Riksdag. The company, however,

> was at its most careful when dealing with internal politics. Parliamentary coverage was managed for many years by TT's man in the Riksdag, Thorvald Sachs. There was no commentary without a summary, in the true TT-style, of what had been suggested, said, and decided in the Riksdagen.
>
> (Hadenius, 1998, p. 66)

More generally,

> as far as internal politics was concerned Radiotjänst solved its common problem with coverage through using the *referat*-form [in which each claim was preceded by its source and repeated almost verbatim]. Referat-journalism was therefore a way to live up to the ideals of factual and impartial coverage which required all parties to have the chance to appear on the same terms, and where every news report should hew as close as possible to the facts. Those within Radiotjänst were not pleased with this, but at the same time afraid of any alternative. *It is therefore appropriate to portray the style of* referat-*journalism as a strategy for avoiding criticism.*
>
> (Djerf-Pierre & Weibull, 2001, pp. 103–104; emphasis added)

Where a *referat*-style could not be employed, and where the risks of being perceived as partisan were too great, the company preferred to "outsource" its journalism: the questions posed to candidates in the election debates between 1946 and 1948 were posed by newspaper journalists, not Radiotjänst employees (Hadenius, 1998, p. 123).

Throughout the pre-war period, and thanks to Radiotjänst's continued attempts to sail closer to the wind, principles gradually developed around the *referat*-style. The election debate of 1932 established that Radiotjänst's impartiality was an impartiality between those opinions which, in virtue of their popular support, had secured representation in the Riksdag. The mid- to late-1930s established the principle that, whilst Radiotjänst would be neutral between Allied and Axis powers in Europe, the last word in a debate or sequence of speeches would not go to those representing dictatorship. Thus, whilst Radiotjänst was able to signal its support for democracy, it was able to do so without disturbing Hitler.

The principles which were being developed in Radiotjänst were thus suffi-cient to ensure that, even if newsmen and programme presenters were being recruited from partisan environments, their final output was unlikely to be parti-san, since it was so heavily constrained by the *referat*-style and certain other rules applying to programmes more generally. Nevertheless, the first Radiotjänst journalists and current affairs programme presenters were not drawn from jour-nalism, partisan or otherwise. Only six of the programme-workers in 1936 had previous experience in journalism (Djerf-Pierre & Weibull, 2001, p. 100). Far from being *murvlar*, or common hacks, they were instead disproportionately likely to be academics: three-quarters of all programme-workers in 1945 had a higher degree.

When, however, journalists who had been active in the party press were recruited to Radiotjänst, opposition within the company was strong, precisely because it was feared that such recruits might pursue the same kind of partisan journalism that they had practised at their previous employer. Lars-Åke Engblom, in his book on recruitment to SR and SVT (Engblom, 1998), cites two cases in which the board split on appointments of programme-workers. In the first case, Erik Hjalmar Linder was appointed as head of the talks division by a 5 to 2 vote; opposition to Linder's candidacy came from those who wanted someone closer to the labour movement dealing with talks. In the second case, Sven Jerstedt was proposed as labour market reporter; in a choice between Jer-stedt and another candidate, Jerstedt won a bare majority of the seven votes (Engblom, 1998, pp. 46–47, 60). Jerstedt had been controversial because he had previously worked on a Social Democratic newspaper, *Lantarbetaren* [The Farmhand]; his nomination led to a complaint from the internal trade union, the RTF. Conversely, Olof Forsén was appointed as the head of the Current Affairs division unanimously: although Forsén had previous journalistic experience, the *Göteborg-Tidningen* had no particular political colouring.

Nevertheless, Radiotjänst's strategy of relying on TT for its news was self-limiting; the company had moreover built up a sufficient reputation that it could begin to build up its own reputation. The first break with TT's monopoly supply of news came through over-enthusiasm when Gunnar Helén reported news of Hitler's death. Understandably, given the circumstances, Helén's reporting brought no official consequences, and Radiotjänst began to build up its own news-team (Djerf-Pierre & Weibull, 2001, p. 76).

1.5 Political interference

Few of the early political controversies involving Radiotjänst concerned pro-gramming or its political impact. The company had effectively prevented certain types of sporadic parliamentary scrutiny. By the late 1940s, the principle was established that the Riksdag would not concern itself with individual Radiotjänst programmes. By the end of the war, the principle was established that ministers would not answer interpellations concerning details of Radiotjänst's activities. Communications minister Sven Andersson stated that the management "worked in full freedom, but responsibly" (Elgemyr, 2005, p. 413). Radiotjänst was therefore able to prevent or minimize two of the legal instruments available to politicians who would influence the broadcaster: parliamentary questioning, and the non-renewal of a concession agreement. Rather, the company was more vulnerable to attacks on its finances. The limited concession period exposed the company to considerable difficulties in this regard. Radio licences sold strongly in pre-war Sweden, with 108 of every 1,000 Swedes owning a radio licence by 1933, compared with 130 in Britain and only 8.8 in Italy (Elgemyr, 1996, p. 268). Although only a part of this revenue went to Radiotjänst, the fecundity of this source attracted unwanted attention. Finance minister Felix Hamrin met with members of the Radiotjänst board, and asked for Radiotjänst to make savings out of solidarity with the country and its deteriorating financial position.

> Board members expressed their full understanding for this goal, and prom-ised to implement savings … According to Manne Ginsburg, at that time the secretary to the director-general, the board had been most irritated by this issue being raised, and viewed it as an order only agreed to under duress.
>
> (Elgemyr, 1996, p. 261)

Savings of 84,000 kronor – around 5% of licence-fee income – were made and passed on to the government as a "surplus", though 103 fewer hours were broad-cast as a result. Radio chief Julius Rabe insisted that a weather eye be kept on listener opinion, lest licence-fee evasion and disappointment rise.

These savings, however, did not succeed in staving off Hamrin, who came back two years later insisting that wages were too high at Radiotjänst, and that the state needed the revenue more than the broadcaster. This time, the threat which had been implicit two years earlier was now explicit: the government threatened not to renew Radiotjänst's concession, and indeed gave the requisite six-month notice that it wished to terminate the agreement with the broadcaster. Consequently, after 1933, Radiotjänst received less than 3 kronor for each 10-kronor licence sold.

The incongruity of a private company "voluntarily" passing on its savings to the state led to some concern in the Riksdag, and a motion was proposed calling for the company to be nationalized. Whether nationalization would have been better or worse for Radiotjänst is difficult to say – the long-term independence of the BBC does not seem to have been affected by the transition from the British Broadcasting Company to the British Broadcasting Corporation – but what matters for my argument here is that the company saw the proposal as a threat to its independence, and fought accordingly. What is even more important from the point of view of professionalization is that Radiotjänst was able to win the parliamentary battle by mobilizing knowledge which only it possessed: the pro-gramme company had – then as now – a clear advantage in convincing parlia-mentarians and departments. They had access to knowledge which was difficult for those outside the company to acquire (Hadenius, 1998, p. 47).

The demands for nationalization – and continuing technical issues surrounding what was still a young medium – led to the appointment of the first Radio Committee in 1933. Again the proposal to nationalize the company was raised – and this time the political members of the committee, who enjoyed a majority, came out in favour of nationalization. The Riksdag debate on the committee's proposal showed no great dissatisfaction with Radiotjänst's output; perhaps as a result, the committee's proposal was unsuccessful. Nationalization was off the agenda, although the method of appointing members to the board was changed, with the state – through the King-in-Council – now appointing four, instead of two, members. "Yet the TT-*Telegrafstyrelse* axis had won a further victory" (Hadenius, 1998, p. 50), for at the same time the group won an extension of the concession period. The board had unsurprisingly recognized that a limited concession period created "feelings of uncertainty" (Elgemyr, 2005, p. 32).

At the end of this period, Radiotjänst came under more serious pressure for its current affairs coverage. The so-called *vetorättskrisen* of 1956 confirmed the wisdom of retaining the *radionämnden* as a buffer between politics and Radiotjänst. The incident concerned two instalments of *Ekot*, the main news and current affairs broadcast. In both cases, parties featured in *Ekot* were annoyed because they had refused to participate in the programme, thinking that this would prevent the programme from going ahead, given Radiotjänst's commitment of *opartiskhet*, giving them a de facto veto over news programming. The first programme involved the Swedish trades union congress, LO, and the financier Torsten Kreuger. The latter had announced his intention to sell two Stockholm papers – *Stockholms-Tidningen* and *Aftonbladet* – to the LO. The sale would have had a marked effect of the political complexion of the Stockholm media landscape, for both papers had previously been close to the People's Liberal Party, and LO had close links to the governing Social Democrats. *Ekot* had managed to secure comment from three experts, but no one from either the LO or the Kreuger concern. The incident had considerable repercussions because of LO's capillary representation on the board of the broadcaster. The second incident involved coalition negotiations following the 1956 elections. The bourgeois parties had secured a working majority in the Riksdag; all commentators wished to know whether the Social Democrats would be able to convince their partners in government, the Agrarian Party, not to jump ship and form a government with their bourgeois colleagues. *Ekot* wanted to cover this rapidly changing situation, and had been in contact with prime minister Tage Erlander. Erlander didn't wish to debate with the leaders of the opposition parties, arguing that they could have little to say about a coalition programme which they had not seen since it had not yet been agreed. Some on the programme thought they had an agreement for Erlander to speak first, followed by the leaders of the opposition parties – but there was confusion within the broadcaster, and the director-general Olof Rydbeck decided that, such was the news value of the piece, the opposition party leaders could be heard only if preceded by a lengthy and rigorously non-partisan analysis of the situation. In both cases Radiotjänst came in for considerable criticism; in both cases the *radionämnden* fudged the issue of whether

Radiotjänst had been right in principle to go ahead with the programmes, prefer-ring instead to deal with the selection of guests. Whilst the *vetorättskrisen* can hardly be taken as an example of the theory presented in this book (there was no conscious deployment of rules concerning output; indeed, some media critics alleged that Radiotjänst's commitment to impartiality implicitly precluded such programming), it does show the usefulness of the kinds of quasi-autonomous complaints units that rules governing output require if they are to be credible. The episode bookmarks a period in Radiotjänst's development, and shows how it sloughed off various restrictions on its reporting in analogous fashion to the BBC's sloughing off the 14-day rule in the early 1950s.

2 Diplomats and exegetes (1955–1969)

2.1 The setting

By the mid-1950s, Sweden had embarked on a prosperous and social democratic trajectory that lasted almost uninterruptedly until the economic crisis of the early 1990s. Thanks to the pioneering Red–Green coalitions of the early 1930s, the Social Democrats had become the dominant party within the party system; the party's leader, Tage Erlander, was prime minister for 23 years, a record amongst parliamentary democracies. Relative political stability did not mean stability at the public broadcaster. In 1957, Radiotjänst changed name and became Sveriges Radio (SR). The change of name came at an important time for the company. Under the duopoly of managing director Erik Mattson and radio-chief Eloh Ehnmark, the company had drifted. The appointment, in the same year, of Olof Rydbeck as both managing director and radio-chief signalled a new start for the company. Rydbeck was an outsider to Radiotjänst, having previously served in the Foreign Ministry. He had no party affiliation, though his upper-class back-ground led some to suspect that he was no social democrat. Nevertheless, his appointment was approved by unanimity on the board, even at the cost of reject-ing one candidate, Walter Åmen, who was well qualified but perceived as too close to the Social Democrats. As Rydbeck put it, "the social democrats didn't wish to 'burn' one of their own on the post of radio chief, and the bourgeois members of the board desired to avoid a social democrat there for entirely differ-ent reasons" (Rydbeck, 1990, p. 123). Whether it was due to his relative inexpe-rience with journalism, or merely the zeal of the convert, Rydbeck took to managing a large cultural and journalistic organization by vigorously creating new structures. His period as director-general is particularly notable for his emphasis on developing rules on programme activity, and his dogged defence of the broadcaster externally, coupled with his equally dogged insistence on the pursuit of impartiality within the company. Rydbeck shepherded the company through a period of robust growth; yet this growth was to be his undoing, as he lost control over escalating costs and personnel matters. This lack of control – aggravated by well intentioned decisions in parliament and by the opposition of Rydbeck's successor Otto Nordenskiöld to the advisory committees Rydbeck had established – eventually led to backlash, with the 1978 reorganization of SR (discussed in the next section) into three different programme companies, each overseen by now more politicized boards of governors.

2.2 Key rhetorical commitments

Shortly after Rydbeck's arrival, a group within the company began work on a series of rules concerning programme output. Part of this involved fleshing out the requirements of impartiality, described as "of fundamental importance". This work went beyond the mere reiteration of the need to *opartiskhet* in all content; it described what *opartiskhet* required in specific cases.

Opartiskhet first meant that SR was not a party to any debates: it had no opinions (although see p. 150). The refusal to take opinions implied restrictions on SR employees: whilst criticism of art and literature might be permissible, employees were not supposed to put forward opinions outside of those areas. This obligation did not cease upon leaving the *Radiohuset*: whilst

> in principle it should be stated that the decision on impartiality applies only to employees' activity in their official function and not their engagements outside of the company, it has nevertheless been shown that SR's impartiality has been called into question with reference to its employees' engagements outside of the company. Such appearances can, insofar as they imply a stand on certain controversial issues, certainly complicate colleagues' work in the company.
>
> (Sveriges Radio AB, 1960, attachment 1, 13)

Second, *opartiskhet* meant that "different opinions may be heard in programmes in order that an appropriate balance be achieved". This was not, however, a commitment to balance in the same sense as the commitment to *pluralismo*, for example, is a commitment to balance. Rather, it is more akin to the BBC's commitment to due impartiality, being moderated in two senses. The rules first state that *opartiskhet* is not a property of individual programmes, but of programme output in its entirety, citing a 1948 board decision. This means that not all parties to a dispute might be represented in the same programme – precisely the issue which has caused an earlier crisis (the so-called "veto rights crisis"). The rules then state that *opartiskhet* should not be considered in isolation, but rather in conjunction with SR's other commitments to truthfulness and "appropriate form". The commitment to truthfulness defeats objections of partiality, for "it is not partial to state the truth". For our purposes, however, the commitment to "appropriate form" is more significant, because it allows criticisms concerning partiality to be met, not with recourse to the facts of the case or the balance of the opinion – facts which can as competently be judged by outsiders as by those inside the company – but rather by reference to the nature of the programme, or the requirements of television or radio, principles which those outside the monopoly broadcaster were, almost by definition, unable to contest. (See, for example, the quotation on p. 153.)

The commitment to impartiality was not unbounded. According to the provisions of its agreement with the state, SR was bound to uphold "democratic values". The rules therefore incorporated a styrelsen decision of August 1958, which stated "anti-democratic strands of thought may only in exceptional cases be heard, and any such speeches should not be given the final word".

2.3 Concrete rules

Discussing the value of impartiality was only part of the work that Rydbeck ordered as new director-general of SR .The decision to develop rules governing programming was taken early in 1960, not long after Rydbeck's appointment. The committee was appointed on 19 March of that year to work out "appropriate rules for radio and television coverage" (Hahr, 1960). The membership of the committee was divided equally between radio news, television news and the legal department of the company. They began work on a collection of rules, eventually comprising five parts: the company's legal responsibilities (primarily directed at ensuring the company did not commit crimes or unduly influence trials); the company's obligations in soft law (principally obligations of *opartiskhet* (impartiality), truthfulness and public service); journalistic rules (the *publiceringsregler*); rules on advertising or product placement; and finally rules concerning political programmes. These guidelines were approved unanimously by the board on 15 December (Sveriges Radio AB, 1960, §2). The impetus for these rules was likely to forestall legislative action by the parliament (Djerf-Pierre & Weibull, 2001, p. 191). Early that year, the Riksdagen had passed a motion[2] calling for an investigation into SR's legal responsibilities, which were not governed by existing freedom of expression legislation, and the section on legal responsibility was one of the first to be finalized by the committee (Rydbeck, 1960b). Thus, the committee worked under the "shadow of hierarchy" (Héritier & Eckert, 2007). The more ambitious plan of moving beyond legal responsibility, however, was possible only thanks to prior experience at formulating rules to govern news coverage. The *publiceringsregler* were, essentially, a slightly altered and carefully annotated version of the *publiceringsregler* published by the Publicistklubben, and committee members had met with the Publicistklubben as well as TT and TU (the publishers' association). These rules contained a set of broad, ordered values which prioritized procedurally fair principles such as impartiality and truthfulness, but which left sufficient room for internal judgements about news-worthiness and appropriateness for the medium so that programme-workers could defend themselves from criticism by citing their professional judgement. Programme-workers' autonomy, did not, however, extend to the expression of their own opinions, nor was their professional judgement unsupervised. The more closely rules affected the coverage of politics, the more detailed and automatic they became, at least as they were applied to the principal parties. The more the rules touched on politics, the more detailed they became. The rules make a distinction between coverage during electoral periods and coverage during "normal" periods. During the former, time in political programmes is divided on an equal basis between parties represented in the Riksdag (thus including the Communist Party), whilst during the latter, time was divided according to news-worthiness. Special considerations were, however, taken: following complaints from the bourgeois parties that government ministers were over-represented on current affairs programmes,

> SR explained that the government, qua government, was newsworthy, yet, to avoid the suspicion of partiality, a rule was nevertheless introduced that the radiochef should be informed if ministers were to appear in programs other than pure newsprogrammes. This rule was in force throughout the 60s.
>
> (Thurén, 1997, p. 121)

Other finely crafted compromises were also to be found.

Should the parties attempt to depart from these compromises, they would be ignored. A key section in the rules read: "No consideration should be taken of attempts from those outside the company to influence the selection or production of news on dubious grounds." Whether this rule was written in order to assure management that journalists would follow such a rule, or in order to give journalists a quotable rule in order to defend rebuffs to politicians, is unclear. Nevertheless, the rules taken as a whole represent a bargain struck between management and journalists: management is prepared and willing to defend journalism within the company, provided that journalists follow the rules and follow certain procedural rules not related to content which help management to deal with tricky issues (for example, the obligation on journalists to refer issues upwards to their editor or to management in case of doubt over interpretation of the programme guidelines; this principle is also to be found in BBC standard operating procedures). The rules were significant within the company both because of what they represented and because of who stood behind them. Copies of the rules were sent out to all employees and to members of the parliament, and the group behind the drafting of the rules became a power in itself. Board chairman Per Eckerberg, dissatisfied with the board's lack of influence within the company, became concerned about the growing group around the committee, who he "contemptuously and angrily described as "exegetes" (Hansson, 1998, p. 34).

The commitment to *opartiskhet* was a restriction on SR's activity that was sought out by the company itself. By committing both itself and successive governments to ensuring *opartiskhet* in broadcasting, the company was able to better marshal itself to face criticism. Conversely, where this commitment wavered, the company sought to strengthen it. Following the radio law of 1966, the government and SR negotiated a renewal of SR's charter. In early versions of the charter, there was no mention of the commitment to *saklighet* ("factualness") and *opartiskhet*, commitments which were found in the radio law. Yet SR lobbied to have these terms repeated in the terms of the charter. The relatively innocuous commitments in the government draft became longer and more detailed. At the same time, SR pushed to insert qualifications that would allow it to nuance *opartiskhet*, such as the requirement that programmes be "appropriate to the medium".[3]

2.4 Structure, organization, recruitment in news

The commitments to *opartiskhet* and *saklighet* were useful to SR because they legitimated certain heavy-handed actions on the part of management to curb content – or at least to ensure that producers were mindful of the potential trouble they could encounter. Two examples demonstrate this, one comic, the other less so. The first comes from Tomas Dillén, who recalled that

> when he edited one of Ulvenstam's debate programs he choose to lock himself in and take the telephone off the hook in order to work undisturbed. The [director-general] tried to phone him, but couldn't get through. He then sent his driver to the editing room on A1. Suddenly, a note was shoved underneath the door. On it there was a reminder from the radiochefen that the program should be edited in accordance with the charter's decisions on *opartiskhet* and *saklighet*.
>
> (Hansson, 1998, p. 170)

The second example is more serious. Rydbeck, dissatisfied with a documentary programme on anti-war protesters, intervened, demanding the removal of certain scenes. When this was not forthcoming, the director of the programme was removed. The decision caused a rift between Rydbeck and the unions. Whether Rydbeck felt he needed to justify his actions is unclear; certainly, his letter in response to the unions was extremely dismissive. Nevertheless, he did justify his decision by noting that "responsibility for the application of laws, the charter, and program-rules lies with the management of the company, and the same obviously concerns program policy in general" (Thurén, 1997).

Rydbeck also ensured more systematic control over coverage by instituting a daily meeting of news chiefs at 11.45 a.m. The meeting had been instituted during the "note crisis" between Finland and Russia; Rydbeck judged that the situation demanded prudence, and asked for a round-up of planned coverage. The crisis was resolved, but the daily meetings remained. These meetings may not have been tremendously useful – each news chief attempted to conceal his key top stories for fear that they would be stolen by the competition – but they ensured Rydbeck's will was felt. "Rydbeck rarely vetoed items – but it happened. When he said no, it was a no without appeal" (Hansson, 1998, p. 238).

This heavy-handedness was possible because "Rydbeck learned quickly the rule which distinguishes all good newsmen: criticise internally, but defend the company and its employees to the outside world" (Hansson, 1998, p. 35). He was able to defend the company to the outside world due to the repeated emphasis on *opartiskhet* and good professional judgement, thus making clearer the implicit bargain between management and journalists.

2.5 Political interference

Amongst the files of SR's *centralkansliet* (director-general's office), one finds a number of letters from smaller or new parties seeking party-political broadcasts or space on debate programmes. These were politely rejected, on the grounds that the parties had no representation in the Riksdag, and thus did not qualify for participation in political programming during electoral periods. They were, however, promised that their events would be considered for inclusion in regular news coverage should they be newsworthy: in essence, nothing more than SR was already committed to do. Such responses, were, for example, given to the Progress Union (Framstegsunionen) and the Skåne-based Medborgerlig Samling. The letters defused the issue without necessarily leading to any coverage. Some parties – like the Vänsterradikala Socialistpartiet – persisted; these requests were again defused both on technical grounds – the party's failure to register with the Interior Ministry – and on equal-treatment grounds – the party was merely receiving the same treatment as the Medborgerlig Samling and Kristendemokratisk Samling.

The concerns of larger opposition parties did not involve their presence or absence from news or electoral period coverage, but rather the quantity of time afforded them. The (perceived) lack of screen-time was usually referred to in the opening paragraphs of party leaders' and capillary associations' letters as "a failure of impartiality"; certain letters – for example, a joint letter of 10 December 1963 – made explicit reference to SR's commitments in its charter. Typical is a joint letter from January 1964 sent by all three secretaries of the centre-right parties (Bertil Ohlin, Gunnar Heckscher and Hansson for the Centerpartiet), complaining about the disproportionate amount of time given over to government spokespersons, especially in television. Rydbeck's seven-page response to the letter defended the company in terms of the news-worthiness of the government:

> In news coverage, whether it be mere wire copy, reportage, or such like, the fact that the news service is based on a factual evaluation of news value, those belonging to the government must in practice be given a quantitative "boost" compared to other parties insofar as the number of appearances on radio and television is concerned. As you well know, a not inessential part of domestic news has its origin in the government ... Sveriges Radio's journalistic line in this respect is *the same as that of the press and naturally cannot be otherwise.*
>
> (Rydbeck, 1964; emphasis added)

That SR had convinced the bourgeois parties to couch their complaints in terms of *opartiskhet* and *saklighet* – terms which could be easily defended by the company given that the company had comparative advantage in interpreting those terms – is perhaps not surprising. What is more surprising is that in-principle agreement on *opartiskhet* spanned the political spectrum to also include the Communist Party, which wrote to Rydbeck later that year complaining about the lack of objectivity in foreign news. Far from contesting the commitments found in the charter, the Västmanlands district party thought the company should go further: "Strict neutrality should be the principle in any commentary" (Västmanlands Kommunistisk Partidistrikt, 1964).

Indeed, of all the parties, the Communist Party seemed to be the most attentive to the development of SR's rules, perhaps seeing in them a way to avoid discrimination: a letter from party representative C. H. Hermansson in 1964 references the "printed rules governing programme activity" in addition to commitments to *opartiskhet*, whilst an earlier letter cited a number of board decisions (Hermansson, 1964). SR's rules served as a justification for the minimal communist presence on screen and on radio. These rules were in principle neutral, but applied with special bite to the Communist Party. Herbert Söderström, in his book *Samhällskritik i radio och tv* (Soderström & Ag, 1962), argues that SR can never formulate clear principles against communist participation, and so discriminates on other grounds.

> The small size of the communist party and its limited political significance is one argument ... The party's limited involvement in domestic politics is another ... Herr Hagberg [Communist Party chair] votes so often with Herr Erlander [Social Democratic prime minister] that a radio debate would hardly deliver any new points of view if a communist were present.
>
> (quoted in Thurén, 1997, p. 156)

The communists were perhaps fobbed off one too many times: the party wrote to Rydbeck stating that

> Rules, in order to have any practical worth, must be clearly formed, so clear that they exclude misunderstandings and incorrect interpretations. The "rules" which Radiotjänst's board has written are formulated so that they can be cited as a defence for any subjective judgement whatsoever.
>
> (Sveriges Kommunistiska Parti, 1963)

The complaint is extremely perceptive: the rules were vaguely formulated, but served to soften responses to the political parties, and to conceal the implicit claim that the company was making, that it had the final say in determining the coverage of political parties through its professional expertise.

The defence of the company's coverage in terms of impartiality and newsworthiness went hand in hand with a rejection of other possible criteria which might allow less room for discretion or professional judgement. Karl-Erik Lundevall signalled the danger to Olof Rydbeck in a letter from 1961 concerning the annual budget debate. The bourgeois parties had complained that they had received insufficient coverage during the annual budget debate: Lundevall wrote to Rydbeck that the complaint should be rejected, since the statistics on screen-time did not bear this out, but noted that nevertheless we want to have a free hand, and not be bound by any quota rules when it concerns such reportage, and that any eventual reference to the distribution of screen-time across the year should not be presented as a promise of a similar division in another year.

(Lundevall, 1961)

Rydbeck was perhaps mindful of Lundevall's warning when, three years later, the opposition parties wrote to request that statistics on the distribution of speaking time be published. They wrote that

in order to facilitate the avoidance of a political imbalance it would, in our opinion, be appropriate if Sveriges Radio itself established retrospective statistics concerning different political speakers' time on radio and television, including, naturally, non-political programmes. Even if such statistics do not give an unambiguous judgement, they may be of help in judging the direction and scope of programmes.

(quoted in Rydbeck, 1964)

Rydbeck in his reply attached a previous letter to one of the opposition parties detailing SR's stance, which, after setting out a list of reasons why an account of appearances or time might be misleading, sets out the most important reason, namely, that such an account would limit the company's discretion and thereby its independence:

In general Sveriges Radio fears that a register [of appearances] of the kind referred to by the *Centerpartiets* national organization ... could unintentionally obstruct the recent and (from the point of view of political education and enlightenment) favourable development according to which SR, with the support of the political parties, has been able to exercise, to an ever greater degree, a more newsworthy and independent judgement in the presentation of political material, without thereby neglecting the demand for impartiality.

(Rydbeck, 1960a)

Even where criticisms were not made to Rydbeck but to individual programme-makers, those within SR could still forestall the criticism by pointing to the *radionämnden*. At the same time, the principle of referral upwards also extended to referring upwards criticism received from politicians, which fortunately means that the following note of a phone call between *Ekot* chief Per Persson and Folkpartiet leader Bertil Ohlin is found in the *centralkansliet* archives:

Herr Ohlin had messaged that he would like me to talk with him. I phoned him around 3 o'clock. He first stated that he wanted to talk about his participation in next Monday's Utsikt, which was to be recorded on Friday with him and Erlander. But first – referring to my recent work – have certain assurances concerning the program. That is to say, I had "wilfully and gravely distorted and falsified his questions to Erlander on Dagens Eko on the 6th October ... I asked whether O[hlin] realised how insulting the accusation that I had willfully distorted was. Herr O[hlin] pointed out that one can never judge others' intentions. I replied that with or without "intentions", accusations of that type belonged with the Radionämnden and that I would rather that he filed his complaint with the Eko piece there. Hr. O[hlin] thought that the Radionämnden "wasn't needed", he thought I had good judgement and that I would rather correct my "mistake". I suggested that we relied on the Radionämnden's judgement and refused to further discuss the matter of the Eko piece.

(Persson, 1961)

The note is not only a wonderful example of how rules can be used to defuse politicians' complaints: it also indicates the comparative rarity of such attempts to influence programme output. One can hardly imagine that attempts such as Ohlin's would be referred upwards in this manner if they were daily occurrences: the absence of similar letters in the archives is not necessarily evidence that no other attempts were made, but does suggest that the kind of interference seen here was rare during the period in question.

3 The centre does not hold (1969–)

3.1 The setting

By the late 1960s, SR had changed almost beyond recognition. Not only had the principal focus of the company changed from radio to television, but television programming was to be split between two separate channels. In autumn 1966 the Riksdagen gave permission for a second television channel. The channel began work in 1969, slightly later than expected due to the enormous difficulties in hiring enough people to staff the new channel. The speed of the hiring process, and a Riksdag-mandated decentralization of power within the company, led to the influx of more radical journalists and documentary-makers who were less willing to follow *opartiskhet*, and less at risk of being sanctioned for failing to do so. This had noticeable differences for content, and led to increased complaints and, ultimately, a tighter grasp on the broadcaster with the reorganization in 1976. This period coincided with the formation, in 1976, of the first non-socialist government in 40 years.

3.2 Structure, organization, recruitment in news

The company needed between 400 and 500 new employees to staff the channel (Engblom, 1998, p. 128), or an increase of one-sixth over its current numbers. Yet concern in the parliament about a too-uniform approach in SR meant that responsibility for hiring would not be central, but rather that each of the channel directors – Håkan Unsgaard (TV1) and Örjan Wallqvist (TV2) – would be responsible for assembling their teams. This posed a threat to Rydbeck's self-appointed status as guardian of *opartiskhet*. In a letter to the selection committee, Rydbeck wrote that

> candidates [should] in different ways throughout the assessment be thoroughly tested on their unconditional preparedness to subject themselves to the terms following on from the radio law, charter with the state, and current program rules. If there is any reason to doubt applicants in this respect, they should not be accepted.
>
> (Engblom, 1998, p. 123)

And again, in his memoirs,

> It was obviously not on to ask after their political opinions, but there was one question which was put to all candidates, and that was: are you prepared, irrespective of your own views, to respect SR's commitment to opartiskhet?... I myself met with various groups after training and put this question to them. I always received a positive answer ... but with such a mass recruitment drive at that time a very one-sided balance of opinions within the group could scarcely be avoided.
>
> (Rydbeck, 1990, p. 218)

Then-chairman Per Eckerberg was, unusually, in full agreement with Rydbeck on this point: "The recruiting process was badly handled ... Put bluntly, we employed men and women from Stockholm University. In those circles there were certain strange political currents which led to certain peculiar incidents."

By their coy terms, Rydbeck and Eckerberg mean that those recruited in 1968 were, or were perceived to be, left-wing radicals. According to Hadenius (1998, p. 224), "no one denies that there was a strong element of left sympathizers amongst radio and TV-workers, either amongst those recruited through testing or those recruited through other means". These new employees were certainly perceived as left-wing radicals: novelist Jan Guillou famously described the crowd at an anti-Vietnam war demonstration as exiting via two paths: one towards SR, the other towards the Swedish Development Ministry. This new influx of younger, better-educated and more political employees might have been successfully absorbed by SR had the company retained its former degree of centralization. But due to the autonomy devolved to the channel directors – and *pari passu* to the individual directors of programme departments – a form of self-selection occurred: younger workers were more likely to move to TV2; TV1 retained older programme-workers who were more used to big-budget productions. Within channels, TV2's Current Affairs unit became a magnet for socially engaged documentary-makers (Hansson, 1998, pp. 172–173). These new employees did not lead radicalization within parts of SR – that role fell to slightly older producers from the 1920s, all "good liberals" – but they provided a critical mass for it.

3.3 Key rhetorical commitments

The year 1969 was thus the start of a five-year-long debate on *vänstervridning* (the left turn) within SR (Hansson, 1998, p. 245). The company found it difficult to defend itself against accusations that it was being partial because (a) it did not have the means to control the new elements within the company, and (b) because these new elements themselves called into question the policies of *opartiskhet* and procedural rules which had shielded the company from criticism. The head of TV2's Current Affairs department, Roland Hjelte, wrote in a 1968 book *Tre Ser På TV* (Hjelte, Krantz & Torell, 1968) that "objectivity … does not exist", and noted that "the Publicist Club has recently struck from its journalistic guidelines the rule that one should distinguish between news and comment".

Whilst Hjelte's comments might have been taken as mere philosophical opposition to the idea of neutrality, other workers within his department were opposed not only in principle, but also to the practice of commitments to *opartiskhet* and *saklighet*, and the institutions which surrounded them. Oloph Hansson cites the following comment from a meeting of the Culture group in TV2 in 1971 as typical:

> It is urgent that we, on all levels, question the prevalent way of looking upon impartiality, where one equivocates between conservative and sometimes very reactionary values, and apolitical, impartial, objectivity. The right balance should be found in the totality of output, and one must anchor this point of view with our viewers, listeners and readers. First, therefore, all opponents – amongst others the radionämnden – must be forced to reevaluate their current perspective.
>
> (quoted in Hansson, 1998, p. 201)

Vänstervridning led to a political backlash which limited the company's room for manoeuvre. Yet *vänstervridning* in itself was not a sign of limited independence, but rather the reverse. Any hope the ruling Social Democrats might have had to fashion the company in their image – the first stirrings of which Rydbeck perceived in the mid-1960s (Rydbeck, 1960b, *passim*) – was futile: programmes like *Från socialism till ökad jämlikhet* (1971) and the satire *Har du hört vad som hänt* (1970/1) were seen as bitter attacks on social democracy from a communist perspective. The left turn had effects on coverage, both in its selection and in the words used therein. At the same meeting which provided the above quotation, programme-workers suggested that the term "employers" (*arbetsutgivare*) be dropped, in favour of the more correct (and Marxist-influenced) term "buyers of labour" (*arbetsköpare*) (Hansson, 1998, p. 202).

Although radicalism was strongest amongst the Current Affairs and Documentary departments, news was also affected by the channel split: workers on TV2's *Rapport* disagreed with the distinction between fact and comment, which had been given official sanction in a 1966 Riksdag proposition. Their mission, as they saw it, was one of "deepening understanding, comment, and analysis"

(Djerf-Pierre & Weibull, 2001, p. 218). Consequently, a gulf developed between news reporting as it was practised by *Aktuellt* (TV1) and *Rapport* (TV2): one estimate from 1973/4 showed that 50–60% of items covered were unique to each programme (Djerf-Pierre & Weibull, 2001, p. 234). Differences in content between the two channels led to a board investigation (Djerf-Pierre & Weibull, 2001, p. 227). Chairman Per Eckerberg argues that the use of news with commentary – understood as a non-normative but not entirely factual analysis of news items based on the reporters' professional judgement – undermined SR in the eyes of the public, and *a fortiori* in the eyes of important interest groups.

> One can say that everything went smoothly between SR and public opinion – including SR's owners – until we started having news programmes with commentary. One can date the great row over television in Sweden to that period. Swedes were not used to reporters' opinions coming through in news.
>
> (Hansson, 1998, p. 287)

Eckerberg's comments find confirmation in the number of complaints sent to the *radionämnden*, which rose from 177 in 1968 to 794 five years later. The most common source of complaints were "current affairs and documentary programs" – precisely the area in which the rejection of the principles of *opartiskhet* and *saklighet* was most widespread – and the commonest grounds for complaint were breaches in *opartiskhet* (33%) and *saklighet* (41%) (Djerf-Pierre & Weibull, 2001, p. 266).

3.4 Political interference

The Social Democratic government under Olof Palme had signalled its discontent with SR and its turn to the left when, in 1973, it cut 40 million kronor from the company's budget. Interpretations of the motivation for the cut differ: Hadenius (1998, p. 244) argues that it was most likely an aid to newly appointed director-general Otto Nordenskiöld, who had proposed budget cuts of just this magnitude; but also notes that the cuts were "perceived by many within the management of the company as a punishment for vänstervridning". The Social Democrats might have taken more thorough measures had they won the 1976 election. SR's charter was set to expire on 1 July 1977 (Tjernström, 2000, p. 237), and a committee had been appointed to examine options for the future structure of the company. Surprisingly, after toying with a number of options, the committee recommended that the current organizational form – a common company for both radio and television engaged in both programme creation and transmission – was preferable to dividing the company into independent companies with responsibility for national and local radio and television respectively (the so-called vertical cleavage), or into programme production and transmission companies (the horizontal cleavage). (This option was the company's own preferred position.) "The rationale was principally the integrity of the organization

– that is to say, its capacity to withstand different types of influence from external sources" (Tjernström, 2000, p. 242).

Yet in the interim the Palme government had fought and lost the 1976 elections, leading to the first non-socialist government in 40 years forming under the Center Party's Thorbjörn Fälldin, with Jan-Erik Wikström as Culture minister. "One of [Wikström's] first measures was to take Per Eckerberg off of the board and appoint his own man, the Liberal party member Erik Huss, replaced after a couple of years by Gunnar Helén." Eckerberg was bitter about what he perceived as punishment for the very same radical turn that he had railed against (Hansson, 1998, p. 374). Yet board appointments were only part of the deeper political involvement in SR that was to come. The ministry took the unusual step of rejecting the advice of the radio commission, preferring instead to suggest that SR be split up into separate programme companies for each of its current activities – that is, local radio, national radio, educational programming and television. In its original form, the proposal called for each of these programme companies to report directly to the department. Hansson (1998, p. 374), at that time head of the director-general's office, railed against the proposal, warning that it would undermine SR's independence; the government eventually adopted the compromise proposal from a Social Democratic member of the Riksdag, that the four programme companies should be united under a single parent company, which would in turn report to the parliament.

The reorganization of the company achieved two things for the bourgeois parties. First, it increased the number of posts within its gift. Although the boards of the daughter companies were in theory appointed by the board of the parent company, these appointments were second-order appointments, in that they merely reflected the political balance of power present at the time the parent board was appointed. An increased number of posts would have been a boon to the bourgeois parties, insofar as it is more difficult to deal out a limited number of posts between three governing parties than it is with one governing (hegemonic) party. Second, the reorganization meant that a new round of jockeying for power within the company could begin, as old responsibilities were divided and new posts created.

Again, the scale of the reorganization meant that the opportunities for influence were much greater than in competition for a single post, where particular candidates often secure the appointment even before its official announcement (compare with Burns, 1977, for the case of the BBC). Board chairman Erik Huss was called to a meeting with prime minister Fälldin, culture minister Wikström and Gösta Bohman (leader of the Moderate party), and a number of names were suggested to him. They were interested in appointments "at all levels", and interest in directors with responsibility for programmes was especially great (Huss). These suggestions had been preceded by a limited number of cross-party consultations: Wikström met with his predecessor as communications minister, Hans Gustafsson, and with Social Democrat leader Olof Palme, to try to secure a compromise on appointments, and thereby achieve a balance of appointments from across the political spectrum (Hadenius, 1998, p. 270).

With the arrival of the new government, some executive appointments within the broadcaster took on a political tinge. Sam Nilsson, a former party secretary in the Moderate Party, became channel director for TV1; Oloph Hansson, "known social democrat", became director for TV2. Magnus Faxén was appointed head of SVT without a clear party political tie (see below), and Britt-Marie Bystedt was appointed head of SR as a generic "bourgeois" nominee (Bystedt had been active in industry).

At the same time, however, there was limited room for manoeuvre for the political parties. "42 of the 45 newly appointed directors within television were internal" (Hadenius, 1998, p. 271), suggesting that politicians could not impose others from outside. Consequently, the involvement of the political parties in the appointments of different directors was hampered by their limited knowledge of the political orientation of those within SR/SVT. Lacking knowledge of individual candidates' party affiliations, party leaders sometimes imputed party affiliation to their nominees in order to save face. As Wikström said in an interview with Oloph Hansson,

> The Center party had no real candidate in the 1978 round of appointments ... PO Sundman rang [Magnus Faxén, later director-general of SVT] on other matters, and then asked him, "you're a Center party supporter, aren't you?" Faxén said no, and the conversation drifted on to other matters. But right before it ended, Sundman said, "Yes, but if I'm going to vote for you tomorrow that means that you're a Center party supporter in any case". That is, he was forced to defend his choice to his party colleagues by saying that Faxén was a friend to the party.
>
> (Wikström, n.d.)

Had Faxén come to SR/SVT through the party press, or had the degree of political parallelism in notionally non-affiliated newspapers been higher, it is less likely that party leaders would have had to guess at Faxén's political orientation. Certainly, it is hard to imagine this scenario happening in Italy.

4 Conclusion

The 1976 split of SR represented the last major organizational reform of Swedish public broadcasting. The structures created by the reform – Sveriges Radio (SR), Sveriges Television (SVT) and Sveriges Utbildningsradio (UR) (Swedish Educational Radio) – continue today, although their legal form has changed over time: in 1993, the three companies were reconstituted as subsidiary units of three different foundations; three years later these foundations were merged to form a single foundation, the Förvaltningsstiftelsen för Sveriges Radio AB. It is this parent foundation which appoints the members of the boards of SR and SVT, and which is in turn appointed by the Riksdag.

The round of nominations which followed the 1976 split also marked the last phase of protracted political debate over SR/SVT. From the 1980s onwards, the attention paid to SR/SVT by politicians diminished considerably. This reduced attention is due to several factors. First, the introduction of commercial television in 1992 meant that SVT was no longer a monopoly provider of television news; courting private companies became, particularly for the bourgeois parties, an important alternative to threatening SVT. Second, the decision of commercial competitors to adopt the same content rules and the same complaints referral process (to the Granskningsnämnden för radio och TV, the replacement for the *radionämnden*) had the effect of legitimating SVT's existing practices. Whilst the bourgeois parties have continued to view SVT as inclined to the left, the degree of conflict between the bourgeois parties and the broadcaster is nowhere near as large as it was prior to the organizational reform of the late 1970s. On occasion the bourgeois parties have been embarrassed in their dealings with the public broadcasters, as when the newly appointed culture minister in the Reinfeldt government, Cecilia Stegö Chilò, was found to have not paid the television licence fee for the past 16 years. Equally, the broadcaster has mis-stepped on occasion. From the time of his appointment as prime minister in 1996 until his retirement 10 years later, Göran Persson had granted SVT journalist Erik Fichtelius regular interviews on a deep background basis. These interviews – which were recorded, and subsequently turned into an extremely successful documentary film, *Ordförande Persson* (Chairman Persson) – continued whilst Fichtelius worked as a political commenter on *Aktuellt*. When, in 2002, news of the *Ordförande Persson* project was leaked, Fichtelius and SVT came under heavy criticism. Critics – including the bourgeois parties – alleged that Fichtelius faced a conflict of interest between his interest in continued collaboration with Persson and his role as an impartial commentator. Fichtelius felt vindicated by the ultimate ratings and sales success of the documentary, but certain of his colleagues insisted that the project had been mistaken from the start.[4] In any case, although the episode did nothing to help relations between the bourgeois parties and SVT, Fichtelius's career did not slow down after the bourgeois parties returned to government in 2006 – in May 2009 he was appointed managing director for UR.

One might argue that the period following 1976 was calm only because nothing happened to provoke serious conflict between the government and the broadcasters. Sweden, after all, was not involved in the Iraq War, and thus SR/SVT were spared the kind of conflicts faced by the BBC and DR (see Chapters 5 and 8). This objection is true, but unhelpful: we only recognize such conflictual episodes because the mechanisms designed to damp down conflict fail in some way, and the argument of this chapter is that SR/SVT's mechanisms to damp down conflict are extremely well developed. If this argument is true, then even had Sweden participated in the Iraq War, and even if SR/SVT's coverage of Swedish participation had proved to be contentious, SR/SVT might have been better able to prevent and/or minimize the political fall-out than either the BBC or DR.

In summary, the extensive and storied development of rules governing content has been the major concern of this chapter. In this chapter, I have demonstrated

- first, that the market for news in Sweden on a per capita basis – and sometimes even on an absolute basis – was extremely well advanced compared to other countries in Europe;
- second, that because of this, journalists' associations started quickly, and quickly started efforts at content regulation through the development of *publiceringsregler*;
- third, that these developments were paralleled by the formation of a monopoly national news agency, TT, which set great store by its impartiality;
- fourth, that both of these developments were incorporated by the first Swedish public broadcaster, Radiotjänst, which sourced all its news from TT and adopted its practices, and which adapted the journalists' association's *publiceringsregler* when writing its own;
- fifth, that the content rules thus developed have been repeatedly cited in communications with politicians to ward off interference;
- and sixth, that when SR has got into trouble with politicians, it has been because these rules were not implemented enough and/or openly challenged, as was the case in the run-up to the *vänstervridning* of the 1960s and 1970s.

Swedish public broadcasting thus conforms well to our expectations of broadcasting in what Mancini and Hallin label a "democratic corporatist" system. The subsequent chapter examines to what extent developments in Sweden are mirrored in its neighbour Denmark.

8 Denmark

Being driven to the left?

1 Establishment until the 1950s (1922–1955)

Just as in Sweden, the early impetus for broadcasting in Denmark came from groups of interested amateurs. Unlike Sweden, and in contrast with the UK or even Ireland, these amateur groups were not quickly displaced by commercial groups. The Danish press, though surprisingly open towards the new medium (see below), was not interested in operating it; nor were other commercial interests – such as radio-set manufacturers – viable candidates for broadcasting concessions. As Brink Lund (1976, p. 37) described the situation,

> Private management [of radio] was no real alternative. The independent radio clubs were internally divided, and private industry was still unclear about the economic possibilities of the medium. Involvement in radio was not immediately profitable in 1920s Denmark, and the radio clubs could not therefore find non-risk-averse sources of private start-up capital.

Nevertheless, the prospect that radio clubs might continue to form, and thereby join the existing Dansk Radioklub and the Bindestregsklub (The Hyphen Club) (Skovmand, 1975a, p. 13), was enough to convince the Socialist Minister for Public Works Friis-Skotte that legislative action was necessary, and that nationalization of the nascent radio industry was the only way of avoiding American-style "chaos": "since so many resourceful individuals ... had established their own receiver sets, such that there are now thousands across the land ... it must, one way or another, be authorised under a new framework" (Skovmand, 1975a, p. 14).

The minister thus secured parliament's consent for a temporary nationalization of the radio industry from 1 April 1925 for a period of one year. This transitory arrangement was subsequently made permanent, and the Statsradiofoni (State Radio) was formed as an independent public body (*selvstændige offentlige* institution). In exchange for their consent to nationalization, the listeners' associations were granted representation on the board of the new organization. This representation was granted not just to the pre-existing associations, but also to any new listener associations which might form. This possibility incentivized the formation of new listeners' associations: the Social Democratic-oriented Arbe-jdernes Radioforbund formed in March 1926, and was followed shortly after by the Christian-inspired Kristelig Lytterforening (Brink Lund, 1976, p. 38). The formation of such listeners' groups, embodying, as they did, thick conceptions of the good, gave the lie to the belief that the Statsradiofoni would be an "apoliti-cal" (*upolitisk*) body. Yet this belief had fared well amongst a sea of ignorance or inadequate foresight on the part of politicians, "since radio until that point had been perceived as a spreader of harmless Talks and Music of an entertaining and educational nature" (Brink Lund, 1976, p. 37). Indeed, the organization of the new body assumed as much: the director-general of the transport ministry stated huffily that "since he would not be a concert leader, it would be necessary to have a board under the ministry, which can organize the programs and take the rap for the choice of music" (Skovmand, 1975a, p. 26; Bild, 1975, p. 199). Con-sequently, the board (*radioråd*) became not just the highest decision-making organ within the authority, it also developed a number of influential sub-committees – a Programmes Committee (*programudvalg*) and an Administrative Committee (*forretningsudvalg*) – which became executive and not supervisory organs. The board's dominance was abetted by the choice of managing director for the station. Emil Holm was a former opera singer who had become pro-gramme manager for the largest Danish radio club (Skovmand, 1975a, p. 375). He held a minimalist view both of the Statsradiofoni's potential – privileging music over literature and drama, and literature and drama over information and politics – and of his role in it, which was purely administrative (Bild, 1975, p. 201). The board's dominance consequently grew with subsequent changes in legislation, which granted political institutions a larger share of the representa-tives on the board (Skovmand, 1975b, p. 64), and with changes in the standing orders of the body.

> Contrary to the organization's standing orders ... there were in 1929 two bodies with executive functions: the program committee [of the råd], which took care of potential political matter, and the general manger himself, who was primarily concerned with the music program.
>
> (Bild, 1975, p. 201)

This situation was subsequently formalized in 1937 with Holm's departure. Despite the board's increased influence, and the formation of politically inspired listeners' groups, the new body retained its claim to neutrality. In effect, however, this neutrality lent itself strongly to the politics of the conservative Madsen-Mygdal government of the time. Bindslev, who replaced Friis-Skotte as transport minister, unabashedly affirmed this interpretation in the Folketing in a debate of 1927: "The neutrality which the management of the radio affirms is, – as far as I have understood it – a neutrality which, if I may say so, aims at pro-tecting the spiritual status quo in the country" (Bild, 1975, p. 197). The Statsradiofoni concurred: when the Socialist listeners' association requested a talk on the possibility of civil marriage ceremonies, the chairman of the board,

Christian Lerche, replied saying that it would not be possible for the Statsradiofoni to "take a broadcast from an association which opposes the Established
Church" (Bild, 1975, p. 197), whilst a previous religious broadcast had included
a vicious attack from a church pastor against the very idea of civil marriages.
Incidents such as this have led one author to conclude that

> it is hard to avoid the conclusion that the Statsradiofoni during the Madsen-
> Mygdal period was a true case of state radio, in which freedom in practice
> lay under narrow boundaries, as decided by the Venstre cabinet's interpreta-
> tion of the purpose of radio broadcasting.
>
> (Bild, 1975, p. 199)

Some independence was preserved. Social Democratic governments were
much more open to the idea of granting the Statsradiofoni full responsibility
over its output, and Friis-Skotte announced that it was the government's policy
that the Statsradiofoni, not the minister, should be responsible for radio broadcasts. Additionally, the news broadcast by the Statsradiofoni was largely unaf-
fected by the decisions of the radioråd. Prior to the Statsradiofoni's foundation,
broadcast news had been supplied on an ad-hoc basis by three Copenhagen-
based newspapers. With the nationalization of radio, the press, through its
umbrella organization Den danske Presses Telegramudvalg, secured guarantees
both from the minister and from the broadcaster itself that it would not only
have a monopoly on the provision of news, but would also have the exclusive
right to decide which news was broadcast and how. Although news broadcasts
in the run-up to the Second World War were occasionally criticized for being
too friendly to Nazi Germany (Brink Lund, 1976, p. 60), the news was not the
principal target of politicians' ire. Like the news supplied by TT in Sweden,
Pressens Radioavis (the name of the broadcast) reported "raw news" without
commentary.

2 The 1950s until Vänstervridning (1957–1974)

After the war, the influence of the political parties and their associated listeners'
associations grew both within and without the broadcaster. This development
was not welcomed by DR employees: "it was hardly surprising that the intellectual workers, as they were called at that time, were not entirely delighted to see
political and religious organizations take care of their own interests in the new
opinion-forming medium" (Nissen 1975, p. 132; see also the listener association
membership figures on p. 117). The rising influence of the listeners' association,
and, more generally, the influence of the radioråd over programme output, led to
an "insurrection" (*oprør*) on the part of DR employees. In 1957, two individuals
– the chairman of the personnel association's negotiating committee, Karl Bjarnhof, and the director of the Talks section, Hans Sølvhøj – were deputized to
speak to the råd. As Nissen writes, the source of the dissatisfaction, and the two
parties' desire for changes, were almost identical.

Briefly, there was dissatisfaction with the way in which the Programme Committee involved itself in the organization of individual programmes. This might have been through a thorough readthrough of the speakers' manuscript, or through their desire to see the speakers' names in advance of the debate programme.

(Nissen, 1975, p. 133)

The "insurrection" demonstrates two things: first, that the råd – the politically appointed part of the broadcaster – exercised a great deal of power within the company, and that it used this power in order to interfere with programme content. Whether this interference was motivated by partisan concerns in a broad or narrow sense we cannot tell from this particular incident, but it is clear that employees did not perceive them as being motivated by concern over the best interests of the company.

Second, the "insurrection" demonstrates the weakness of management relative to the board. Management could not prevent or dissuade employees from circumventing them and presenting their concerns directly to the board; indeed, one of the most senior division chiefs (Sølvhøj) was making the case. Presumably employees did not believe that management was capable or willing to wrest power from the board. Consequently, strong centralized control became identified with interference motivated by concerns external to the company. For such interference to be eliminated or reduced, the company would need to be decentralized, and control given to individual programme workers or division chiefs. The insurrection was followed by an easing of control: preventive viewing was formally ended in 1959 (Brink Lund, 1976, p. 40), and there was a thoroughgoing decentralization of power within the broadcaster five years later. Yet the decision to decentralize responsibility was largely pragmatic, and had little to do with employees' demand for greater freedom: simply put, the råd did not have enough time to oversee the company's increasing output (Bild, 1975, p. 232). In decentralizing, however, the råd did not grant authority to the director-general; rather, authority was devolved directly from the råd to the programme chiefs.

The decentralization of 1964 caused severe problems in attributing responsibility within DR. Emblematic both of this and of the cultural changes taking place at this time is the case of *Weekend 66*, a magazine-style programme which had interviewed sex experts Inge and Sten Hegeler to a predictable chorus of outrage. A majority on the board agreed that DR had made a mistake in broadcasting the programme, but the board was divided on the question of where responsibility lay: whether with the director-general or the programme director (Bild, 1975, p. 236). It did not help that the director-general at the time, Erik Carlsen, was serving in a merely temporary capacity, awaiting the return of Hans Sølvhøj, who had taken leave of the broadcaster between 1964 and 1967 in order to become culture minister in the second Krag government.

At the time of the 1964 decentralization, a number of board members recognized that diminished *ex ante* control at the centre had to be compensated for by the adoption of rules on the part of programme-makers themselves. "What guarantee was there", it was asked, "that departments would not take criticism and run with it"? The problem concerned not so much with the news department – which had adopted its own content rules following the end of the agreement with *Pressens Radioavis* – but the other departments, including those supplying news commentary. Even board members themselves were troubled by their lack of action: Peder Nørgaard admitted that whilst the board's statement of general principles was "adequate", he had assumed when agreeing to decentralization that the report implied the adoption a "moral codex" to cover all of DR's departments. However, as Tage Bild (1975, p. 236) has noted,

> this task was not taken up by the board. In practice the program committee's post hoc criticism found success through more or less causal and superficial remarks on individual programmes. It was hard to see what general principles could be drawn from these rather loose discussions.

The board's inability to develop general principles is unsurprising given that in general it met only once a month; the development of general principles has, in other broadcasters, been the preserve of management, which has outlined general principles that have subsequently been ratified by the board. Given, however, the decentralization at work, and the strong influence of the individual departments, management's input into these discussions was minimal. Even had the board adopted general principles – or some sort of moral codex – it might have had difficulty in getting it accepted by employees due to the growing mutual distrust between these two groups. Board members continued to behave "like politicians as much as like board members" (Bild, 1975, p. 219) – including voicing their concerns outside the broadcaster, to the detriment of relationships within the broadcaster. Remarks like those of board member Svend Aage Olsen, who complained about certain unnamed circles within the ranks of the producers, cannot have helped relationships between the board and the programme-makers (Bild, 1975, p. 238). In truth, it is not even certain that a call to general principle would have helped the board in reining in programme-makers. The most important regulatory value for DR at the time was the value of *alsidighed*, the literal translation of which is "the property of being many-sided", but which can also be translated as "balanced" or "varied". The law concerning DR has always included a demand for *alsidighed*, but the demand has never been clearly articulated. Moreover the concept of *alsidighed* has never been clearly articulated even by DR itself. Willy Johannsen has, in an excellent contribution to the debate, shown that the concept of *alsidighed* was only ever treated by the board in a cursory way, and with much confusion: "*alsidig* and neutral were often used in the same fashion, when what was meant was, for example, that a broadcast should not have a particular political slant" (1975, p. 258).

Absent a strong and convincing interpretation of *alsidighed* on the part of DR, it was left to the politicians to set the terms of the debate. Here, however, differences of interpretation developed. In general, politicians on the left argued for an expansive interpretation of *alsidighed* as involving a duty to represent all strands of debate present in society. In more expansive interpretations still, this duty required the broadcaster not merely to permit all strands of debate to broadcast, but to seek them out. A moderate interpretation of *alsidighed* was given by Social Democrat minister Julius Bomholt in the 1950s: "It is here that the Stat-sradiofoni's biggest intellectual challenge lies: to bring in entirely different out-looks on life, entirely different constellations of values, into daily life, and thereby show that there is another world outside the window" (Johannsen, 1975, p. 249). A more expansive interpretation was given by Morten Lange, member of the Socialist People's Party: "In being *alsidig*, DR has a duty to bring about a renewal" (Johannsen, 1975, p. 250). Conversely, members of conservative parties argued, first, against the active search for minority opinions, which would represent a gift to extremists of all stripes – as M. Hartling (Venstre) put it:

> It certainly can be *alsidig*, but it must be at a certain level. The one-sided, the fanatics, the agitators – these one has to look out for. One wouldn't simply invite into your home any agitator who happened to pass by.
>
> (Johannsen 1975, p. 249)

Second, they argued for an interpretation of *alsidighed* as representing views in proportion to their uptake in the population. The classic exponent of this view was Erhard Jacobsen, who initially started as a social democratic politician only to move to the centre over the course of his political career. Jacobsen in a parlia-mentary debate started his contributing by quoting the director-general Hans Sølvhøj's statement that "no interpretation or position should be excluded", and continuing by stating that this led directly to the main question, "in what relation the different interpretations and positions should be presented on radio and television".

> He gave the statistics that, according to him, 80–90% of the population was happy with the role of the monarchy, with NATO, civil defence and the home guard, the scout movement, religious services, trade unionism and other things, old Danish folk music, and much much more, and that DR should represent this.
>
> (Johannsen, 1975, p. 252)

Jacobsen believed that many of the programmes broadcast by DR were influ-enced by radical left elements within the workforce, and although he cited "majority opinion" in defence of his arguments, his concerns about DR were typically minority concerns: a 1967 survey of viewers showed that 53% of respondents believed radio and TV coverage in the field of domestic politics to be truthful and impartial, whilst 11% noted a left orientation, 5% a right orienta-tion and 31% took no position on the matter (DR, 1967 Yearbook). At the same time, however, there was concern even amongst board members who did not share Jacobsen's cultural outlook. Their concern was concretized in a plea from Bernhard Baunsgaard to programme directors – in particular those in children's programming – to consider the effects of trying to expand the boundaries of the possible. Board member Bernhard Baunsgaard appealed to programme directors to understand "what is at play. If one oversteps certain boundaries, one may create a situation whereby others step in and change the conditions here". He underlined that he did not want to call for censorship, but, he continued, "there might not be many more broadcasts before one started to feel a hand around the neck" (Bild, 1975, p. 239).

In part, this concern could have been read as a threat – Bernhard Baunsgaard was brother to prime minister Hilmar Baunsgaard, and no doubt the programmes that Jacobsen was concerned about were equally unpalatable to the centre-right government Baunsgaard led. Nevertheless, Bernhard Baunsgaard's comments were prescient, for soon afterwards the communications minister Kristen Helveg Petersen questioned whether DR's control structures were adequate for the task at hand. In such a context, the board was forced to take some action, and it did so by reversing many of the decentralizing decisions taken just a decade ago. The centralizing reforms of 1971–1973 cannot be depicted as a response to pressure purely from the centre-right of the Danish political spectrum, for they were undertaken during periods of both conservative and social democratic government. Nor were they necessarily perceived by workers in party-political terms: their opposition was instead opposition towards what they saw as a request "to give power from themselves and be lorded over in a pyramidal chain of command with the director-general at the top". Thus, "referring to the general 'democratizing tendency' in society, the program chiefs proposed an array of collective responsibility and management structures" (Bild, 1975, p. 240). The centralization did not, however, represent a return to the status quo ante prior to the decentralization of the early 1960s: the radioråd had realized that the previous degree of control it had exercised was still untenable for purely practical reasons. The intention of the control was thus that the figure of the director-general should regain power within the organization previously ceded to the *programcheferne*, and that he should have control over the "general policy" of the company (Bild, 1975, p. 241). The survey figures quoted above show that there was no great public concern about the coverage of domestic politics. In part, this may be because the concerns articulated by Jacobsen and his viewers' and listeners' association were blown out of proportion. In part, it may be because coverage of domestic politics – unlike children's programming or dramatic programming – still enjoyed the heritage of a more regulated past. The contract between DR and the national press had been abandoned in 1964 at the same time as the decentralization of the company (Brink Lund, 1976, p. 238), and yet DR did not lose all of the rigour which had applied to the raw news supplied in *Radioavisen*: the company decided to draft its own editorial guidelines (*redaktionelle retningslinier*) to replace those which had previously been drafted and backed by the Pressens Telegramudvalg. These guidelines applied with greater force to the "raw news" broadcast by the organization, in the form of the *Radioavisen* and later the *TV-Avisen*, than to the news commentary found on *Aktuelt Kvarter* (radio) and *Tv-Aktuelt*, a news round-up with commentary. *Aktuelt Kvarter* had initially been authored in collaboration between DR employees and journalists from *Radioavisen*, but the two programmes were split in the 1950s in order that the latter could be perceived as transmitting raw news and raw news only, and thus pristine. (The decision was reversed in the 1970s, with *Radioavisen* and *Aktuelt Kvarter* brought together again.) Yet long reliance on the *Pressens Radioavis* had also left the company without the control structures necessary to deal with news in a consistent fashion across media and across programmes. The same internal working group which proposed editorial guidelines to replace those written by the Pressens Telegramudvalg also proposed that the different news teams be united under a single news-desk; yet this recommendation was rejected. The decision not to build a central news-desk was justified "by the management, and by the divisions and the board with the need to create news coverage which was as pluralistic as possible" (Brink Lund, 1976, p. 62). Consequently, the division within the broadcaster between those who practised "raw news" and those who gave "news commentary and analysis" grew, and led to concern both within the board and within the national daily press. Indeed, an internal report of 1973 described sections of the commentary and analysis section as practising "committed journalism", a description shared by numerous board members: for Viggo Knudsen (Radikale):

"in the news commentary the aim was always to have pluralistic, personally argued journalism. We were out on stormy seas with Christian Winther and Frank Oswald, who were often extremely personal in their commentaries and analysis..." A large part of the daily press also viewed these expressions with some skepticism. One feared, amongst other things, that the trustworthiness of the station would be undermined by, for example, "Vedel-Petersen's red army faction". The press complained that news analysis didn't resemble the "good old *radioavis*", but rather that ... those of a social-democratic or more left-wing oriented tendencies were often first to come to the microphone.

(Brink Lund, 1976, p. 73)

Again, some of this criticism could be perceived as partisan – the partisan balance which had hitherto characterized the Danish press was coming undone, with left-oriented newspapers failing, leaving right-wing voices dominant (Siune, 1987). By comparison, DR now appeared as a left-of-centre voice. Once again, the problem led to ministerial attention, with the minister reported as now being

in her own words, exceptionally angry. It was DR's *Orientering* programme which had stuck in her throat. Not without reason ... It could hardly be doubted that often there were gross and unacceptable cases of manipulation against the good people, be they politicians or others, who came to the microphone.

(quoted in Brink Lund, 1976, p. 73)

And thus centralization of the news services followed the more general centralization of 1971–1973. In both cases, DR had come under fire and had chosen to respond by centralizing its operation and attempting to ensure greater uniformity of output.

3 The professionalization turn? (1980–)

The re-centralization of the 1970s led to an end to formal hostilities, but low-intensity squabbles over the broadcaster and continued discontent with its politicization continued. This discontent led the Four-Leaf-Clover cabinet of Poul Schlüter to reform the broadcaster's governance, abolishing the radioråd and replacing it with a board (*bestyrelse*) of 11 members. Abolishing the radioråd was supposed to send a signal that politicized management of the broadcaster was at an end; the new *bestyrelse* members were supposed to behave more "professionally", and in a more business-like fashion: though this may have been an excuse for appointing more members drawn from business circles. Since these changes are largely dealt with in the chapter concerning appointments, I skip over them here.

The 1990s were characterized by two processes: continued centralization of the broadcaster, carried out by director-general Christian Nissen (1996–2006), and the continuation of politically influenced decision-making on the board. Towards the end of the 1980s and in the beginning of the 1990s, DR was an effective dyarchy, with power divided between the heads of radio and television services, with a weak co-ordinating role for the director-general, and news services split between the two media. This division of power within the organization was so extreme that the "Swedish option" of splitting DR into two formally separate entities dealing with radio and television was seriously considered. With a tightening of funding in the beginning of the 1990s, and the appointment of Christian Nissen as director-general, this course was reversed. In a trope which obviously appeals to those who write on public broadcasters (cf. p. 45), Nissen described DR as

> not a state-within-a-state, as some critics maintained. Far from being a "state", or even a federation, it was closer to a loosely organised empire [*kejserrige*] consisting of highly independent and mutually antagonistic principalities, which in DR were called program divisions.
>
> (Nissen, 2007, p. 76)

Nissen's plan for reform of the broadcaster was initially welcomed (with some reservations from two left-leaning board members), but opposition grew over time, particularly when the merger of radio and television news was concerned. Internal opposition to centralization was aggravated by the continued political character of board decision-making. The board had divided along party-political lines in appointing Nissen; party-political voting continued in a limited fashion with the labour representative on the board often voting together with the Socialistisk Folkeparti member Preben Sepstrup. Staff members who complained about centralization initiatives made sure that their complaints were circulated also to board members, and in at least one instance a board member may have encouraged head of television programming Hans Jørgen Skov to lobby parliamentarians to return to the "Swedish model" (Nissen, 2007, pp. 71, 97). Centralization in news was particularly strongly resisted on the basis that radio and television each had their own methods of working and of recounting facts. But although Nissen and the board were in favour of centralization, both of the organization and of news-gathering, Nissen in particular, and the programme directors to an even greater extent, were sceptical of board demands for greater written regulation of news:

> The interesting point in this field is that one cannot draft rules of the game which are clear and always-binding. Just as with tax law, for each new rule, two new cracks emerge about which one can have doubts, or which could lead individuals to circumvent the rules. It was more important for me that all program workers should, whilst starting with a limited set of rules, be participants in an ongoing discussion of programme ethics, which could serve as a magnetic north-pole for their inner journalistic compass.
>
> (Nissen, 2007, p. 187)

Where such rules did exist, Nissen's approach was hardly marked by caution: Nissen had announced that he would give a case of good red wine to any news-team which brought him to court to represent DR in its reporting:

> My rationale for putting up this prize out front was to say to all the news-desks, that whilst we should certainly uphold the press ethics and the law of the land, but that if we didn't sometimes overstep these lines, we would never know where the boundaries lay.
>
> (Nissen, 2007, p. 187)

This view is largely shared by Nissen's successor as director-general, Kenneth Plummer,[1] and by the first director of the unified news department, Lisbeth Knudsen, who had made clear her opposition to the adoption of codified rules and the appointment of a listeners' and viewers' editor (Skovbjerg, 2007, p. 197). Ultimately, the adoption of written rules and some structure with which to apply these rules was forced on the company by a relatively minor incident which nonetheless was a precursor of future developments. In 2003 a documentary programme on childcare in the municipality of Morsø was broadcast. The film and soundtrack of the documentary made it appear as if an agency childcare worker had struck a child and that the child had subsequently had to go to hospital. Following complaints to the police about the childcare worker's conduct, and an official request from the police for the raw footage of the incident (turned down by DR), it transpired that the footage of the blow – offscreen, but clear from the soundtrack – and the footage of the hospital visit

had been edited together from two different shots. The incident led to the codi-
fication of DR's rules on journalistic ethics in the summer of 2003, and the
subsequent appointment, one year later, of a viewers' and listeners' editor,
Jakob Møllerup, a former DR journalist. Møllerup's appointment was initially
resisted, and there was much internal criticism (voiced in the company news-
letter *DRåben*) about Møllerup's mixed roles as both a participant in the drafting and revision of DR's ethical rules, and as an arbiter of the same rules.[2]
Unfortunately (from the point of view of the theory articulated in Chapter 2),
the position of viewers' and listeners' editor is not analogous to comparable
structures at either the BBC or SVT, largely because the decisions of the
viewers' and listeners' editor compete with at least two other bodies which
also reserve the right to judge DR's output: the Radio- og tv-nævnet, established in 2001, and the Pressenævnet. The former was established in order to
ensure that DR and the private TV2 live up to their public service obligations.
They are therefore primarily concerned with output in its broadest sense. The
Pressenævnet, by contrast, is a uniquely Danish compromise – a self-regulatory
organ with press representation, established by a law of 1993 (Vignal-Schjøth,
2007, p. 57). The listeners' and viewers' editor has thus felt it necessary to
advertise the advantages of directing complaints to him instead of the Presse
or Radio- og tv-naevnet.[3] Ironically, the most controversial item of DR programming was not strictly speaking a news-item, but rather a documentary,
Den Hemmelige Krig (The Secret War), which alleged that Danish forces had
handed Afghan prisoners over to the US Army for interrogation and subsequent torture. The chairman of the Conservative group in the Folketing,
Helge Adam Møller, announced an appeal to the Pressenævnet, and DR dared
prime minister Anders Føgh Rasmussen and defence minister Søren Gade to
do likewise, but the matter was never ultimately taken up by the nævnet.
However, by the time of *Den Hemmelige Krig*, the government's relations with
the broadcaster had already deteriorated considerably, particularly concerned
coverage of war in Iraq and Afghanistan. In March 2003, the culture minister
Brian Mikkelsen wrote to the chairman of DR's board criticizing DR's coverage of the Iraq War, and making crude threats about privatization:

> Purely for your information I wanted to note that DR's coverage of the gov-
> ernment and especially the Iraq war was on the agenda at cabinet today, first
> at breakfast with a number ministers and subsequently during the formal
> meeting. There is very great dissatisfaction with DR's coverage, which is
> extremely one-sided – many have been especially angry with a number of
> female hosts and Ole Sippel (who many mentioned as an extreme in his
> opposition to the coalition). After that the Foreign Minister remarked that
> we should not privatize TV2, which was fair in its coverage, but rather that
> we should privatize DR.
>
> It's precisely this argument which is the strongest argument the centre-
> right has against the privatization of TV2. Many [members of the right-wing
> parties] think that we ought to privatise DR, which is against the government,

and do not understand why we are privatizing TV2, when it has been only positive vis-à-vis the government. I know well that it's difficult for you – today I was in the line of fire for it suddenly became my responsibility – but you needed to be informed about the government's position. I mentioned to the prime minister that I had had a confidential discussion with you about the state of things. And that I had impressions of that the management and Nissen took it very seriously, but the problem lay with Lisbeth Knudsen [director of news].

(Nissen, 2007, p. 210)

Continued government dissatisfaction with DR's coverage of the war was one of the reasons suspected in the 2004 dismissal of director-general Christian Nissen. Ostensibly Nissen was fired because of cost over-runs concerning DR's new headquarters in the Ørestad district of Copenhagen, but it is known that there was an email exchange between the board vice-chairman, Ersling Aaskov, and culture minister Brian Mikkelsen, the week before the decision.[4] Nissen states in his autobiography of his time at DR that the board gave him no formal reason for his dismissal, but the linkage between DR's coverage of the Iraq War and Nissen's dismissal was made by numerous commentators and raised in the Folketing.[5]

4 Conclusion

The Danish situation is therefore somewhat paradoxical, because any summary of the chapter must start with two contrary notes: that,

- despite a market for news that was (on a per capita basis) comparatively advanced, and
- despite the supply of news from a press consortium functionally analogous to the *Tidningarnas Telegrambyrå*,
- first, neither Danish journalists as a whole, nor DR have ever adopted thorough-going rules governing output, nor adopted any rhetorical commitments capable of being cashed out in concrete terms;[6]
- consequently, complaints initiated by the government are rarely passed through either the Radio- og tvnævnet or the viewers' and listeners' editor, meaning that complaints rapidly escalate;
- second, that the absence of thorough-going rules governing output can perhaps be explained by the lack of strong management;
- third, that this, in turn, may be a result of the "solution" to an excessively interfering and political board during the 1950s and 1960s – namely, excessive decentralization of the company and a split in news reporting between raw factual analysis and more interpretative fare.

DR may therefore be the obverse of the British case. Unlike in Britain, where the absence of leadership from the National Union of Journalists was compensated for by the presence of strong managers like Reith and Hugh Greene, in the Danish case the absence of any readily adapted codes was compounded by the absence of any strong managerial figure willing to fulfil the demand – already expressed by the radioråd in the 1960s – for some kind of guiding lines capable of protecting the broadcaster.

Part III

Comparisons and conclusions

9   Comparing the six broadcasters

Chapters 3 to 8 offered the reader concise political histories of the six public service broadcasters (PSBs) studied here. These political histories were not comprehensive: instead, they dedicated special attention to the key concerns of my argument, namely the recruitment of programme-workers, the development of written rules governing content and the broadcasters' relationship with politics. The reader will hopefully be able to perceive how my argument applies to each of the countries studied in virtue of the facts presented in the country specific chapters. At the same time, however, the need to present information in rough chronological order, and to present background information concerning the respective broadcasters, has obscured the argument somewhat. Here, I present the argument taking the information presented in Chapters 3 to 8 as read, though the argument can be followed without having read these chapters. This chapter is also an opportunity to fulfil the promissory note issued in Chapter 2. In that chapter, I developed a statistical model of PSB independence which showed that the independence of the broadcaster depended on the degree of legal independence it enjoyed and the size of the market for news. I argued there that the size of the market for news was an adequate proxy of the degree of professionalization of the news corps, and that this would have effects on the independence of the broadcaster through the possibilities for the development of written rules concerning output. Having spent much of the preceding chapters describing the state of the market for news, I can now make that argument more concrete. I therefore start with an overview of the various markets for journalism and their degree of professionalization (1), before discussing the stock of journalists (2) and managers (3), before, in the final section, discussing the development (4.1) and deployment (4.2) of rules governing content. A summary of the main points can be found in Table 9.1.

1 The market and professionalization

Earlier I argued that a larger market for news would have beneficial effects on the independence of the broadcaster, via its effects on journalistic professionalization and the development of "news whole-salers", or press agencies. We would therefore expect Sweden and the United Kingdom to have the greatest

Table 9.1 Comparison of countries

Country	Per capita market for news	Press monopoly on broadcast news?	Internal codes?	Ombudsman or complaints board?	Independence
Sweden	Large	Yes	Yes – from 1960	Yes – from 1933	High
United Kingdom	Large	Yes	Yes – from 1987	Yes – from 1971	High
Ireland	Moderate	No	Yes – from 1989[a]	No[b]	Moderate
Denmark	Moderate	Yes	Yes – from 2003[c]	Yes – from 2004	Moderate
Italy	Small	Yes (EIAR); No (RAI)	No	No	Low
Spain	Small	No	No	Yes – from 2007	Low

Notes

a Reference to written codes in RTÉ is a reference to *Broadcasting Guidelines for RTÉ personnel*, first published 1989.

b RTE has a complaints process, but there is no autonomous complaints unit.

c Reference to written codes in DR is a reference to *DR's programetik: etiske retningslinjer for DR's programmer og medarbetare*.

journalistic professionalization and most influential press agencies, followed by Denmark and Ireland, and then by Italy and Spain. This order is roughly correct, although Spanish journalism looks to have overtaken Italian journalism in its professionalization.

1.1 The agencies

In both the United Kingdom and Sweden, dedicated news agencies obtained a monopoly on the supply of broadcast news. In the British case, this was through a consortium of press agencies; in the Swedish case, through a sole agency, TT. In both cases, the monopoly was insisted upon by the government bureaucracy, conscious of the twin needs to ensure that coverage was impartial and that it was not prejudicial to national security. One of the BBC's principal contributors, Reuters, had a secret government share with special rights; TT, by contrast, could be relied upon by the Swedish state to be neither pro- nor anti-German, born, as it was, out of a merger of two competing news agencies which had supported opposing sides during the First World War. The need for the agencies to guarantee impartiality was explicitly noted. The Swedish Telegrafstyrelsen judged TT's participation to be a "guarantee against misuse"; the British Post Office judged the agencies provided "some sort of assurance ... of uncoloured news". In Denmark and Ireland, news agencies were not so influential. In the Danish case, a monopoly of supply on broadcast news was granted by the government, but it was granted not to the Danish press agency Ritzaus, but to a joint project of several Danish newspapers. Though this monopoly ultimately turned out to be longer-lasting than the monopolies of the British or the Swedish press agencies, this may have been because of an early lack of interest in news, perhaps caused by the appointment of an opera singer as first managing director. Similar lack of interest in news was shown in Ireland: this choice, however, may have been *faute de mieux*, as there was no Irish press agency.

Finally, whilst press agencies did exist in Italy and Spain, they were much closer to the state, and did not enjoy a monopoly of supply of broadcast news. Spanish news agency EFE was closely controlled by the same ministry that supervised RTVE; Ansa was more independent, but still subject to government influence through considerable government subsidies. Consequently, only the BBC and Radiotjänst (and to some extent DR) were really in a position to benefit from the kind of shield that sourcing agency news copy provided. This was particularly the case with the BBC, where Reuters' influence extended also to giving advice on the BBC's news style. RTÉ was able to benefit indirectly, through repeating BBC news broadcasts, but neither RTVE nor Rai could have shielded themselves by sourcing news copy exclusively from EFE or Ansa, since this would not have satisfied those who viewed those agencies as closely tied to the regime of the period.

1.2 Professionalization

As far as professionalization is concerned, whilst it is true that those countries with larger markets for news formed journalists' associations first (see Figure 2.2), it is not obviously the case that there was more professionalization in the UK than in Denmark, or in Ireland than in Spain. Additionally, the impact of professionalization on the broadcaster took different routes in each country.

The clearest case of high circulation leading to early professionalization and subsequent adoption of rules on the part of the broadcaster comes from Sweden. Here, journalists professionalized early, with the explicit aim of maintaining their status, and established rules and a structure by which to arbitrate those rules. Those rules were subsequently adopted by the broadcaster with the aim of forestalling a legislative intervention by the parliament. In the UK, Denmark and Ireland, the picture was less clear. Here, although journalists unionized, they did not draw up rules to govern their conduct or content; consequently there was no codified expression of the idea that journalists' output should in some way conform to certain rules. Efforts in the UK (and, *a fortiori*, in Ireland) to establish a more professional direction for journalism failed. Consequently, expressions of professionalism took less institutional forms, as when groups of like-minded journalists came together to grant journalism a mission or vocation, as was the case with purveyors of analytic journalism in the UK.

Where, however, a limited market did impede the formation of journalists' associations, the state was liable to step in. In the Italian case, this meant the establishment of a journalists' union which granted journalists the objective of the professionalization project – restricted entry to the profession – without the need to first demonstrate the possession of specialized or technical knowledge to the state. Thus, the Order of Journalists not only did nothing to construct written codes governing output (until 1993), but may actually have retarded such a development. This development was not seen in Spain, despite the Fascist regime having similar ideas about the media. There, the government invested in further education for journalists, resulting in considerable disparities between the Spanish and Italian journalistic corps. That this increased professionalization in Spain has resulted in benefits for the broadcaster can be seen from the experience of the committees which formed to protest against government interference.

2 The journalists

Earlier, I claimed that the overall level of partisanship in the journalism of a given country would not necessarily affect the independence of the broadcaster, since normally there would be no incentives for management to select for partisan journalists (other things being equal), whilst there would be incentives to select against such journalists. This, in most countries, was the case. Most obviously, in Sweden, where numerous newspapers did have clear partisan affiliations, Radiotjänst either recruited journalists from outside journalism with strong academic backgrounds or employed journalists from unaffiliated newspapers, such as *Göteborg Tidningen*; where the broadcaster did appointed journalists from affiliated newspapers, there was concern. Similarly, in Britain, the BBC at first selected from high-quality newspapers and when, from the 1980s onwards, those high-quality newspapers also began to manifest a clear editorial line, management switched to recruiting from other newspapers (the influx of *Financial Times* journalists), or recruiting internally. The insistence on avoiding recruiting "engaged" journalists can be seen in the Board of Governors' concern that BBC News should not employ those who "created" rather than "reported" news. As a result, politicians in these countries were very often unsure about the "true" partisan affiliations of the journalists who covered them: the instinctual Conservative Grace Wyndham Goldie was taken to be a socialist; and Magnus Faxén was imputed a party affiliation when he refused to disclose one. More often, however, partisan affiliations were simply not known: directors-general of the BBC could not without risk be assumed to be either Conservative or Labour voters, until Greg Dyke's appointment.

The situation is slightly different in Italy, where the overall level of journalistic partisanship was high both overall and within the broadcaster. Had management had a free choice in hiring, it is difficult to know how they would have circumvented the high level of journalistic partisanship in Italy: the most prudent hiring strategy would probably have involved numerous hires from *Il Sole 24 Ore*, which, despite being owned by Confindustria, does not demonstrate a clear political line. Yet what is important to note is that management has not had a free hand: in the 1950s and 1960s, agents of the Christian Democrats recruited fellow Christian Democrats from Christian Democratic newspapers; in the 1960s and 1970s, managers recruited from all political parties in order to maintain political consensus; and in more recent years, managers have perforce been obliged to pick from a limited pool of qualified candidates who, as a result of previous decades' hiring policies, have clearly identifiable partisan affiliations. Thus, although partisanship is high both outside and within Rai, the former has not caused the latter.

3 Management

I attributed to management a key role in creating and preserving the independence of the broadcaster. Management was to be an intermediary between politicians on the one hand, capable of defeasing or defusing their interventions, and on the other hand, journalists. In order to be a trusted mediator, management had to demonstrate to journalists that the rules they set would be capable of deflecting criticism. To do so, they had to convince journalists that their tenure in office would not be too short; otherwise, the incentive to the journalist to adapt to the new rules would have an uncertain pay-off. What is clear from the case studies here is that precedents and rules which have stuck have been put in place by long-lasting directors-general; conversely, directors-general or boards which are in office for only short periods cannot hope to set rules which will be followed by journalists. Thus, figures like Reith, Birt and Rydbeck have been directors-general who have imposed written rules to govern content which have persisted over time; at the same time, they have also been amongst the longest-serving directors-general of their respective organizations. This does not imply that these rules have not been developed outside of periods of rule by "strong" directors-general, but rather that their initial implementation and any subsequent reinventions of these rules owes much to such strong directors-general.

Conversely, where executives' expected term in office is short, the chance of implementing new rules and having them obeyed in the long run is slight. This has been the case for Rai, throughout its history. The first post-war Rai board which hailed impartiality and objectivity as its catchphrases was, shortly after that acclamation, replaced by a board which was more congenial to the government. The Rai board which was most vocal in its intent to impose new rules on Rai and a new style of journalism – the board of the Professors – failed in its attempts because it was in office for just one year. Although this argument principally applies at the board level, it is true also at the level of director-general. Where there have been long-lived directors-general, such as Ettore Bernabei and Biagio Agnes, rule-development of some limited kind has gone ahead. For Bernabei, this rule-development was never formally codified. Agnes, by contrast, did implement some of the first codified documents establishing a coherent schedule for Rai and a direction for its programming. This reasoning applies with even greater force to RTVE, where the turnover of directors-general has been extremely high, and where the board has had limited powers which preclude it from giving a strategic impetus, even were it to serve in office for a long time.

Between these two extremes, the Irish and Danish broadcasters have never had directors-general which truly marked the respective companies. Directors-general in DR were, until the 1980s, heavily reliant on the directors of television and radio respectively; consequently, they lacked the power to push forward rules on their own design. Whilst there was a demand for the board for some kind of codified rule governing content, the board itself was not willing to design such a code nor see through its implementation; the channel directors, in defence of their territory, insisted that each service had special requirements which made the development of unified guidelines for content not advisable.

4 Rules

4.1 Rule development

The link between journalistic professionalization and rule-development, and between news agencies and rule-development, was a simple one: the management of the PSB was assumed to be more likely to develop rules where journalistic associations or wire agencies had already developed similar rules. Direct evidence of learning from journalistic associations and wire agencies, however, is limited to three cases: the Swedish case, where Sveriges Radio essentially adopted the rules previously drafted by the Publicistklubben, adapting them to the demands of radio and television and accompanying them with guidance on the legal position of the broadcaster; the Danish case, where the broadcaster was obliged to adopt rules for the *Radioavis* and *TV-avisen* after the involvement of Den danske Presses Telegramudvalg ceased; and in the British case, where, at a much earlier stage in the broadcaster's development, Reuters aided the BBC in developing some initial rules for news-reading.

Of these examples, however, only the first gives strong support to my theory, insofar as rules were "borrowed" quite openly, and were subsequently developed with the intent of protecting the broadcaster from interference. The Danish case is less helpful, since the rules established following the development of DR's own news broadcasts do not seem to have been developed over time, or to have had much impact. The British case is partially relevant, but this episode of learning antedates considerably the much more important waves of rule development which took place in the late 1930s and early 1980s. There is one further instance of learning about the beneficial impact of rules: the Irish broadcaster's agreement with the party whips seems to have been modelled on the similar agreement which held between the BBC and party whips in the UK; here learning took place not between media, but rather between two different countries. This, therefore, hints at an extension to the theory: broadcasters may learn either from journalistic associations, news agencies or similarly situated broadcasters which are nearby.

4.2 The use of rules

Despite the paucity of concrete examples of rule-transfer or learning between journalistic associations and the broadcaster, we do in fact find greater rule-development in those countries in which we would expect most professionalization: rules were most developed in Sweden and Britain, less developed in Ireland and Denmark and scarcely developed at all in Spain and Italy (save for manuals of style). Equally it seems clear that these rules do play the role that theory demands of them in defeating and defusing intervention. As far as the values of the broadcaster were concerned, both the BBC and SR committed themselves to certain values which were only subsequently written into legal regulations. Thus, the BBC's commitment of impartiality was developed first by the Corporation and only later incorporated into legislative language, and only became binding upon the BBC with the passage of the 1990 Communications Act. The story in Sweden is similar, where SR amended the government's charter proposal to make the requirement of impartiality more demanding, not less.

This strategy of self-binding serves as a highly visible signal to politicians that the broadcaster has rules in place to which it is committed, and from which it could not easily retreated. Committing oneself to achieve impartiality, or objectivity, is an important signal, and is also very different from committing oneself to achieve pluralism. Objectivity and impartiality belong to a family of journalistic values which imply that content produced will never stray very far from the kind of content which would be produced by an ideal observer.

Consequently, by committing themselves to these values, broadcasters signal to politicians something about the way they produce output.

Conversely, the commitment to pluralism, whilst it might be observed extremely faithfully, and be extremely demanding of the journalists who uphold it, does not necessarily signal to politicians that content will be of the type produced by an ideal observer, but rather that content will be dependent on the particular viewpoint of those who produce it, and that consequently, different types of content can be achieved by changing the set of journalists who produce that content. More often, however, the commitment to pluralism is a commitment which results *faute de mieux*, as previous commitments to objectivity and/or impartiality are found to be too onerous. (This, I would suggest, is the lesson of Chapter 3.)

A second strategy which emerges from the historical chapters is that of substituting internal controls for external impositions, or the threat of such. In the Irish case, an external imposition – a ban under Section 31 of coverage of Sinn Féin – was in place, and had already caused much trouble for the broadcaster, as when the Fianna Fáil government dismissed the entire RTÉ Authority in 1973. The external imposition was removed only after the intervention of a sympathetic minister (Michael Higgins) and after the Authority showed Higgins guidelines which it promised to follow were the external imposition to be removed. A similar attempt was made by the BBC when it attempted to substitute the 14-day rule with guidelines that would meet the spirit, if not the letter, of the rule.

More commonly the external imposition is merely mooted. Thus, a proposed motion in the Riksdag to clarify SR's editorial responsibilities, which could potentially have acted as a constraint on the broadcaster, was avoided by the development, within SR, of a comprehensive set of codes covering the broadcaster's legal responsibilities and its responsibilities in news coverage. Equally, the proposal made to the Annan committee, of a dedicated complaints commission covering both the BBC and ITV, could have represented another external constraint on the broadcaster – but was again pre-empted by the creation of an internal complaints committee. Where the creation of new structures follows criticisms of the broadcaster, we can describe these criticisms as having been defused. That is, in such cases, the broadcaster implicitly admits that its output was at fault, but revises structures so as to convince politicians that sanctioning is unnecessary. This, to some degree, was the case with the BBC's guidelines on violence, which followed criticism in the press by the Home Secretary Jim Callaghan. The BBC archives suggest that Callaghan did not wish to sanction the BBC formally, but was instead playing to the gallery; in any case, the revision of written rules was sufficient to "get Callaghan off the hook".

Defusing strategies, however, are a distinctly second-best solution, since they do require the broadcaster to constrain itself further, even when, as in the Callaghan case, these constraints were carefully calibrated to be as unintrusive as possible. Far better, however, is to defease complaints by showing that the object of the complaint was in conformity with some rule, and as such is eminently defensible. The best example of defeasing a complaint – and, incidentally, of how to trap politicians in knots – comes from Ireland, following the National Farmers' Association case. The politicians involved believed that the invitation extended to the head of the NFA breached the Whips' Agreement – but RTÉ was able to show the politicians that the Agreement did not in fact extend to non-politicians, and thus that they had nothing to object to. A more recent attempted example at defeasing a complaint was given in the chapter on the BBC, where BBC executives attempted to demonstrate that their coverage of the run-up to the Iraq War was in conformity with their Editorial Guidelines, and thus that the government had nothing to object to. Again, I note that citing this case as an example of defeasing may appear strange given that ultimately both the director-general and the Chair of the BBC were forced to resign over this same coverage, but I believe that the chapter shows that prior to the suicide of David Kelly, the BBC had succeeded in narrowing down to grounds of disagreement between the broadcaster and the government to minutiae of the Editorial Guidelines; had the much more rigorous scrutiny of the Hutton Inquiry not intervened, the BBC's dogged defence of its coverage might have seemed, or might have continued to seem, principled, or at least sufficiently so to convince the government that their complaints were ultimately counterproductive. The Hutton case was so protracted because of the considerable passion evoked by the decision to go to war.

One of the less easily demonstrated advantages of internal rules and complaints-handling procedures is their ability to reduce tempers concerning disputes over broadcast output. Where disagreement breaks out between broadcaster and government, or between the broadcaster and a political party, that disagreement may be of considerable public interest, and may be covered extensively by other media, so as to draw both broadcaster and politician(s) into further controversy and an escalation of contrasting claims, eventually leading to greater risk of sanctioning. Asking that the controversy be adjudicated by a complaints panel set up to adjudicate on the rules followed by the broadcaster can be a method of sidelining the controversy, or at least reducing to a minimum the risk of escalating claim and counterclaim. Such a strategy was attempted by DR following controversy over the *Secret War* documentary, but government ministers declined to make a formal complaint; the lack of resolution of this affair, and the subsequent dismissal of Christian Nissen, cast doubts over the degree of independence of DR. Indeed, DR seems, of the four "northern" broadcasters, to be the broadcaster with the least well developed body of rules for governing content and for adjudicating disputes. In part, this is predicted by our theory, insofar as the Danish media market was smaller (on a per capita basis) than either the Swedish or British media markets; that the Irish broadcaster should have better developed rules, and should have been able to deploy them already by the 1950s to defuse political complaints, is not predicted by theory, but is likely to be a positive consequence of RTÉ's (geographic and cultural) proximity to the BBC, and the possibilities for learning from the latter.

Nevertheless, the delay with which DR has developed rules for governing content and arbitrating disputes may have been accentuated by another aspect of

DR's history, namely the prolonged absence of a strong central executive capable of imposing rules of this nature. The demand for such rules was frequently expressed by the board of the broadcaster, but the board was not capable either of drafting or of imposing such rules. This rationale applies with greater force to the two southern broadcasters, Rai and RTVE, which have, in recent years, rarely had chief executives who have enjoyed significant ongoing power within the organization. We would expect these broadcasters to have limited rule-development in any case, such are the low level of professionalization and the ties between the state and news wholesalers, but the limited term in office of directors-general makes imposition of such rules much more difficult. It is not that broadcasting executives are unaware of the potential beneficial effects of such rules on independence, as Biagio Agnes' complaint ("Give me a document I can hold on to, and from which I can give instructions") demonstrates. Rather, executives simply did not have the time to implement such rules, and this expectation was diffuse amongst programme-workers.

5 Conclusion

In this chapter I have briefly demonstrated the chain of processes that leads from the market for news to the greater independence of the public service broadcaster. Not all of the links in this chain are equally well demonstrated. In particular, although there is an association between greater professionalization and press agency dominance, on the one hand, and greater rule-development on the other hand, this association is not often manifested through concrete examples of broadcasters borrowing or learning from journalistic associations or agencies. It seems at least possible that the impact of professionalization and news agency influence is the kind of process which is not seen in individual events, but is rather one of those processes which is "big, slow-moving, and invisible" (Pierson, 2003). In any case, the most proximate link in the chain – the use of rules to defend the broadcaster against attempted intervention – seems well demonstrated, with multiple examples of how broadcasters use such rules both to defeat and to defuse intervention.

10 Conclusions

I began my argument about the political independence of public broadcasters with a theory and associated statistical model, which were corroborated by quantitative measures of independence, market size and legal protection. Having followed that statistical analysis with more nuanced historical analysis, as well as some comparative statistics, it is wise to ask how our prior beliefs, formed on the basis of the statistical model of Chapter 2, should be revised in light of the findings of Chapters 3–8. I start by reassessing my proxy measurement of independence (1), and my measure of legal protection (2), before examining the causal chain stipulated (3). I conclude by looking at the implications of my work for the reform of real-world broadcasters (4).

1 Reassessing independence

Since independence from politics is a scale variable, and since previous literature on central bank independence had found the (political) turnover of chief executives to be a valuable indicator of de facto independence, I constructed a proxy indicator of independence to use in the statistical model of Chapter 2. I demonstrated that my indicator has concurrent validity insofar as it matched the results of a limited number of opinion polls, and showed that according to the proxy, the BBC would be more independent than DR, which would be more independent than RTÉ, SVT, Rai and RTVE. Based on the preceding chapters, it seems that this rank ordering is very approximate. First, the proxy misleadingly suggests that Rai became less politically independent after 1993, when in fact it became more independent: although the reforms implemented within the broadcaster at the beginning of the 1990s were only partially successful, they did considerably reduce the parties' influence over hiring decisions. This suggests either that the proxy over-estimates Rai's independence prior to 1993, or under-estimates Rai's independence after 1993, or both. I suggest that the former is most likely: with the exception of Biagio Agnes, most directors-general between 1975 and 1993 were not strong figures. If they stayed in their job for very long, it was only because the heavily politicized board of that time allowed the political parties to pursue influence through other means, or because of conflict between different sources of pressure on the broadcaster. Recall that

Agnes continued so long as director-general precisely because the parties could not agree on nominations to the board, leaving the board led by Sergio Zavoli to continue in a caretaker capacity. This incident shows how strong political pressure can coexist with limited turnover, creating misleading values for our proxy.

Second, the position of DR seems to be undeserved. In Chapter 2, I noted that whilst 42% of respondents to a British survey judged the BBC to be independent, 38% of respondents to a Danish survey judged DR to be independent, and therefore that DR was likely to be only slightly less independent than the BBC. It seems, however, that the gap between the BBC and DR is slightly more than these figures would suggest. Indeed, given that the poll concerning the BBC was conducted shortly after the Hutton Inquiry, and the poll on DR shortly before the firing of Christian Nissen, it seems plausible that public perception of the BBC's independence was slightly depressed, and public perception of DR's independence slightly inflated. Certainly, the extent of political involvement at board level in DR greatly exceeds the political involvement found in the Board of Governors; and whilst directors-general of both organizations were forced to resign shortly after coverage of the Iraq War, in the British case this was achieved only after a judicial inquiry, whilst in the Danish case it was achieved by the board acting alone. Equally, the position of DR seems unmerited compared to the various Swedish broadcasters. Whilst both DR and SR suffered from a political backlash after episodes of left-wing driven coverage, the structural reform of SR was followed by a dissipation of those tensions; by contrast, the much-vaunted professionalization of DR and the abolition of the programme council in 1980 has been followed by continued intervention and struggles over DR's programming. One of the reasons why the figures presented in Table 2.1 may over-estimate DR's independence is that they are calculated on the basis of turnover of the chief executive, and thus on the assumption that the chief executive is the most important individual within the organization, the individual whom any government would wish to appoint in order to direct coverage. Where instead the chief executive is weak, governments may choose to influence the broadcaster by influencing the composition of the board. This does not preclude government-induced changes in the chief executive – and indeed Italy combines high turnover both at board and chief executive level – but does reduce the incentives for it.

The low position of SVT in Table 2.1 may result in part from increases in turnover which had little to do with political independence, and more to do with secular changes in the organization relating to the upheaval of the 1976 reforms. Indeed, we saw that the independence score for Rai dipped sharply following the reforms of 1993. Whilst Rai's average score over the two periods is merited, and gives a rough indication of its true independence over this period, it may be that in both cases some element of turnover was caused by changes unrelated to the degree of political independence. Consequently, a better proxy of independence would be likely to place the BBC and SR/SVT close to the top of the ranking, followed by RTÉ and DR, with Rai and RTVE bringing up the rear.

2 Reassessing legal protection

At the same time as providing a proxy for independence, I constructed an index of legal protection based on previous work on the independence of regulatory agencies. How should this index be revised in the light of the preceding chapters? First, the index seems comprehensive. In the historical chapters there were no legal means by which politicians intervened in the broadcaster which could have been included in the index. Although in certain instances legal proceedings and inquiries did provide politicians with an opportunity to chastise the broadcaster, the decision, for example, to hold an inquiry like the Hutton Inquiry, cannot easily be incorporated into an index of legal protection that has any pretence to generality.

Second, it seems that the index may be more than comprehensive, and include some index items which are not necessary. Strictly speaking, the evidence of the preceding chapters is not enough to demonstrate that one particular aspect of legal protection does not contribute to independence – politicians always have a variety of legal options to intervene in the broadcaster, and the fact that one legal option for intervening was not used could result either from (a) that option being an irrelevant or ineffective option, or (b) from that option being inferior to other, more effective options. Thus, the fact that governments did not seem to use their power over the licence fee may either mean that control over licence-fee funding has no connection to independence, or that governments in these five countries always preferred to use their power of appointment over their power over licence fees. Nevertheless, it seems that in the cases examined here, the power of the purse counts little in explaining the independence of the broadcaster. Equally, the power to appoint individuals to the board of the broadcaster does not explain the broadcaster's independence – or at least not as originally expected. Where executives appoint board members with few constraints, they tend not to appoint fellow partisans. Executives in these countries which decide to interfere in the public broadcaster do so independently of the composition of the board. Even the Thatcher government, which was strongly critical of the BBC, and which desired to bend it to its will, appointed former Labour supporters or trade unionists to the board. Conversely, where parliaments appoint board members with considerable constraints, they do tend to appoint partisans. These partisan boards are rarely partisan in a single direction. Rather, the mix of clashing partisans on the board enfeebles the broadcaster, and, in the worst case, ably demonstrated by Rai, leads to managers who cannot either get the board to lay down the law, or to fully support the director-general. In other research, I have shown that provisions on appointment are unrelated to the bundle of items used in many indices of legal protection (Hanretty & Koop, 2011).

Nevertheless, it would be wise to retain the item on the method used to appoint the chief executive of the broadcaster, rather than the board. Indeed, the importance of a strong chief executive is a recurring theme in many of the country chapters. Executives in relatively low-independence broadcasters lament the absence of a single figure capable of uniting the competing fiefdoms of the broadcaster. Whilst the presence of a chief executive is no guarantee of independence, independence for some broadcasters has been attained (to some degree), or consolidated, only with strong chief executives – one thinks, for example, of the beneficial impact of Olof Rydbeck on SR/SVT, or of Ettore Bernabei on Rai. This connection is no coincidence – only in relatively centralized broadcasters is one likely to get the same coherence of output and same rule-following behaviour that was described in Chapter 2 as forestalling politicians' objections to "partisan" journalism.

3 Reassessing the causal chain

In the previous chapter I noted that not all links in the causal chain which runs from the market to news, to the degree of independence, were equally well substantiated. In particular, whilst rules in the broadcaster did develop earlier in countries with larger markets for news, there were few conspicuous examples of borrowing from professional associations or from wire agencies. I have already suggested that this may be because this process was "big, slow-moving, and invisible" – that a bigger market for news creates the conditions for rule-development, but that it does so invisibly. Thus, the presence of powerful press agencies might favour the development of rules within the broadcaster not because of direct transfer, but rather because the idea of news produced by these agencies – a product which, in structural terms, is relatively homogeneous, and which in any case deserves to be considered as a commodity rather than as a craft product – percolates through other media organizations, and disposes both journalists and managers to consider journalism as the kind of thing which can be either regulated or, if not regulated, at least guided. Equally, however, this link might be weakly demonstrated because it relies on an ideal of professionalization which only applies in certain circumstances. That is, the formation of a journalists' association with the primary aim of an increase in status and partial limitations on entry into the profession is quite a specific institutional feature, and may not be universally applicable, for professionalization may take place through other methods. Few would contest that American journalism is highly professionalized, but this professionalization has not taken place through the formation of a single journalists' association; and whilst the American Association of News Editors does produce guidelines on news content, it is hardly these which have shaped the profession.

Ideally, future research would be able to identify the determinants of professionalization in its different guises, and identify how these different guises are affected by different contexts. Thus, one relatively easy way to tap the kind of "institutionalized" professionalization we saw in Sweden would be to examine the percentage of journalists in each country who are affiliated to a journalists' union; this figure would presumably depend not only on features specific to the media system, such as the size of the media market, but also to wider features of society, such as the rate of union density overall.

4 Implications for reform

The preceding sections examine the academic validity of my hypothesis. In the real world, however, the only "valid" hypotheses might be those which can be cashed out in terms of real prescriptions for policy. If what I have hypothesized is true, my findings have three principal implications for reform of existing PSBs – that is, for efforts to improve the degree of political independence of low-independence PSBs in established democracies. First, journalists who wish to increase the degree of independence of the PSB should consider whether their work is regular and consistent in style and form across the broadcaster, or whether instead different journalists would report different stories differently depending on where they sit in the organization. If their work varies in style and form across the broadcaster, they should consider whether this variation is determined by considerations of the medium and the intended audience, or whether instead it would cause politicians to believe that journalists operating within the broadcaster are not reporting events as an impartial spectator would. If, having concluded that their work does vary across the broadcaster in ways that are not suggested by considerations of medium and intended audience, journalists should consider the adoption of a self-regulatory code, or should in any case display a willingness to accept procedural constraints on their output in exchange for greater independence of the agency as a whole, and a lesser likelihood of arbitrary or partisan hiring decisions in the future.

Second, managers – and in particular the chief executive of the broadcaster – should be aware of the key role they play in reforming the broadcaster, and in acting as a mediator between politicians and journalists. Journalists will be unlikely to accept the kind of constraints on output found, in example, in Editorial Guidelines, without some benefit in exchange. It is the task of the chief executive of the broadcaster to convince journalists that she or he can provide both short-term benefits to journalists, perhaps in terms of an increased investment in training and professional development, as well as guarantee the long-term benefits of increased independence that will result from adherence to procedural constraints on output. Additionally, where journalists have not displayed a movement towards the acceptance of constraints on output, or greater self-regulation, the chief executive should be able to win the consent of journalists for proposed changes. S/he should in all cases guard against the risk that attempts at developing self-regulatory codes on output will be seen as a form of "censure". Managers of the broadcaster must also convince politicians that they enjoy sufficient control over the broadcaster to ensure that self-regulatory codes, once imposed, will be followed; and that subsequent breaches of that code will be treated seriously. Mediating between these two groups is not easy: early breaches of the code, or an impression that the broadcaster is "out of control", may lead the chief executive to sanction journalists in highly visible fashion, and thus further weaken journalists' incentives to self-regulate. Instead, devices that allow the chief executive to temporize – such as the establishment of committees to consider complaints and subsequently deliver reasoned judgements – will be useful in mediating between the two groups.

Third, politicians who sincerely desire greater independence for the broadcaster should act on that desire and pass legislation granting the broadcaster greater legal protection. In light of the preceding remarks, particular attention should be paid to the term length and possibilities for dismissal of board members and chief executives – only where term lengths are long and (politically initiated) dismissal is difficult will the difficult mediation act of chief executives be likely to succeed. Greater legal protection may take different forms in different countries. Considered in abstract, therefore, politicians might readily assent to granting greater legal protection.

Considered concretely, reform efforts may involve the abolition of posts for politicians and the limitation of certain opportunities for interference. In the case of Italy, reform to grant Rai greater legal protection would likely involve a number of specific measures which have not been addressed either in the most recent reform law (the legge Gasparri), nor in proposals for reform (ddl Gentiloni; proposta di iniziativa popolare, senatrice Tana de Zulueta ed altri). First, effective reform would likely reduce the current excessive degree of parliamentary supervision. This could be achieved either by the abolition of the Commissione parlamentare per l'indirizzo generale e la vigilanza dei servizi radiotelevisi (CPIV) or by the elimination of the majority of functions assigned to it by law 103/75, which, despite having been superseded in other respects, remains the primary normative reference for the committee's work. Those functions which do not directly pertain to Rai – the fourth, fifth and ninth clauses of article 4, concerning public access programming, party-political broadcasts, and misleading advertising respectively – could easily be reassigned to the parliamentary committee on transport and communications (clauses 4 and 5) and to Agcom (clause 9). Second, reform would involve a new system of appointing board members. (This would be necessary if the parliamentary committee were abolished, since it currently appoints seven of the nine board members and ratifies the two remaining choices.) The current system of parliamentary nomination has produced highly partisan Rai boards; throughout the country chapters we have seen that parliamentary nomination (as in Denmark and Italy, and latterly also in Sweden) is associated with more partisan appointments to multi-member boards, and that nomination by the executive is associated with less partisan appointments. Nomination of Rai board members by the government is probably unwise and perhaps unconstitutional in the Italian case. The Constitutional Court has repeatedly underlined that the management of Rai should not reflect the influence of the executive. Nomination could therefore only be carried out by other quasi-governmental office holders. One option would be to return to the system of nomination used between 1993 and 2004, where board members were nominated by joint decision of the presidents of the two chambers. This system – also used for the competition watchdog – could be complemented by parliamentary ratification of these nominations, should some form of parliamentary involvement be held desirable.

Third, reform of the system of appointment of board members should be accompanied by an increase in the length of term. Members of the board of the competition watchdog are appointed for a seven-year, non-renewable term; the same would lessen the likelihood that the PSB's managerial cycle and the politico-electoral cycle would overlap. Fourth, the system used for appointing the director-general should also be changed. Currently the Treasury, as majority shareholder in Rai, ratifies the board's choice of director-general; in practice, this leads to extensive ministerial "soundings" prior to the choice. If the current company structure of Rai as a *società per azioni* is to be preserved, the Treasury should pre-commit itself to approving the board's choice. If not, and to the extent compatible with the civil code, the choice of director-general should be the exclusive competence of the board. The director-general's term should also be increased in line with the board's.

5 Continued relevance

These recommendations are only worthwhile if PSBs have a future. Yet there are reasons to believe that public service broadcasting has reached its peak. PSBs were created in a period of spectrum scarcity, which justified state intervention given concerns about natural monopolies, leading to producer surpluses and a deleterious impact on the terms of national debate. Spectrum scarcity is no longer an issue, and so much of the justification for public broadcasting has gone (even if arguments about state provision of merit goods remain). Additionally, given spectrum abundance and the multiplicity of channels, PSBs must compete for audiences in a way that they have not had to before. Politicians may therefore be unwilling to countenance further state support for public service broadcasting if PSBs attract only niche audiences.

Figure 10.1 shows the average audience share of PSBs across 36 European countries. The solid line represented the simple average; the dashed line represented the average weighted for the population of each country. Both lines show a decline in the average share of audience held by PSBs, but the dashed line declines faster, suggesting that the pattern of overall decline is heavily influenced by considerable decline in larger markets. This is indeed the case: there have been large declines in PSB audience share in Germany (4%), France (7.2%) and Spain (14%). Even accounting for this, however, the population weighed average shows a general pattern of decline, though the trend is small: PSBs lose audience share at a rate of around 1% every four years. It is also worth noting that this small decline in audience share does not necessarily mean a smaller impact on the public. In most media markets in Europe, television viewing time has increased over the period 1998–2008. Consequently, even broadcasters with smaller audience shares may speak to more people, more of the time. Concentrating on television viewership ignores other media; and one of the most significant threats to PSBs – and indeed traditional broadcasters in general – is the Internet. If viewers were to switch from watching television to streaming media over the Internet, the first-mover advantage had by PSBs might disappear, and their hold over the public would be considerably diminished. It is difficult to tell whether public broadcasters will be harmed by the emergence of the Internet as

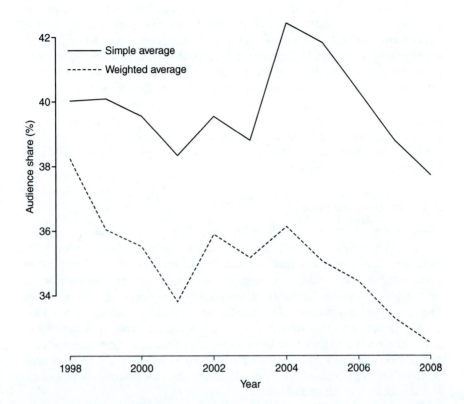

Figure 10.1 PSB audience shares, 1998–2008.

a delivery mechanism for audiovisual content. Presently it seems that Internet-use and television-use are not rivalrous; rather, users make use of multiple media, often at the same time. However, if the Internet does represent an existential threat for PSBs, it is low-independence broadcasters which will be worst hit. Alexa/Netcraft traffic reports show that PSBs in the north of Europe tend to attract much more traffic (relative to other websites located in their respective countries) than PSBs in the south of Europe: the websites of the BBC, DR and RTÉ are the fifth, ninth and tenth most-visited websites in the UK, Denmark and the Republic of Ireland respectively; Rai's website is only the 44 most visited Italian website, and is beaten by the website of *Repubblica* (#10) and by its television rival Mediaset (#16). RTVE's website is the 53 most visited Spanish website, behind Telecinco (#42) and El Mundo (#10).[1] Consequently, greater political independence, if secured now, might free PSBs to face future threats to their existence.

Notes

1 Introduction

1 "Fråga 2004/05:1073 av Gustav Fridolin (mp) till utbildnings- och kulturminister Leif Pagrotsky om vikten av kritiskt granskande medier", Riksdagen, 24 February 2005.
2 "Svar på frågorna 2004/05:1073 om vikten av kritiskt granskande medier och 1124 om SVT:s kampanj och regeringens utrikespolitik", Riksdagen, 8 March 2005.
3 This distinguishes PSBs from official external services such as the BBC World Service or surrogate domestic services like Radio Free Europe or Radio Marti (Head, 1985, pp. 342–365).
4 The fact that Italian PSB Rai is often described as the *televisione di stato* (state television) may therefore give pause.

2 The broad picture: testing rival theories of independence on 36 public broadcasters

1 Article 10 of Law no. 4 of 10 January 1980 ("De estatuto de la radio y la television"); §31, comma 2 of the Broadcasting Act of 19 May 1994.
2 The Pearson's r for the two measures is 0.675, suggesting that the two indicators tap the same concept, but that neither is a copy of the other.
3 Some politicians seem to be pure policy-seekers, and act towards the broadcaster so as to give expression to their views on the ideal polity. This is often the case with right-wing parties espousing traditional moral values. Criticism of the broadcaster based on such values often seems like an unadulterated expression of the politician's policy position: often, however, such stances are additionally very popular amongst the party's core support group. It therefore may resemble vote-seeking behaviour in effect, if not in intention. In any case, the following arguments about independence hold whether politicians seek votes or policy. These distinctions between vote-, office- and policy-seeking politicians come from Strom (1990).
4 It is possible to think of counterexamples to this assumption: if broadcast output were consistently close to a certain ideal point in political space irrespective of the flow of events (see below), then that broadcaster might lose credibility entirely, and would thus be entirely discounted by voters and not lead to an increase in votes. This counterexample, however, is drastic, and would require a degree of control over the broadcaster which is not seen in any of the broadcasters studied here.
5 From the description given above, it might seem that the figure of the ideal observer produces the kind of "objective" output which has widely been derided as psychologically and practically impossible. This kind of output may indeed be impossible, and consequently the ideal observer may be chimeric, but it is a useful chimera, since it helps focus attention on what does matter, namely that we commonly believe we can

recognize "a deviation from an unattainable but theoretically conceivable condition of unbias" (Williams, 1975, p. 191).

6 A response in terms of direct evidence about journalistic partisanship might also be tactically foolish, as it may invite further queries from politicians concerning individual journalists or groups of journalists.

7 The Italian *par condicio* demonstrates both reasons: see pp. 69–71.

8 By the size of the market for news, I do not mean the total profitability of the sector, but rather the total consumption. Although news can be consumed in a number of formats, historically the most important of these has been the printed daily newspaper. Accordingly, the exposition that follows is cast in terms of newspaper readership and production.

9 Although journalism courses now include large elements of the law on copyright, libel and protection of sources.

10 See p. 33 for an explanation of why 1975 data is used.

11 Australia: www.atua.org.au/ptta/038.html; Austria: Hallin & Mancini (2004, pp. 171–172); Belgium: www.agjpb.be/ajp/ajp/histoire.php; Britain: Delano (2002); Denmark: personal communication from Hans-Henrik Holm; Estonia: Høyer et al. (1993, p. 134); Finland: Hallin & Mancini (2004, pp. 171–172); France: www.snj.fr; Germany: Retallack (1993); Greece: www.esiea.gr; Iceland: www.press.is/page/adalkjarasamningur; Italy: www.fnsi.it; Japan: Huffman (1997); Latvia: Høyer et al. (1993, p. 154); Netherlands: Hallin & Mancini (2004, pp. 171–172); New Zealand: Elsaka (2004); Norway: Hallin & Mancini (2004, pp. 171–172); Portugal: www.jornalistas.online.pt/canal.asp?idselect=0&idCanal=51&p=0; Spain: www.fape.es/index.php?option=com_content&task=view&id=262&Itemid=136; Sweden: p. publicistklubben; Switzerland: www.icom-info.ch/p.php?ID=897.

12 These cases were Latvia, Lithuania and Slovakia. Results from the regression without imputation did not differ significantly.

13 Data for the Baltic countries were taken from Høyer et al. (1993); data for the Czech Republic, Slovakia, Flanders and the French-language community in Belgium were imputed from parent countries. It is likely that the model fit would have improved had separate 1975 data for these latter four areas been available; the Belgian French-language broadcaster has lower levels of independence than predicted, and the French-language community reads fewer newspapers than Flanders; the same is true for Slovakia compared to the Czech Republic.

14 It might be thought that this control variable is in fact an independent variable in its own right, reflecting either the legacy of a Leninist philosophy of the press (cf. Milton, 2001) or turbulence related to processes of democratization. First, for all that they were under Soviet influence, it would be a mistake, however, to think that a Leninist philosophy of the press applied equally well in Poland, Estonia and Russia; or to think that stated commitments to such a philosophy were incompatible with the development of professional norms (on which point, see Curry, 1990). Second, it is not the case that democratization-related turbulence led to inflated values of TOR or VUL: of the shortest-serving executives in each of the nine post-communist countries included in the analysis, six started as chief executive after 1999; the remaining three started between 1991 and 1994.

15 In some cases, where the number of members was large and the methods used to appoint them divergent, I have assigned different scores for some part of the board, and averaged these methods. For example: in Italy following the passage of the 1975 reform of Rai, six members of the 16-member administrative council were nominated by the majority shareholder (the state, coded here as the executive), whilst the remaining 10 members were nominated by a parliamentary committee. The score for "appointing body for first executive group" is therefore equal to $[(6 \times 0.25)+(10 \times 0.75)]/16$.

16 It is incorrect to apply veto players theory in this way, since a focus on institutional veto points may mislead if those veto points are occupied by the same players, or if

putative extra veto players have ideal points which fall inside the unanimity core (Tsebelis, 2002, pp. 26–30). Nevertheless, this faulty application is only likely to bias downwards the effects of the index of legal protection.

17 The law is the Portuguese Television Broadcasting Act, Law no. 32/2003.

3 Italy: the absence of Caesars

1 The acronym stuck when Radio Audizioni Italiane became Radiotelevisione Italiana.
2 D.Lgs.C.P.S. 3 aprile 1947, n. 428.
3 Sentenza no. 59 del 1960.
4 Sentenza no. 225/74; all subsequent section references are to the part of the judgment *Considerato in diritto*.
5 In particular, decision no. 59 of 1960.
6 Relazione della Commissione presentata il 7 marzo 1975, on progetto di legge AC3448, "Nuove norme in materia di diffusione radiofonica e televisiva".
7 Debate of 13 March 1975, col. 20903; emphasis added.
8 Sentenza no. 59/60.
9 Deputy Baghino (MSI-DN), debate of 24 March 1975.
10 The report was authored by Giuliano Amato and Enzo Cheli. Amato would later become prime minister in the period leading up to the second great reform of Rai (1993). Cheli would be appointed as president of Rai seven years later. Critics of objectivity and impartiality thus playing leading roles in Rai's future.
11 The division of posts within the broadcaster amongst the political parties.
12 Interview with author, Rome, summer 2005.
13 "Calcetti all'Annunziata", *Prima Comunicazione*, February 2004.
14 Interview with Claudio Cappon.
15 Interview with Rubens Esposito.
16 USIGRAI press release of 27 October 2004.
17 www.odg.it/elenco_scuole.
18 A possible exception might be made for Ettore Giovanelli, who is the technical commentator for Rai's excellent Formula 1 coverage.
19 Legge no. 60/1953.
20 *Resoconto della Commissione parlamentare per l'indirizzo generale e la vigilanza dei servizi radiotelevisivi*, 24 October 2007, pp. 273–274.
21 Walter Veltroni's decision to nominate author Giorgio Van Straten caused discomfort within the Partito Democratico, not least because a former parliamentary colleague of Veltroni's, Carlo Rognoni, was obliged to leave the board to make room for Van Straten.
22 See, for example, his editorial of 3 October 2009 attacking those protesting about freedom of the press in Italy; or his February 2010 criticism of investigations of corruption amongst government ministers.
23 "Rai, Garimberti porta il caso Tg1 in Cda", *La Repubblica*, 24 June 2009.
24 See, for example, Paul Ginsborg's account of the left's attempt at reform, in Ginsborg (2004).

4 Spain: huge steps forward?

1 There was one exception: Radio Cadena Española merged with RNE to form a single public radio service.

5 The United Kingdom: "treading delicately like Agag"

1 The reference is to 1 Samuel 15:32. Agag was king of the Amalekites; he trod delicately before Samuel, and pleaded before him, but Samuel "hewed Agag to pieces". The wisdom of following Agag's example is thus unclear.

2 Co-operation also made easier the unified treatment of news, as we shall see below.
3 Booklet BP5, "The Broadcasting of Controversial Matter (Excluding Religious Broadcasts): History and Present Practice" (November 1942), in BBC WAC file R34/317/2 – POLICY – CONTROVERSIAL BROADCASTING 1929, 1932, 1935, 1942–3, 1957.
4 Ibid., Appendix 2b.
5 Ibid.
6 H.S. to D.X.B., 28 January 1957, in connection with Lord Strang's motion, 6 February 1957.
7 Ibid., emphasis added.
8 Ibid., emphasis added.
9 Minutes of a meeting of Tuesday, 24 March 1953, WAC.
10 Ibid.
11 "The Closed Fortnight", note by the director-general, 27 May 1953, emphasis added.
12 Charles Hill, who would subsequently be appointed BBC Chairman (1967–1972).
13 Now kept as WAC (R34/518) – "POLICY FILE".
14 Undated 1958 letter from H. Casey to DH Clarke, BBC WAC file "R34/612 – POLICY: PROGRAMME POLICY BOOK – 1945–1963".
15 "Companion to the Standing Orders and guide to the Proceedings of the House of Lords", §§4.83–4.85.
16 WAC R78/1,217/1 "Violence in Programmes – General" (1960–1969).
17 "WAC R78/1,218/1 Violence in Programmes, General – Part 2, Jan. 1970"; emphasis added.
18 Excerpted in ibid.; emphasis added.
19 Letter from J. M. G. Best to Anne-Marie Hellerström, 16 September 1960. BBC WAC E1/2388/2 – Sveriges Radio 1960.
20 Including Neil Hamilton MP, later found guilty of perjury in an unrelated court case.
21 Interview with Will Wyatt.
22 Interview with Patricia Hodgson.
23 Ibid.
24 Evidence submitted to the Hutton Inquiry, BBC/4/0144.
25 BBC/5/0172.
26 Hoon: CAB/1/0408; Bradshaw: BBC/5/0170.
27 BBC/6/082.
28 BBC/14/0127.
29 BBC/5/068.
30 Minutes of the Board meeting of 6 July 2003, BBC/6/100.

6 Ireland: importing experience

1 For Finland, see Pine (2002, pp. xii–xiii); for France, McLoone (1991, p. 13).

7 Sweden: "disturbing neither God nor Hitler"

1 The established non-socialist parties in Sweden are often described as *borgerlig*, which translates as bourgeois, but which does not have the pejorative overtones of that word in English. The bourgeois parties are the Moderate Party (formerly the Right Party, Höger), the Christian Democrats, the Centre Party (formerly the Agrarian party, Bondeförbundet), and the Liberal People's Party (Folkpartiet).
2 Första Kammaren no. 127, Herr Ollén.
3 The initial government version read:

> Programmen skall utformas så att olika åsikter kan framföras och balanseras på ett rättvist sätt. Sakuppgifter och påståenden i ett program skall vara sanna och

ämnes- val och framställning ta sikta på vad som är väsentligt. Den enskildes rätt till privatliv skall respekteras. Felaktig sakuppgift skall utan dröjsmål beriktigas, när det är påkallat...

SR suggested a much expanded version, which read:

Programverksamheten skall präglas av opartiskhet och saklighet och av en strävan att se programmen en för medierna lämplig form. Kravet på opartiskhet innebär bl.a. att olika åsikter får komma till uttryck i programmen, och att berörda eller jämförliga parter blir företrädda på lika grunder. Olika åsikter kan dock få framföras vid skilda tillfällen, förutom att programverksamheten som helhet präglas av balans. Av kravet på saklighet följer bl.a. att i program fram- förda sakuppgifter och påståenden skall underkasta nog- gran kontroll och att ämnesval och framställning tar sikte på vad som kan bedömas som väsentligt. Den enskildes privatliv skall respekteras därest icke oavvisligt allmänintresse annat kräver. Felaktig sakuppgift skall beriktigas när det är påkallat ... Reglerna om opartiskhet och saklighet bör tillämpas med beaktanade av att en vidsträckt yttrande och infor- mationsfrihet skall råda i rundradion.

These versions are found in Unsgaard (n.d.).
4 Mats Carlbom, "'Aktuellt'-chef försökte stoppa Fichtelius", *Dagens Nyheter*, 19 March 2007.

8 Denmark: being driven to the left?

1 Interview with Plummer.
2 Møllerup has asked that his successor be spared this dual role.
3 See, for example, "Mollerup: Flere bruger DRs ankesystem i stedet for Pressenævnet", www.dr.dk/OmDR/Lytternes_og_seernes_redaktoer/Klummer/2009/0324103102.htm.
4 Svar til Spørgsmål nr. S 230.
5 2004–05, 1. samling – §20-spørgsmål: Om fyring af DR's generaldirektør Christian Nissen, S. 228, af Søren Søndergaard.
6 Unless one includes *alsidighed*, which resembles Italian *pluralismo* in its ineffability.

10 Conclusions

1 All data from Alexa.com as of 29 November 2010.

References

n.a. (2008). Il cda Rai salva Saccà: no al licenziamento. *Repubblica*, p. 9.

Aldridge, M., & Evetts, J. (2003). Rethinking the concept of professionalism: The case of journalism. *British Journal of Sociology*, *54*(4), 547–564.

Asor Rosa, A. (1981). Il giornalista: appunti sulla fisiologia di un mestiere difficile. In C. Vivanti (Ed.), *Storia d'Italia* (vol. IV, pp. 1227–1260). Torino: Einaudi.

Bagge, G., Lundberg, E., & Svennilson, I. (1935). *Wages in Sweden* (vol. 2). Stockholm: Institute for Social Sciences, University of Stockholm.

Balassone, S., & Guglielmi, A. (1995). *Senza rete: Politica e televisione nell'Italia che cambia*. Milano: Rizzoli.

Banks, A., & Databases International (2007). Cross-national time-series data archive. Electronic Database.

Barile, P. (1989). Vecchi e nuovi motivi di incostituzionalità dell'Ordine dei Giornalisti. *Problemmi dell'informazioni*, *14*(1), 7–17.

Barnett, S., Curry, A., & Chalmers, A. (1994). *The battle for the BBC: A British broadcasting conspiracy*. London: Aurum Press.

Baumgartner, J., & Morris, J. (2006). The Daily Show effect. *American Politics Research*, *34*(3), 341.

Becchelloni, G. (1991). *L'obiettività giornalistica: un'ideale maltrattato*, chap. "Preface". Napoli: Liguori.

Bild, T. (1975). Programstyringen i Danmarks Radio. In R. Skovmand (Ed.), *DR50* (pp. 195–244). Copenhagen: Danmarks Radio.

Bischoff, C. S. (2006). *Political competition and contestability: A study of the barriers to entry in 21 democracies*. Ph.D. thesis, European University Institute, Florence.

Born, G. (2005). *Uncertain vision: Birt, Dyke, and the reinvention of the BBC*. London: Vintage Books.

Brancati, D. (1984). Ecco la strada per diventare giornalista Rai. *Repubblica*, p. 5.

Brancati, D. (1988a). Ai consiglieri Rai i tg e i giornali radio piaccioni come sono. *Repubblica*.

Brancati, D. (1988b). Ora la Rai ha un piano editoriale. *Repubblica*, p. 37.

Briggs, A. (1979). *Governing the BBC*. London: BBC.

Briggs, A. (1995). *The history of broadcasting in the United Kingdom*, Vol. I, *The birth of broadcasting (1896–1927)*. Oxford: Oxford University Press.

Brink Lund, A. (1976). *Magten over Danmarks Radio: en analyse specielt med henblik på forholdene omkring lydradioens nyhedsformidling 1970–1976*. Århus: Publimus.

Bruzzone, M. G. (2007). Rai, Staderini e Urbani pronti a lasciare il Cda. *La Stampa*, p. 11.

Budge, I., Klingemann, H.-D., Volkens, A., & Bara, J. (2001). *Mapping policy preferences: Estimates for parties, electors, and governments, 1945–1998*. Oxford: Oxford University Press.

Budge, I., Woldendorp, J., & Keman, H. (1998). Party government in 20 democracies: An update (1990–1995). *European Journal of Political Research, 33*(1), 125–164.

Burns, T. (1977). *The BBC: Public institution and private world*. London: Macmillan.

Bustamante, E. (2007). *Storia della Radio e della Televisione in Spagna (1939–2007)*. Roma: Rai-ERI.

Canel, M. J., & Piqué, A. M. (1998). Journalists in emerging democracies: The case of Spain. In D. M. Weaver (Ed.), *The global journalist*. Cresskills, NJ: Hampton Press.

Cannistraro, P. (1975). *La fabbrica del consenso*. Roma: Laterza.

Cardini, F., & Riccio, G. (1995). *Il cavallo impazzito. Una stagione di polemiche alla Rai*. Florence: Giunti Editori.

Castronovo, V., Giacheri Fossati, L., & Tranfaglia, N. (1979). *La stampa italiana nell'eta liberale*. Bari: Laterza.

Caviglia, S. (2001). Zaccaria: Per Berlusconi un anno da record sul video. *Repubblica*.

Cesareo, G. (1970). *Anatomia del potere televisivo*. Milano: Franco Angeli.

Chiarenza, F. (2002). *Il cavallo morente. Storia della Rai*. Milano: Franco Angeli.

Cipolla, C. M. (1969). *Literacy and development in the West*. London: Penguin.

COMPAS (1999). Attitudes toward broadcast issues, Canadian content and the CBC. Survey carried out for the Friends of Canadian Broadcasting.

Coppedge, M., & Reinicke, W. H. (1991). Measuring polyarchy. In A. Inkeles (Ed.), *On measuring democracy* (pp. 47–68). New Brunswick, NJ: Transaction.

Coppens, T., & Saeys, F. (2006). Enforcing performance: New approaches to govern public service broadcasting. *Media, Culture & Society, 28*(2), 261.

Costner, H. L. (1969). Theory, deduction, and rules of correspondence. *American Journal of Sociology, 75*(2), 245–263.

Crossman, R. (1977). *The diaries of a cabinet minister*, Vol. 3, *Secretary of State for Social Services 1968–1970*. London: Hamish Hamilton.

CSA, & Marianne (2003). L'image des journalistes et l'objectivité des médias. Retrieved from: www.csa-fr.com/dataset/data2003/opi20030227c.htm.

Cukierman, A. (1992). *Central bank strategy, credibility, and independence: Theory and evidence*. Cambridge, MA: MIT Press.

Cukierman, A., & Webb, S. (1995). Political influence on the central bank: International evidence. *World Bank Economic Review, 9*(3), 397–423.

Curry, J. L. (1990). *Poland's journalists: Professionalism and politics*. Cambridge: Cambridge University Press.

Curzi, A., & Mineo, C. (1994). *Giù le mani dalla Tv*. Milano: Sperling and Kuper.

Dahl, R. A. (1971). *Polyarchy: Participation and opposition*. New Haven, CT: Yale University Press.

Danmarks Radio (DR). (various years). *Årbog* [Yearbook]. Copenhagen.

Danmarks Radio. (2006). Resultat om uafhængighed fra DRs public service image undersøgelse 2006. Personal communication from Bente Hansen, DR.

Delano, T. (2002). *The formation of the British journalist, 1900–2000*. Ph.D. thesis, University of Westminster, London.

DellaVigna, S., & Kaplan, E. (2007). The Fox News effect: Media bias and voting. *Quarterly Journal of Economics, 122*(3), 1187–1234.

Djerf-Pierre, M., & Weibull, L. (2001). *Spegla, granska, tolka. Aktualitetsjournalistik i svensk radio och TV under 1900-talet*. Stockholm: Prisma.

Dod's (2006). *Dod's parliamentary companion*. London: Dod's.

Donsbach, W., & Patterson, T. (2004). Political news journalists: Partisanship, professionalism, and political roles in five countries. In F. Esser & B. Pfetsch (Eds.), *Comparing political communication: Theories, cases, and challenges* (pp. 251–270). Cambridge: Cambridge University Press.

Dowling, J., Doolan, L., & Quinn, B. (1969). *Sit down and be counted: The cultural evolution of a television station*. Dublin: Wellington Publishers.

Elgemyr, G. (1996). *Radion i strama tyglar: om Radiotjänsts tillblivelse, teknik och ekonomi 1922–1957*. Stockholm: Norstedt.

Elgemyr, G. (2005). *Får jag be om en kommentar?: yttrandefriheten i svensk radio 1925–1960*. Stockholm: Norstedt.

Elgie, R., & McMenamin, I. (2005). Credible commitment, political uncertainty or policy complexity? Explaining variations in the independence of non-majoritarian institutions in France. *British Journal of Political Science, 35*(3), 531–548.

Elsaka, N. (2004). *Beyond consensus?: New Zealand journalists and the appeal of "professionalism" as a model for occupational reform*. Ph.D. thesis, University of Canterbury, New Zealand.

Engblom, L.-A. (1998). *Radio- och TV-folket: rekryteringen av programmedarbetare till radion och televisionen i Sverige 1925–1995*. Stockholm: Stiftelsen Etermedierna i Sverige.

Etzioni-Halevy, E. (1987). *National broadcasting under siege: A comparative study of Australia, Britain, Israel, and West Germany*. London: Macmillan.

Evans, J. (2002). In defence of Sartori. *Party Politics, 8*(2), 155–174.

Farinelli, G., Paccagnini, E., Santambrogio, G., & Ida Villa, A. (1997). *Storia del giornalismo italiano: dalle origini ai giorni nostri*. Torino: UTET.

Firth, R. (1952). Ethical absolutism and the ideal observer. *Philosophy and Phenomenological Research, 12*(3), 317–345.

Fisher, D. (1978). *Broadcasting in Ireland*. London: Routledge.

Fontanarosa, A. (1998). Rai, An torna all'attacco. *Repubblica*, p. 22.

Fragola, A. (1983). *Elementi di diritto della comunicazione sociale*. Roma: GEA.

Freedman, D. (2001). What use is a public inquiry? Labour and the 1977 Annan Committee on the Future of Broadcasting. *Media, Culture & Society, 23*(2), 195–211.

Garnham, N., & Inglis, F. (1990). *Capitalism and communication: Global culture and the economics of information*. London: Sage.

Gentiloni, P. (2007). Linee guida per la riforma della Rai. Retrieved from: www.comunicazioni.it.

Gilardi, F. (2002). Policy credibility and delegation to independent regulatory agencies: A comparative empirical analysis. *Journal of European Public Policy, 9*(6), 873–893.

Gilardi, F. (2005). The formal independence of regulators: A comparison of 17 countries and 7 sectors. *Swiss Political Science Review, 11*(4), 139–167.

Ginsborg, P. (1990). *A history of contemporary Italy: Society and politics, 1943–1988*. London: Penguin Books.

Ginsborg, P. (2004). *Silvio Berlusconi: Television, power and patrimony*. London: Verso.

Gismondi, A. (1958). *La televisione in Italia*. Roma: Editori Riuniti.

Glasgow University Media Group (1976). *Bad news*. London: Routledge.

Glasgow University Media Group (1980). *More bad news*. London: Routledge.

Gran, B., & Patterson, R. (2006). Law and weak links of independence: A fuzzy-sets analysis of children's ombudspersons. Unpublished working paper, Case Western Reserve University.

Greene, H. (1969). *The third floor front: A view of broadcasting in the sixties*. Oxford: Bodley Head.

Griffiths, D. (2006). *Fleet Street: Five hundred years of the press*. London: British Library.

Groseclose, T., & Milyo, J. (2005). A measure of media bias. *Quarterly Journal of Economics, 120*(4), 1191–1237.

Hadenius, S. (1998). *Kampen om monopolet: Sveriges radio och TV under 1900-talet*. Stockholm: Prisma.

Hahr, H. (1960). Letter to Olof Rydbeck. SR Arkiv – Kommittén för publiceringsregler: Seriebeteckning F 1; Volym nr 1; T65.

Hallin, D., & Mancini, P. (2004). *Comparing media systems: Three models of media and politics*. Cambridge: Cambridge University Press.

Hanretty, C. (2006). *Yes Minister? Political interference in the BBC and RAI, 1996–2006*. M.Phil, St. Anne's College, University of Oxford.

Hanretty, C. (2007). The gospel truths of Italian media bias. *Comunicazione Politica, 8*(1), 31–48.

Hanretty, C., & Koop, C. (2011). Measuring regulators' statutory independence. *Journal of European Public Policy*. Forthcoming.

Hansson, O. (1998). *Intresset ljuger aldrig. Striden om makten i och över Sveriges Radio*. Stockholm: Ekerlids.

Head, S. W. (1985). *World broadcasting systems: A comparative analysis*. Belmont, CA: Wadsworth.

Héritier, A., & Eckert, S. (2007). New modes of governance in the shadow of hierarchy: Self-regulation by industry in Europe. *Journal of Public Policy, 28*(1), 113–138.

Hermansson, C.-H. (1964). Letter to Olof Rydbeck. Sveriges Radio Dokumentarkiv. Centrala Kansliet, Handlingar rörande programverksamheten, policyfrågor. F4 CB Vol. 9.

Hjelte, R., Krantz, L., & Torell, C. (1968). *Tre på TV ser på TV. Ett inlägg om programpolitiken inför TV2*. Uddevalla: Zindermans.

Ho, D., & Quinn, K. (2008). Measuring explicit political positions of media. *Quarterly Journal of Political Science, 3*(4), 353–377.

Horgan, J. (2002). *Irish media: A critical history since 1922*. London: Routledge.

Horgan, J. (2004). *Broadcasting and public life: RTÉ news and current affairs*. Dublin: Four Courts Press.

Horrie, C., & Clarke, S. (1994). *Fuzzy monsters: Fear and loathing at the BBC*. London: Heinemann.

Høyer, S., Hadenius, S., & Weibull, L. (1975). *The politics and economics of the press: A developmental perspective*. London: Sage.

Høyer, S., Lauk, E., & Vihalemm, P. (Eds.) (1993). *Towards a civic society: The Baltic media's long road to freedom*. Tartu: Baltic Association for Media Research/Nota Baltica.

Huber, J., & Inglehart, R. (1995). Expert interpretations of party space and party locations in 42 societies. *Party Politics, 1*(1), 73–111.

Huffman, J. (1997). *Creating a public: People and press in Meiji Japan*. Honolulu: University of Hawaii Press.

Humphreys, P. (1996). *Mass media and media policy in Western Europe*. Manchester: Manchester University Press.

Hutton, B. (2004). *Report of the inquiry into the circumstances surrounding the death of Dr. David Kelly C.M.G.* London: The Stationery Office.

International Institute for Management Development (2006). *IMD world competitiveness yearbook*. Lausanne: International Institute for Management Development.

Iseppi, F. (1998). *Il ruolo e la missione del servizio pubblico radiotelevisivo e l'etica d'impresa*. Roma: Rai-ERI.

Istituto Eurisko, & Montesi, M. P. (1988). Immagine della RAI. Internal company document.

Johannsen, W. (1975). Alsidighed – hvordan og for hvem? In R. Skovman (Ed.), *DR50*. Copenhagen: Danmarks Radio.

Johansson, B. (2004). Mass media, interpersonal communication or personal experience? Perceptions of media effects among Swedish politicians. *Nordicom Review, 25*(1–2), 259–276.

Katz, R. S., & Mair, P. (1995). Changing models of party organization and party democracy. *Party Politics, 1*(1), 5–28.

Krauss, E. (1998). Changing television news in Japan. *Journal of Asian Studies, 57*(3), 663–692.

Kumar, K. (1975). Holding the middle ground: The BBC, the public and the professional broadcaster. *Sociology, 9*(1), 67–88.

Leapmann, M. (1986). *The last days of the Beeb*. London: Allen & Unwin.

Lerner, J., & Tetlock, P. E. (1999). Accounting for the effects of accountability. *Psychological Bulletin, 125*(2), 255–275.

Lieberman, E. (2005). Nested analysis as a mixed-method strategy for comparative research. *American Political Science Review, 99*(3), 435–452.

Lindahl, E., Dahlgren, E., & Kock, K. (1937). *National income of Sweden 1861–1930*. London: PS King & Son.

Lloyd, J. (2005). *What the media are doing to our politics*. London: Constable.

Locke, E. (2000). Motivation, cognition, and action: An analysis of studies of task goals and knowledge. *Applied Psychology, 49*(3), 408–429.

Lundevall, K.-E. (1961). Letter to Olof Rydbeck. Sveriges Radio Dokumentarkiv. Centrala Kansliet, Handlingar rörande programverksamheten, policyfrågor. F4 CB, Vol 9.

Lundström, G., Rydén, P., & Sandlund, E. (2001). *Det moderna Sveriges spegel (1897–1945)*. Den Svenska pressens historia. Stockholm: Ekerlids.

MacDonald, K. (1995). *The sociology of the professions*. London: Sage.

Manca, E. (1987). Agnes è il mio profeta. *Repubblica*, p. 1.

Mancini, P. (2009). *Elogio della lottizzazione*. Bari: Laterza.

Marletti, C. (1988). Parties and mass communication: The RAI controversy. *Italian Politics: A Review, 2*, 167–178.

Matteucci, N., Bobbio, N., & Pasquino, G. (Eds.) (1976). *Dizionario di Politica*. Torino: UTET.

Mauri, M. (1984). Differenze tra le linee editoriali delle testate. In R. Zaccaria (Ed.), *Rai: La televisione che cambia* (pp. 267–275). Torino: Società Editrice Internazionale.

Mazza, M., & Agnes, B. (2004). *Mauro Mazza intervista Biagio Agnes: TV: moglie, amante, compagna*. Roma: Rai-ERI.

Mazzanti, A. (1991). *L'obiettivita giornalistica: un'ideale maltratto*. Napoli: Liguori.

McLoone, M. (1991). Inventions and re-imaginings: Some thoughts on identity and broadcasting in Ireland. In M. McLoone (Ed.), *Culture, identity and broadcasting in Ireland: Local issues, global perspectives* (pp. 2–30). Belfast: QUB Institute of Irish Studies.

McNally, F. (2002). Burke intervened "not in public interest but to serve promoters". *Irish Times*.

Miall, L. (1994). *Inside the BBC: British broadcasting characters*. London: Weidenfeld & Nicolson.

Milton, A. (2001). Bound but not gagged: Media reform in democratic transitions. *Comparative Political Studies*, *34*(5), 493–526.

Moe, T. M. (1990). Political institutions: The neglected side of the story. *Journal of Law, Economics, & Organization, 6*, 213–253.

Montano, A. G. (2006). *La manipulación en televisión*. Madrid: Espejo de Tinta.

Monteleone, F. (1999). *Storia della radio e della televisione in Italia*. Venezia: Marsilio.

MORI (2004). Quantitative research to inform the preparation of the BBC charter review 2004. Report of a Research Study conduct on behalf of the Department for Culture, Media and Sport.

Müller-Rommel, F., Fettelschoss, K., & Harfst, P. (2003). Party government in Central Eastern European democracies: A data collection (1990–2003). *European Journal of Political Research, 43*(6), 869–894.

Murialdi, P. (1980). Dalla Liberazione al centrosinistra. In G. De Luna (Ed.), *La stampa italiana dalla Resistenza agli anni Sessanta* (pp. 169–301). Roma: Laterza.

Murialdi, P. (1994). *Maledetti "professori". Diario di un anno alla Rai*. Milano: Rizzoli.

Nilsson, A., Pettersson, L., & Svensson, P. (1999). Agrarian transition and literacy: The case of nineteenth century Sweden. *European Review of Economic History, 3*(1), 79–96.

Nissen, C. S. (2007). *Generalens veje og vildveje: 10 år i Danmarks Radio*. Copenhagen: Gylendal.

Nissen, H. S. (1975). Politikere eller kulturpersonligheder. In R. Skovmand (Ed.), *DR50*. Copenhagen: Danmarks Radio.

Nordmark, D., Johanesson, E., & Petersson, B. (2001). *Åren då allting hände (1830–1897)*, vol. 2 of *Svenska pressens historia*. Stockholm: Ekerlids.

Ó Broin, L. (1976). The mantle of culture. In *Written on the wind* (pp. 1–16). Dublin: RTÉ.

Olsson, O., Wagnsson, R., Nyblom, G., Ljungqvist, S., & Reuterswärd, G. (1935). Rundradion i Sverige. *Statens offentliga utredningar, 1935*(10).

O'Malley, T. (1994). *Closedown? The BBC and government broadcasting policy 1979–1992*. London: Pluto Press.

O'Neill, B. (1991). Conflict moves in bargaining: Warnings, threats, escalations, and ultimatums. In H. Peyton Young (Ed.), *Negotiation analysis* (pp. 87–107). Ann Arbor, MI: University of Michigan Press.

Orlando, R. (1954). Letter to Harman Grisewood, Director, BBC Spoken Word. In BBC Written Archives Centre File E1/1008/3.

Ortoleva, P. (1994). La televisione tra due crisi. In *Storia della stampa italiana* (vol. 7, pp. 89–118). Bari: Laterza.

Ottone, P. (1969). Le notizie con la maschera. *Espresso*.

Ottone, P. (1996). Il decalogo del giornalista. *La Repubblica*.

Padovani, C. (2005). *A fatal attraction: Public television and politics in Italy*. Oxford: Rowman & Littlefield.

Persson, P. (1961). Minnesanteckningar från telefonsamtal med Bertil Ohlin. Sveriges Radio Dokumentarkiv. Centrala Kansliet, Handlingar rörande programverksamheten, policyfrågor. F4 CB Vol. 9.

Petersson, B. (2006). *Från journalist till murvel: Journalistyrkets professionalisering från 1900 till 1960-talet*. Nordicom Sverige.

Pierson, P. (2003). Big, slow-moving, and … invisible: Macro-social processes in the study of comparative politics. In J. Mahoney, & D. Rueschmeyer (Eds.), *Comparative historical analysis in the social sciences*. Cambridge: Cambridge University Press.

Pine, R. (2002). *2RN and the origins of Irish radio*. Dublin: Four Courts Press.

Pini, M. (1978). *Memorie di un lottizzatore*. Milano: Feltrinelli.

Pinto, F. (1980). *Il modello televisivo: professionalita e politica da Bernabei alla Terza rete*. Milano: Feltrinelli.

Porter, T. M. (1995). *Trust in numbers: The pursuit of objectivity in science and public life*. Princeton, NJ: Princeton University Press.

Putnis, P. (2008). Share 999. *Media History, 14*(2), 141–165.

Qualter, T. (1962). Politics and broadcasting: Case studies of political interference in national broadcasting systems. *Canadian Journal of Economics and Political Science, 28*(2), 225–234.

Quinn, B. (2001). *Maverick: A dissident view of broadcasting today*. Dublin: Brandon Press.

Raunio, T., & Wiberg, M. (2003). Finland: Polarized pluralism in the shadow of a strong president. In K. Strøm, W. C. Müller, & T. Bergman (Eds.), *Delegation and accountability in parliamentary democracies* (pp. 301–325). Oxford: Oxford University Press.

Reith, J. (1924), *Broadcasting over Britain*. London: Hodder & Stoughton.

Reith, J. (1949). *Into the wind*. London: Hodder & Stoughton.

Retallack, J. (1993). From pariah to professional? The journalist in German society and politics, from the late enlightenment to the rise of Hitler. *German Studies Review, 16*(2), 175–223.

Ricci, M. (1989). Gelosi, concorrenti, uguali: i tg. *Repubblica*, p. 7.

Ronchey, A. (1988). Il modello della Rai, pochi pregi, tanti guai. *Repubblica*, p. 10.

Rumphorst, W. (1999). *Model public service broadcasting law*. Geneva: UNESCO.

Rydbeck, O. (1960a). Letter to Centerpartiets riksorganisation. Sveriges Radio Dokumentarkiv. Centrala Kansliet, Handlingar rörande programverksamheten, policyfrågor. F4 CB Vol. 9.

Rydbeck, O. (1960b). Letter to styrelsen. SR Arkiv – Kommittén för publiceringsregler: Seriebeteckning F 1; Volym nr 1; T65.

Rydbeck, O. (1964). Letter to Bertil Ohlin, Gunnar Heckscher, Hanssom. Sveriges Radio Dokumentarkiv. Centrala Kansliet, Handlingar rörande programverksamheten, policyfrågor. F4 CB Vol. 9.

Rydbeck, O. (1990). *I maktens närhet. Diplomat, radiochef, FN-ämbetsman*. Stockholm: Bonniers.

Sani, G., & Legnante, G. (2001). Quanto ha contato la comunicazione politica? *Rivista italiana di scienza politica, 31*(3), 481–502.

Sartori, G. (2005). *Parties and party systems*. ECPR Press.

Savage, R. (1996). *Irish television: The political and social origins*. Westport, CT: Praeger.

Sävström, A., Berger, A., Hugo, Y., Hökerberg, E., Johansson, J., Linder, E., & Sterky, H. (1946). Rundradion i Sverige. Dess aktuella behov och riktlinjer för dess framtida verksamhet. *Statens Offentliga Utredningar, 1*.

Scannell, P., & Cardiff, D. (1991). *A social history of British broadcasting*, Vol. I, *1922–1939, serving the nation*. Oxford: Basil Blackwell.

Scotto Lavina, E. (1984). Il ruolo del palinsesto. In R. Zaccaria (Ed.), *Rai: La televisione che cambia*. Torino: Società Editrice Internazionale.

Seaton, J. (1997). Yesterday's men. *Contemporary British History, 11*(2), 87–107.

Seaton, J., & Curran, J. (2003). *Power without responsibility: The press, broadcasting, and new media in Britain.* London: Routledge.

Seaton, J., & Hennessy, P. (1997). Reassessing yesterday's men. *Contemporary British History, 10*(3), 87–107.

Selznick, P. (1949). *TVA and the grass roots: A study in the sociology of formal organization.* Berkeley, CA: University of California Press.

Sigelman, L., & Yough, S. N. (1978). Left–right polarization in national party systems. *Comparative Political Studies, 11*(3), 355–379.

Siune, K. (1987). The political role of mass media in Scandinavia. *Legislative Studies Quarterly, 12*(3), 395–414.

Skovbjerg, A. (2007). Intern regulering, etik og kontrol. In O. Jørgensen, H. Nissen Kruuse, A. Skovbjerg, & H. Vignal-Schjøth (Eds.), *Styring eller frihed? Regulering, etik og kontrol* (pp. 233–270). Aarhus: Ajour.

Skovmand, R. (1975a). De første år. In R. Skovmand (Ed.), *DR50* (pp. 11–50). Copenhagen: Danmarks Radio.

Skovmand, R. (1975b). De ledende krafter. In R. Skovmand (Ed.), *DR50* (pp. 51–114). Copenhagen: Danmarks Radio.

Smith, A., & Ortmark, A. (1979). *Television and political life: Studies in six European countries.* Basingstoke: Macmillan.

Soderström, H., & Ag, L. (1962). *Samhällskritik i radio och tv.* Stockholm: Bonnier.

Sparks, M. (1981). Government review of broadcasting 1974–81: Outcome and expectations. *Political Quarterly, 52*(4), 467–481.

Sterzel, F. (1971). *God publicistik sed.* Stockholm: Allmänna Förlag.

Strom, K. (1990). A behavioral theory of competitive political parties. *American Journal of Political Science, 34*(2), 565–598.

Sveriges Kommunistiska Parti (1963). Letter to Olof Rydbeck. Sveriges Radio Dokumentarkiv. Centrala Kansliet, Handlingar rörande programverksamheten, policyfrågor. F4 CB Vol. 9.

Sveriges Radio AB (1960). Styrelseprotokoll med bilagor. Sveriges Radio Dokumentarkiv.

Taylor, D. (1975). Editorial responsibilities. *BBC Lunchtime Lectures, 10,* 3–14.

Thatcher, M. (1993). *The Downing Street years.* London: HarperCollins.

Thurén, T. (1997). *Medier under blåsväder: den svenska radion och televisionen som samhällsbevarare och samhällskritiker.* Stockholm: Norstedt.

Tjernström, S. (2000). *En svårstyrd skuta. Företagsledning i det svenska public service-företaget.* Stockholm: Prisma.

Tracey, M. (1998). *The decline and fall of public service broadcasting.* Oxford: Oxford University Press.

Tsebelis, G. (2002). *Veto players: How political institutions work.* Princeton, NJ: Princeton University Press.

Tversky, A., & Kahneman, D. (1973). Availability: A heuristic for judging frequency and probability. *Cognitive psychology, 5*(2), 207–232.

Ufficio Stampa della Rai (Ed.) (1976). *Pluralismo.* Roma: Rai Radiotelevisione Italiana.

Unsgaard, H. (n.d.). Promemoria. SR Arkiv – Kommittén för publiceringsregler: Seriebeteckning F 1; Volym nr 4.

Västmanlands Kommunistisk Partidistrikt (1964). Letter to Olof Rydbeck. Sveriges Radio Dokumentarkiv. Centrala Kansliet, Handlingar rörande programverksamheten, policyfrågor. F4 CB Vol. 9.

Veltroni, W. (1990). *Io e Berlusconi (e la Rai).* Roma: Editori Riuniti.

Vespa, B. (2002). *Rai: la grande guerra, 1962–2002: quarant'anni di battaglie a viale Mazzini*. Roma: Rai-ERI.

Vignal-Schjøth, H. (2007). Kontrol og klagesystemer. In O. Jørgensen, H. Nissen Kruuse, A. Skovbjerg, & H. Vignal-Schjøth (Eds.), *Styring eller frihed? Regulering, etik og kontrol* (pp. 233–270). Aarhus: Ajour.

Volcansek, M. L. (2000). *Constitutional politics in Italy: The constitutional court*. New York: St. Martin's Press.

Wadsworth, A. (1954). Newspaper circulations, 1800–1954. *Transactions of the Manchester Statistical Society, IV*, 1–41.

Weber, M. (1991). Bureaucracy. In H. H. Gerth, & C. Wright Mills (Eds.), *Max Weber: Essays in sociology* (pp. 196–244). London: Routledge (1948 edn).

West, W. (1987). *Truth betrayed*. London: Duckworth.

Wikström, J.-E. (n.d.). Hansson, Oloph. Sveriges Radio Dokumentarkiv.

Williams, A. (1975). Unbiased study of television news bias. *Journal of Communication, 25*(4), 190–199.

Wyatt, W. (2003). *The fun factory: A life in the BBC*. London: Aurum Press.

YouGov (2004). Greg Dyke and the case for war with Iraq. *Mail on Sunday*. www.yougov.com/archives/pdf/DBD040101002.pdf.

Zaccaria, R. (1984). I rapporti tra la Rai e il sistema politico. In R. Zaccaria (Ed.), *Rai: La televisione che cambia*. Torino: Società Editrice Internazionale.

Zaccaria, R. (1998). *Diritto dell'informazione e della comunicazione*. Padova: CEDAM.

Zeno-Zencovich, V. (1983). Natura giuridica del canone radiotelevisivo e suggellamento dell'apparecchio TV nella giurisprudenza più recente. In R. Zaccaria (Ed.), *Il Servizio Pubblico Radiotelevisivo* (pp. 397–414). Napoli: Jovene Editore.

Index

Note: Page numbers in *italic* denote tables, those in **bold** denote figures. References to notes are prefixed by *n*.

2RN 125–7
14-day rule 96–7
'76 group 113

Aaskov, Ersling 175
AB Radiotjänst 141–2
Adam, Kenneth 100, 110–11
Addison Rules 109
advertising campaign: "Fri Television" 3
AGCOM (Autorità per le garanzie nelle comunicazioni) 70, 78
Agenzia Stefani 48
Agnes, Biagio 50, 65, 68, 184, 188, 189–90
Aktuelt Kvarter 170–1
Albertini, Luigi 47
alsidighed 168–9
Alvaro, Corrado 49
Amato, Giuliano 199*n*10
Åmen, Walter 148
Amor, Fernando Lopez 86
AN (National Alliance – Alleanza Nazionale) 69
Andersson, Sven 145–6
Annan Report 114, 115, 186
Annunziata, Lucia 78
anti-Establishment programmes 112
anticipated reactions 15
appointments 25, 74–7, 191–2
Arato, Rodolfo 51
Arbejdernes Radioforbund 165
Attenborough, David 105
Attlee, Clement 96
audience share 8, 195, **196**
Autorità per le garanzie nelle comunicazioni (AGCOM) *see* AGCOM

Balbín, José Luis 85
Baldassare, Antonio 71
Barnett, Joel 118, 120
Baunsgaard, Bernhard 169–70
Baunsgaard, Hilmar 170
BBC (British Broadcasting Corporation): and 2RN 126; (1922–1955) 89–104; (1954–1979) 105–15; (1979–2005) 115–23; conflict with government 112–16; controversy 91–2; expertness 95; formation 91; and the General Strike 102–3; impartiality 93–5, 98; independence 123–4; News Department 99–102; news structure 97–102, 111; organization 111; partisanship 183; political interference 102–4, 111–15; polls of independence perception 13; press agencies 97–9, 181; professionalism 105–8; professionalization 106–8, 182; as public broadcaster 4; recruitment 111, 183; reputation 89, 123; rules 96–7, 105, 108–11, 185; Suez controversy 103–4; timeline **90**; website 196
BBC Bristol 109
BBC directors-general 13
BBC Editorial Guidelines 120, 124, 187
BBC Producers' Guidelines 120, 121–2
BBC Programmes Complaints Commission 114–15
BBC World Service 197*n*1.3
Benn, Tony 109, 113
Berlusconi, Silvio 58, 59, 69, 77–8
Bernabei, Ettore 45, 51, 53, 55, 184
Beveridge Report 100, 102
Biagi, Enzo 53, 55–6, 63, 77

bias 20, 113, 133
Bild, Tage 165, 166, 168
Birt, John 115, 119–20, 184
Bjarnhof, Karl 166
Black, Conrad 119
Blaney, Neil 127
Board of Governors, UK 116–17
Bohman, Gösta 160
Bomholt, Julius 169
bourgeois parties: Sweden 137, 147,
    154–5, 160, 162
Bradshaw, Ben 122
Brancati, D. 65
Briggs, A. 95, 96, 102, 103, 104, 112,
    114–15
Brink Lund, A. 171
British Broadcasting Corporation (BBC)
    see BBC
British Gazette 102, 103
British Worker 102
Brittan, Leon 118
broadcast output: definition 19; and
    politicians 19–20
broadcasters: definition 4–5
Broadcasting Authority Act: Ireland 127
Bryant, Chris 123
Budge, I. 12
bureaucratic partisanship 16, 32
Burke, Ray 132–3
Burns, Tom 105, 106
Burrows, Arthur 99
Bustamante, E. 82, 83–4, 87
"Butskellism" 105
Bystedt, Britt-Marie 161

Callaghan, James 110
Campbell, Alastair 121, 122, 123
Canadian Broadcasting Corporation (CBC)
    see CBC
Canel, M. J. 85
Cappon, Claudio 72
Cardiff, D. 92, 95, 99, 100
Cardini, Franco 45, 74, 77
Carlsen, Erik 167
Carty, Michael 129, 130
Castedo, Fernando 84
CBC (Canadian Broadcasting
    Corporation): polls of independence
    perception 13
censorship 83–4
central bank independence: literature on 12
Central News 89, 98
Century Radio 132
Cesareo, G. 17, 51, 55

Channel 4 4
Checkland, Michael 119
Cheli, Enzo 199*n*10
Chesi, Vittorio 51
Chiarenza, F. 48, 49, 51, 62, 64
chief executives: turnover as proxy
    measure 11–15
Childers, Erskine 127
children: and television 110
Chilò, Cecilia Stegö 162
Christian Democratic party (Democrazia
    Cristiana – DC) *see* DC
Churchill, Winston 96, 102
Clandillon, Séamus 126
Clark, Kenneth 104
Clark, R. T. 100
Clarke, D. H. 99, 120
Clarke, S. 118
CLNAI (Comitato di Liberazione
    Nazionale per l'Alta Italia) 48
coalition negotiations: Sweden 147
Coatman, John 99, 100, 101
"Code of Practice on the Use of Violence
    in Television Programmes" 110–11
codes: BBC 109–11, 119–20; of ethics 72,
    86, 139; Rai 49–50, 78–9
Columbia Broadcasting System 82
Comhairle Council 127
Comitato di Liberazione Nazionale per
    l'Alta Italia (CLNAI) *see* CLNAI
commercial broadcasters 4
committee (1933): Sweden 143
Communist Party: Sweden 154
comparative studies: politics of public
    broadcasting 15–18
complaints: Sweden 159
complaints handling procedures 109–10,
    114–15, 187
Compton, Edmund 115
Conservative Party 115, 116
controversy: avoidance 91–2, 126–7
Controversy Committee 96
Corporation for Public Broadcasting
    (USA) 15
Corriere della Sera 63
corrupt practices 6–7
corruption scandals: Italy 68
Cosgrave, W. T. 126
country comparison *180*
Crawford Committee 102
Crossman, Dick 113, 114
Cukierman, A. 12
Cumann na nGaedheal government 127
Curran, J. 101

Curzi, Sandro 73, 77

Daggar, George 92
Daily Telegraph 100, 119
Damazer, Mark 123
Davies, Gavyn 115, 121
Day, Robin 107, 108
DC (Christian Democratic party –
   Democrazia Cristiana) 49, 50–2, 56,
   60–1, 68
de Valera, Éamon 127
decentralization: DR 167
defeasing strategies 26–8, 186–7
defusing strategies 28, 186
Delano, T. 106
democracy: and political independence 6
democratic regimes: and PSB 4
democratization: of the media 112–14
Den Hemmelige Krig (The Secret War)
   174, 187
Denmark: (1922–1955) 164–6;
   (1957–1974) 166–72; (1980–) 172–5;
   country comparison *180*; DR *see* DR;
   management 184; mispredictions 40;
   press agencies 32, 181; rules 185
Dickens, Charles 90
Dillén, Tomas 152
Djerf-Pierre, M. 144
Donsbach, W. 21
Doolan, Lelia 129, 130
Dowling, J. 129
DR (Dansmark Radio): *alsidighed* 168–9;
   centralization 170–3; decentralization
   167; editorial guidelines 170–1;
   governance reform 172; independence
   187, 190; insurrection within 166–7;
   polls of independence perception 13;
   press agencies 32, 181; recruitment 172;
   rules 167–8, 173–4, 185, 187–8
DS (Left Democrats – Democratici di
   Sinistra) 69
Dyke, Greg 115, 120–1, 183

Eckerberg, Per 151, 157, 159, 160
Eco, Umberto 63
economic independence 8
Eden, Anthony 103–4
Edwards, Donald 100
Ehnmark, Eloh 148
EIAR 48
Ekot 147
Elgemyr, G. 146
Elgie, R. 35
Engblom, Lars-Åke 145

Erlander, Tage 147, 148
Estonia: terms of chief executives 13
ethics code 72, 86, 139
Etzioni-Halevy, E. 16
events 20
ex ante controls 34–5
Exchange Telegraph 89, 98
expertness 95
external impositions: and internal controls
   186; *see also* 14-day rule; Annan
   Report; Callaghan, James; Fianna Fáil

Fälldin, Thorbjörn 160
Fanfani, Amintore 53
Farinelli, G. 49
Farrell, Brian 130
Fava, Nuccio 65
Faxén, Magnus 161, 183
Feeney, Peter 132
Feo, Italo de 57
Fettelschoss, K. 12
Fianna Fáil 127, 132
Fichtelius, Erik 162
Financial Times 119
Fine Gael-Labour coalition 131
Fini, Gianfranco 69
Finland: polarization 17
Firth, Roderick 20
Floris, Giovanni 75
Fontanarosa, A. 71
formal interventions 25
Forsén, Olof 136, 145
Forza Italia 69
14-day rule 96–7
France Télévisions 5, 13
Freivalds, Laila 3
"Fri Television": advertising campaign 3
Fridolin, Gustav 3
Friis-Skotte, J. F. N. 164, 166
funding cutting: as sanction 35, *36*, 191
funding sources 8; *see also* licence fee
   funding

Gabilondo, Iñaki 84
GAC (General Advisory Council) 93, 102
Gadda, Carlo Emilio 50
Gade, Søren 174
Gaitskell, Hugh 103, 104
Gasparri law 76
Gater, George 102
General Advisory Council (GAC) *see*
   GAC
General Strike 102–3
Germany: journalism 29–30

Gilardi, F. 35
Gilligan, Andrew 121, 122
Ginsburg, Manne 146
Giovanelli, Ettore 199*n*18
Glasgow University Media Group 114
Glisenti, Paolo 74
Goldie, Grace Wyndham 109, 183
Gonella, Guido 55
Gorham, Maurice 127, 128
Grade, Michael 119
Graham, William 103
Gran, B. 37
Greene, Hugh 94, 100, 108, 112
Grisewood, Harman 104, 111
Guala, Filiberto 45, 50, 79
Guidance Index 99, 111
guidelines: BBC 99, 111, 115, 120, 121–2,
    124, 187; DR 170–1; Ireland 132; SR 150
Guillou, Jan 157
Guzzanti, Sabina 79

Hadenius, S. 136, 141, 144, 157, 159
Haines, Joe 112–13
Haley, William 100
Hallin, D. 17, 43, 140
Hamrin, Felix 146
Hansson, Oloph 152, 158, 159, 160, 161
Harfst, P. 12
Harris, Eoghan 130
Hartling, M. 169
Haughey, Charles J. 133
Havas 140–1
Hegeler, Inge and Sten 167
Helén, Gunnar 145, 160
Hermansson, C. H. 154
Higgins, Michael D. 132, 133, 186
Hill, Charles 114–15
Himmelweit, Hilde 110
Hjelte, Roland 158
Hoare, Leslie 102
Hole, Tahu 101–2
Holm, Emil 165
Hoon, Geoff 122
Horgan, J. 126–7, 128, 129, 130, 132
Horrie, C. 118, 120
Huber, J. 32
Hughes, Séamus 127
Humphrys, John 122
Huss, Erik 160
Hussey, Duke 118, 120
Hutton Inquiry 115–16, 121, 187

Ida Villa, A. 49
impartiality: BBC 93–5, 98, 106;

commitment to 185–6; and independence
    5–6; Ireland 130–1, 131–2; and press
    agencies 181; and professionalism 106;
    Rai 48–9, 58, 61–4, 69–70, 74; RTÉ 128;
    and rules 185–6; Spain 83; Sweden
    139–42, 144, 149–50, 158
independence: conclusion 189–90; model
    of 37–40; political *see* political
    independence
Independent Television (ITV) *see* ITV
Independent Television Authority (ITA)
    see ITA
Independent Television News (ITN) *see*
    ITN
index of protection 35–7
industrial disputes: portrayal of 114
informal interventions 25
Inglehart, R. 32
insurrection: DR 166–7
interference: BBC 102–4, 111–15;
    definition 5; motives 8; opportunities 8;
    Rai 56–7, 68, 77–8; Spain 83–4;
    Sweden 145–8, 153–6, 159–61
the Internet 195–6
interventions: defeasing 26–8, 186–7;
    definition 5; defusing 28, 186; pre-
    empting 25–9; types of 25
Iraq war coverage 121, 174–5, 187
Ireland: (1926–1960) 125–7; (1960–1976)
    128–31; (1976–) 131–4; country
    comparison *180*; management 184;
    press agencies 32, 181; RTÉ (Radio
    Telefís Éireann) 40, 128–34, 181
IRI (Istituto per la Ricostruzione
    Industriale) 48
Iseppi, Gianfranco 72
Istituto per la Ricostruzione Industriale
    (IRI) *see* IRI
ITA (Independent Television Authority)
    104
Italian Socialist Party (Partito Socialista
    Italiano – PSI) *see* PSI
Italy: country comparison *180*;
    mispredictions 40; news broadcasts 53,
    55, 58–9; partisanship 183; polarization
    17; press agencies 32, 181;
    professionalization 47–8, 182; Rai *see*
    Rai; reform 79; and SVT 3
ITN (Independent Television News) 108
ITV (Independent Television) 105, 107–8

Jacob, Ian 97, 102, 111
Jacobsen, Erhard 169
Jay, Peter 119

Jerstedt, Sven 145
Johanesson, E. 139
Johannsen, W. 169
Jones, Roderick 98
journalism: Germany 29–30
journalism courses 75, 82
journalistic partisanship 20–6
journalists: British 90; and implications for
  reform 193; management of 24–5;
  production functions 21–4;
  professionalization project 29–32; types
  of 20–1

Kaufman, Gerald 121
Kelly, C. E. 127
Kelly, David 115–16, 121, 123, 187
Keman, H. 12
Kennedy, Ludovic 107, 108
Knudsen, Lisbeth 173
Knudsen, Viggo 171
Kreuger, Torsten 147
Kristelig Lytterforening 165
Kumar, Krishnan 106–7

Labour Party 103, 113, 114, 115, 116
Lange, Morten 169
Lavina, Scotto 66
Left Democrats (Democratici di Sinistra –
  DS) *see* DS
legal protection: conclusion 191–2; and
  implications for reform 194; and
  independence 8–9; index 35–7, 191; and
  interventions 25; of public broadcasters
  3–4; sanctions and rewards 33–7; and
  strategic issues 7
legislation: Rai reform 57–9, 59–60, 66
Lémass, Sean 128, 129
Lerche, Christian 166
ley Fraga 82
licence fee funding 4, 116, 146, 191
Linder, Erik Hjalmar 145
listeners' associations 164–5, 166
literacy: Italy 47; Sweden 138
literature: politics of public broadcasting
  15–18
Ljungqvist, Seth 139
Lloyd, John 119
local television: Italy 58
Locatelli, Gianni 74, 75
Longhi, Albino 76
lottizzazione 67–8
Lübeck, Sven 142
Lund, Brink 164
Lundevall, Karl-Erik 154–5

McAleese, Mary 130
MacDonald, Ramsay 92
McMenamin, I. 35
Macmillan, Harold 112
Maconachie file 96, 97, 109
Maconachie, Richard 97
Madsen-Mygdal government 165
Maggie's Militant Tendency 117–18
management: of broadcasters 24–5; and
  implications for reform 193; and
  independence 183–4
Manca, Enrico 65, 67, 68
Manchester Guardian 100
Mancini, P. 17, 43, 140
Marano, Antonio 76
market for news: and causal chain 192;
  growth 3; size 29, 32, 123–4, 134,
  179–82; Sweden 138
market size: union formation and **31**, 32
Marsh, Kevin 123
Marxists 61–2
Matheson, Hilda 97
Mattson, Erik 148
Maybray-King, Lord 114–15
Mazza, M. 50
Mazzanti, A. 63
media markets: and legal protection 9
media output *see* broadcast output
media system types 43
Mediaset 58
Menzies, Robert 103
Merli, Gianfranco 59–60
Miall, Leonard 101, 108, 109
Mikkelsen, Brian 174, 175
Milano, Emanuele 74
Milne, Alasdair 115, 116–19
Mimun, Clemente 76
Mineo, Corradino 73
Minzolini, Augusto 76, 78
model of independence 37–40
Møller, Helge Adam 174
Møllerup, Jakob 174
Monteleone, F. 52
Moratti, Letizia 75
Moro government 60
Movimento Sociale Italiano - Destra
  Nazionale (MSI-DN) *see* MSI-DN
MSI-DN (Movimento Sociale Italiano -
  Destra Nazionale) 61, 62, 69
MTV: (Hungary) 12
Müller-Rommel, F. 12
multivariate regression analysis 37–40
Murdoch, Rupert 119
Murialdi, Paolo 72, 73, 74, 75

National Alliance (Alleanza Nazionale –
    AN) *see* AN
National Association of Journalists 90
National Union of Journalist 90
Nervo, Nino Rizzo 65, 77
news agencies *see* press agencies
newspaper sales 138
newspapers 100
Newsreel 102
NFA (National Farmers' Association)
    dispute 129
Nilsson, Sam 161
Nissen, Christian 172, 173, 174–5, 187
Nissen, H. S. 167
non-partisan journalists 20–4, 26
Nordenskiöld, Otto 148, 159
Nordiska Presscentralen 140–1
Nordmark, D., 139
Nørgaard, Peder 168
Northern Ireland 131

Ó Broin, Leon 127
objectivity: BBC 93; commitment to
    185–6; Ireland 131–2; Rai 48–9, 58,
    61–4, 69–70; RTÉ 128, 130; and rules
    185–6; Spain 83, 85
Office de Radiodiffusion Télévision
    Française 5
Ohlin, Bertil 155–6
Olsen, Svend Aage 168
O'Malley, T. 116–17
O'Neill, B. 27
opartiskhet 149, 151–2, 153–4, 158, 159
Order of Journalists 47, 49
Orlando, R. 17
Ortoleva, P. 67
Oswald, Frank 171
Ottone, P. 45, 63–4

Paccagnini, E. 49
Palme, Olof 159
Panorama 108
par condicio 70
Parker, Lord 114
partiality 5–6; *see also* impartiality
Partido Popular (PP) *see* PP
Partido Socialista Obrero Español (PSOE)
    see PSOE
partisan journalism 144–5
partisan journalists 20–4, 182–3
partisanship: of the bureaucracy 16; and
    independence 182–3; of journalists 20–6
Partito Comunista Italiano (PCI) *see* PCI
party-system polarization 17–18

Patterson, R. 37
Patterson, T. 21
PCI (Partito Comunista Italiano) 60, 62,
    68, 69
Persson, Göran 162
Persson, Per 155–6
Petersen, Kristen Helveg 170
Petersson, B. 139
Petruccioli, Claudio 77
Phillips, F. W. 91
Pine, R. 125, 126
Pinto, F. 54
Piqué, A. M. 85
Pizzorno, Alessandro 60
Plummer, Kenneth 173
pluralism: commitment to 185–6; Rai 46,
    58, 59–61, 66, 70–1; Spain 83, 85
polarization 32
polarized pluralism 17–18, 88
policy-seeking politicians 197*n*2.3
political independence: argument 8–10;
    conclusion 189–90; definition 5–6;
    proxy measure 11–15; significance of
    6–7
political pressure 5
politicians: and broadcast output 19–20;
    definition 18; goals 18–20; interventions
    25–9
polls: of independence perception 13
Post Office: and press agencies 98
Potter, Dennis 115
PP (Partido Popular) 86–7
press agencies 32, 48, 89–90, 97–9, 136,
    140–2, 179–81, 192
Press Association 89, 98
Pressenævnet 174
Pressens Telegramudvalg 170
pressure, political 5
preventative censure: Spain 82
Preziosi, Antonio 75
Prima Comunicazione 72
Prodi, Romano 75
Producers' Guidelines 99
professionalism: BBC 105–8
professionalization: BBC 106–8; country
    comparison 179–81, 182; degree of 3–4;
    future research 192; Italy 47–8, 53–4;
    and rule development 185
professionalization project 29–32
propaganda 48, 52
Protheroe, Alan 117, 118
PSBs (public service broadcasters): audience
    share 195, **196**; definition 4–5; future of
    195–7; independence of *14*, 189–90

PSI (Italian Socialist Party – Partito
Socialista Italiano) 53
PSOE (Partido Socialista Obrero Español)
83, 84–5
psychological sanctions 33–4, 37
public: role of 18
Public Broadcasting Commission 113
Public Institution and Private World 105
public opinion 7; polls on independence 13
public service broadcasters (PSBs) *see*
PSBs
Publicistklubben 138, 139, 150, 184–5

Quinn, Bob 129, 133

Rabe, Julius 146
radio: UK 91
Radio- og tv-nævnet 174
Radio Audizioni Italiane (Rai) *see* Rai
Radio Committee 147
Radio Éireann 127
Radio Free Europe 197*n*1.3
radio licences 146
Radio Marti 197*n*1.3
Radio Nacional de España (RNE) *see* RNE
Radio Telefís Éireann (RTÉ) *see* RTÉ
Radioavisen 170–1
radionämnden 143, 147–8
Radiotelevisione Italiana 199*n*1; *see also*
Rai
Radiotjänst 16, 136, 142–8, 181
Rai (Radio Audizioni Italiane):
(1924–1960) 47–52; (1961–1974) 53–7;
(1975–1992) 57–68; (1993–2008)
68–78; appointments 198*n*15;
background 45–7; ethics code 72;
financial problems 69; impartiality
48–9, 61–4, 69–70; and implications for
reform 194–5; independence 51–2,
189–90; management 184; news output
reform 72–4; news structure 50–1, 55–6,
65–8, 72–7; objectivity 48–9, 61–4,
69–70; organization 50–1, 55–6, 65–8,
72–7; outlook 80; pluralism 59–61,
70–1; political interference 51–2, 56–7,
68, 77–8; polls of independence
perception 13; press agencies 181; as
PSB 4; and public protests 7;
recruitment 51, 55–6, 65–8, 74–7; and
role of the public 18; rules 49–50, 54,
64–5, 71–2, 188; as state television
197*n*1.4; timeline **46**
Rasmussen, Anders Føgh 174
rate of turnover (TOR) *see* TOR

Real Lives 117–18
reappointment refusal: as sanction 35
referat-journalism 144
reform: implications for 193–5; Rai 57–68
regional public service broadcasters 5
regulatory values 46
Reith, John 5, 89, 91–3, 102–3, 126, 184
Rendina, Massimo 51
la Repubblica 62–3
research: politics of public broadcasting
15–18
Retallack, J. 29
Reuters 89, 98, 140–1, 181, 185
rewards 25
Riccio, G. 74
Ridomi, Cristiano 51
Rizzoli group 63
RNE (Radio Nacional de España) 81
Rognoni, Carlo 199*n*21
Roth, Edward J. 128
RTBF: (Belgium) 4–5
RTÉ (Radio Telefís Éireann) 40, 128–34,
181
RTÉ Authority 128, 131
RTVE 39, 81, 82–3, 84–5, 86–7, 184, 188
Rugheimer, Gunnar 128, 129, 130
rules: BBC 96–7, 105, 108–11; of
broadcasters 23–4; of conduct 78–9;
development 184–5; DR 167–8, 173–4;
and politicians 27–9; Rai 49–50, 54,
64–5, 71–2; Sweden 143, 150–2; use
185–8
Ryan, Patrick 100
Rydbeck, Olof 18, 102, 136, 147, 148,
150, 152, 153, 155, 157, 184

Saccà, Agostino 77
Sachs, Thorvald 144
saklighet 151, 152, 153, 158, 159
Sambrook, Richard 121, 122
Samhällskritik i radio och tv 154
sanctions 25, 33–7
Sandén, John 143
Sandulli, Aldo 57
Santambrogio, G. 49
Santoro, Michele 77
Scannell, P. 92, 95, 99, 100
Scelba, Mario 49
Schlüter, Poul 172
SCoB (Standing Committee on
Broadcasting) *see* Standing Committee
on Broadcasting
Scott, C. P. 63
Seaton, Jean 101, 115

Secret Society 117–18
Secret War documentary 174, 187
Segni, Antonio 51
Selznick, Philip 18
Sepstrup, Preben 173
Serenari, Lidia 62
Sinn Féin 131, 132
Sippel, Ole 174
SJF (Svensk Journalistföreningen) 138, 139, 140
Skov, Hans Jørgen 173
Social Democrats: Sweden 137, 148, 159
Söderström, Herbert 154
Solana, Javier 85
Solana, Luis 85
Sølvhøj, Hans 166, 167, 169
Spain: (1923–1977) 81–2; (1977–1996) 82–5; country comparison *180*; government influence 83–4; press agencies 32, 181; rules 185; terms of chief executives 12; Zapatero government 38–9
Spallino, Lorenzo 52
Sparks, M. 115
Spataro, Giuseppe 51
SR (Sveriges Radio) 18, 148–61, 184–5
SRG-SSR directors 13
Standing Committee on Broadcasting (SCoB) 113
state broadcasters 4
Statsradiofoni (State Radio): Denmark 164, 165–6
Stella, Piccone 49
Stockholms-Tidningen 138
Storace, Francesco 71
strategic issues: and political influence 7
Straten, Giorgio Van 199*n*21
Strom, K. 197*n*2.3
Suárez, Adolfo 82
Suez controversy 103–4
Svensk Journalistföreningen (SJF) *see* SJF
Svenska Telegrambyrån (Swedish Telegram Bureau) 140
Sveriges Radio (SR) *see* SR
SVT (Sveriges Television) 3, 16, 190
Swann, Michael 109
Sweden: (1922–1955) 138–48; (1955–1969) 148–56; (1969–) 156–61; background 136–8; country comparison *180*; impartiality 139–42; news structure 143–5, 152; organization 143–5, 152; partisanship 182–3; political interference 145–8, 153–6, 159–61; press agencies 32, 181;

professionalization 182; recruitment 145, 156–7, 182–3; rules 143, 150–2, 184–5; timeline 137

Tambroni government 51, 53
Taylor, D. 21
Telefís na Gaeilge 133
Telegrafstyrelse *see* Telegraph Board
Telegraph Board 16, 139–40
Television Española (TVE) *see* TVE
Tennessee Valley Authority 18
terrorism: Spain 86
Tg1 78
That Was The Week That Was (TW3) 112
Thatcher, Margaret 120
Thatcherism 115
Thurén, T. 151, 154
Tidningarnas Telegrambyrån (TT) *see* TT
Time to Spare 92
timelines: BBC **90**; Rai **46**; Sweden 137
The Times 100, 119
Tjernström, S. 16
Today 121, 122–3
TOR (rate of turnover) 12–15
totalitarian regimes: and PSB 4
trade union model 90
trade unions: USIGRAI 72
trades union congress: Sweden 147; UK 102
training: BBC 105–6; Greene on 108; Rai 75; Spain 80, 82, 87, 182
Tre Ser På TV 158
Trethowan, Ian 116
Trevelyan, Charles 103
the Troubles: Northern Ireland 131
TT (Tidningarnas Telegrambyrån) 136, 140–2, 143–4, 181
TUC (Trades Union Congress): UK 102
TV1: Denmark 157, 158–9
TV2: Denmark 4, 157, 158–9
TVE (Television Española) 81
two-source rule 24

UCD (Unión de Centro Democrático) 83
UK (United Kingdom): (1922–1955) 89–104; (1954–1979) 105–15; (1979–2005) 115–23; BBC *see* BBC; country comparison *180*; market for news 89; polarization 17; press agencies 32, 181
Ullswater committee 93–4
Unión de Centro Democrático (UCD) *see* UCD
union formation: and market size **31**, 32

Unione Radiofonica Italiana (URI) *see*
    URI
United Kingdom (UK) *see* UK
United Press International 82
Unsgaard, Håkan 157
Urdaci, Alfredo 86
URI (Unione Radiofonica Italiana) 48
USIGRAI 72

vänstervridning 158
Veltroni, Walter 52, 68, 69, 199*n*21
Vespa, Bruno 68
violence, code of practice 110–11, 186
Viva Zapatero! 79
vote-seeking politicians 18–20
VRT: (Belgium) 4–5
VUL (vulnerability index) 12–13

Wallqvist, Örjan 157
Walsh, J. J. 126
Webb, S. 12
Weber, M. 27, 30–1
websites 196
Weekend 66 167

Weibull, L. 144
Wenham, Brian 117, 119
West, W. 100
Wheldon, Huw 120
White, Jack 129
Whitelaw, Willie 116
Whitley, Oliver 17
Whittle, Stephen 122
Wikström, Jan-Erik 160, 161
Wilson, Harold 112–13, 114
Winther, Christian 171
Woldendorp, J. 12
Wolff 98, 140
World Service 103–4

Yesterday's Men 112–13, 114
YLE: Finland 17
Young, Stuart 118

Zaccaria, Roberto 59, 66, 70–1
Zapatero government 38–9, 86–8
Zatterin, Ugo 64
Zavoli, Sergio 57
Zircon spy satellite documentary 118